Establishing Cyber Security Programs Through the Community Cyber Security Maturity Model (CCSMM)

Gregory B. White
CIAS, The University of Texas at San Antonio, USA

Natalie Sjelin
CIAS, The University of Texas at San Antonio, USA

A volume in the Advances in
Information Security, Privacy, and
Ethics (AISPE) Book Series

Published in the United States of America by
　　IGI Global
　　Information Science Reference (an imprint of IGI Global)
　　701 E. Chocolate Avenue
　　Hershey PA, USA 17033
　　Tel: 717-533-8845
　　Fax: 717-533-8661
　　E-mail: cust@igi-global.com
　　Web site: http://www.igi-global.com

Library of Congress Cataloging-in-Publication Data

Names: White, Gregory B., author. | Sjelin, Natalie, 1967- author.
Title: Establishing cyber security programs through the community cyber
　security maturity model (CCSMM) / by Gregory B. White and Natalie
　Sjelin.
Description: Hershey, PA : Information Science Reference, an imprint of IGI
　Global, [2020] | Includes bibliographical references and index. |
　Summary: "This book explores how to establish a cyber security program
　through the use of the community cyber security maturity model"--
　Provided by publisher.
Identifiers: LCCN 2019059582 (print) | LCCN 2019059583 (ebook) | ISBN
　9781799844716 (hardcover) | ISBN 9781799851585 (paperback) | ISBN
　9781799844723 (ebook)
Subjects: LCSH: Computer networks--Security measures. | Community
　information services--Security measures. | Computer security.
Classification: LCC TK5105.59 .W534 2020 (print) | LCC TK5105.59 (ebook)
　| DDC 352.3/79--dc23
LC record available at https://lccn.loc.gov/2019059582
LC ebook record available at https://lccn.loc.gov/2019059583

This book is published in the IGI Global book series Advances in Information Security, Privacy, and Ethics (AISPE) (ISSN: 1948-9730; eISSN: 1948-9749)

British Cataloguing in Publication Data
A Cataloguing in Publication record for this book is available from the British Library.

For electronic access to this publication, please contact: eresources@igi-global.com.

Advances in Information Security, Privacy, and Ethics (AISPE) Book Series

ISSN:1948-9730
EISSN:1948-9749

Editor-in-Chief: Manish Gupta, State University of New York, USA

MISSION

As digital technologies become more pervasive in everyday life and the Internet is utilized in ever increasing ways by both private and public entities, concern over digital threats becomes more prevalent.

The **Advances in Information Security, Privacy, & Ethics (AISPE) Book Series** provides cutting-edge research on the protection and misuse of information and technology across various industries and settings. Comprised of scholarly research on topics such as identity management, cryptography, system security, authentication, and data protection, this book series is ideal for reference by IT professionals, academicians, and upper-level students.

COVERAGE

- Information Security Standards
- Data Storage of Minors
- Technoethics
- Security Information Management
- Risk Management
- Cyberethics
- IT Risk
- Device Fingerprinting
- CIA Triad of Information Security
- Privacy-Enhancing Technologies

IGI Global is currently accepting manuscripts for publication within this series. To submit a proposal for a volume in this series, please contact our Acquisition Editors at Acquisitions@igi-global.com or visit: http://www.igi-global.com/publish/.

Titles in this Series

For a list of additional titles in this series, please visit:
http://www.igi-global.com/book-series/advances-information-security-privacy-ethics/37157

Privacy Concerns Surrounding Personal Information Sharing on Health and Fitness Mbile Apps
Devjani Sen (Independent Researcher, Canada) and Rukhsana Ahmed (University at Albany, SUNY, USA)
Information Science Reference • © 2020 • 300pp • H/C (ISBN: 9781799834878) • US $215.00

Safety and Security Issues in Technical Infrastructures
David Rehak (VSB – Technical University of Ostrava, Czech Republic) Ales Bernatik (VSB – Technical University of Ostrava, Czech Republic) Zdenek Dvorak (University of Zilina, Slovakia) and Martin Hromada (Tomas Bata University in Zlin, Czech Republic)
Information Science Reference • © 2020 • 499pp • H/C (ISBN: 9781799830597) • US $195.00

Cybersecurity Incident Planning and Preparation for Organizations
Akashdeep Bhardwaj (University of Petroleum and Energy Studies, Dehradun, India) and Varun Sapra (University of Petroleum and Energy Studies, India)
Information Science Reference • © 2020 • 300pp • H/C (ISBN: 9781799834915) • US $215.00

Blockchain Applications in IoT Security
Harshita Patel (KLEF, Vaddeswaram, Guntur, Andhra Pradesh, India) and Ghanshyam Singh Thakur (MANIT, Bhopal, Madhya Pradesh, India)
Information Science Reference • © 2020 • 300pp • H/C (ISBN: 9781799824145) • US $215.00

Modern Theories and Practices for Cyber Ethics and Security Compliance
Winfred Yaokumah (University of Ghana, Ghana) Muttukrishnan Rajarajan (City University of London, UK) Jamal-Deen Abdulai (University of Ghana, Ghana) Isaac Wiafe (University of Ghana, Ghana) and Ferdinand Apietu Katsriku (University of Ghana, Ghana)
Information Science Reference • © 2020 • 302pp • H/C (ISBN: 9781799831495) • US $200.00

IGI Global
PUBLISHER of TIMELY KNOWLEDGE

701 East Chocolate Avenue, Hershey, PA 17033, USA
Tel: 717-533-8845 x100 • Fax: 717-533-8661
E-Mail: cust@igi-global.com • www.igi-global.com

Table of Contents

Preface..vii

Acknowledgment.. x

Introduction... xi

Chapter 1
The Community Cybersecurity Maturity Model (CCSMM).............................1

Chapter 2
The Two-Dimensional CCSMM...32

Chapter 3
The Three-Dimensional Model for a Community 55

Chapter 4
Awareness 75

Chapter 5
Information Sharing 104

Chapter 6
Policies..131

Chapter 7
Plans..151

Chapter 8
The NIST Cybersecurity Framework.......................................171

Chapter 9
Building Your Community Cybersecurity Program 193

Chapter 10
Incorporating Other Models and Technology Into the CCSMM........................210

About the Authors...219

Index...220

Preface

Over the last decade, states, cities and counties have increasingly become the target of cyber-attacks. This is not only true in the United States but around the world as well. It is not uncommon to come across headlines such as:

- Hit by Ransomware Attack, Florida City Agrees to Pay Hackers $600,000
- 1,852 Cyber Attacks Hit India Each Minute Last Year; Mumbai, Delhi Most Affected
- Crippling ransomware attacks targeting US cities on the rise
- Cyber attack forces Jackson County to pay $400K ransom
- Alarm in Texas as 23 towns hit by 'coordinated' ransomware attack
- Baltimore estimates cost of ransomware attack at $18.2 million as government begins to restore email accounts
- City of London Hit by One Million Cyber-Attacks Per Month

Several of these headlines mention ransomware. Around 2012 ransomware attacks took an evolutionary step forward as the targets of attacks moved from individuals to cities. It would seem that the attackers had spent time perfecting their attacks and had decided to turn to more lucrative targets rather than individuals. From an individual you might be able to extort a few hundred dollars. As the headlines above indicate, with cities that number becomes several hundred thousand dollars. While ransomware is seen in the media more often than other attacks because of the demand for money, attacks have also occurred on the critical infrastructures of communities. At this point no city has been identified as having had some critical infrastructure brought down by a cyber attack but it is only a matter of time.

The Department of Homeland Security (DHS) is tasked with the cybersecurity of the nation. When DHS was first created and given this charge, they treated the mission as protecting the federal government and the critical infrastructures. This was a logical approach at the time as attacks on the government or any of the critical infrastructures could have had a severe impact on the entire nation. This mission still is the major focus of the Cybersecurity and Infrastructure Security Agency (CISA) – the portion of DHS now charged with the nation's cybersecurity. The federal government and the critical infrastructures are still targets of foreign adversaries but, as the headlines above indicate, states and cities are increasingly becoming targets of cyber-attacks. DHS was slow to develop capabilities to assist State, Local, Tribal, and Territorial (SLTT) governments but their pace has picked up and CISA now has a number of services that they offer, free of charge, to SLTTs. States also have begun to establish ways to assist communities when they are hit with a cyber-attack. While these are tremendous steps forward, there is a problem that often goes unmentioned by either DHS or the states. There simply are not enough resources at either the federal or state levels, even if combined, to be able to address all cities in the nation. There are over 19,000 incorporated entities (such as cities) in the nation. If the unincorporated are added the number approaches 35,000. There will never be enough either federal or state funding to be able to assist all states communities. Looking at the list of headlines listed previously one sticks out as critical to this discussion – "Alarm in Texas as 23 towns hit by 'coordinated' ransomware attack". Fortunately for the communities in Texas the ransomware attack was the same for all of them. This meant that an organization assisting the communities only had one piece of malware to analyze. What would happen if instead of one piece of malware, a dozen had been used? Or if multiple attack vectors were employed? If the attacks occurred against Dallas, Houston, San Antonio, Austin, Del Rio, Johnson City, Brownsville, and Dime Box (an actual town in Texas) and the available resources could only assist with 4 cities, which 4 would receive help and which would not? Most likely assistance would be provided to the 4 most populace cities so that the largest number of citizens could benefit from the help. For the citizens of Del Rio, Johnson City, Brownsville, and Dime Box this would mean their communities would take longer to restore to full operations and if the attacks impacted a critical infrastructure, such as power, and it was in the middle of the summer, the citizens of these smaller communities would go without air conditioning for an extended period of time until help could finally be provided to them.

This is one of the reasons for this book. The message to communities across the country is that they need to be prepared to handle cyber-attacks affecting them on their own and not count on outside resources to help. If a community is the only one attacked and resources can be provided, then that is great. Accept the resources, but you can't rely on this happening. You must be prepared to deal with whatever cyber event occurs on your own.

This book introduces the Community Cyber Security Maturity Model (CCSMM). It is a 3-dimensional model that is designed to help communities prepare in a systematic way to be able to address cyber incidents with little or no outside help. It is not uncommon to see a city become motivated to improve their cybersecurity after they, or a close neighboring community, is hit with a cyber-attack. Vendors may rush in willing to sell the community services and products to help them with their security issues. The problem with this is that are the products and services being sold the most important ones for the community at that time? What is the ultimate goal for the community, and do they have a plan to develop a comprehensive cybersecurity program? Without an underlying cybersecurity program much of what communities may be tempted to purchase will not be as effective as it could be because the community is not ready for it. The CCSMM is designed to help communities systematically develop their own cybersecurity program at a pace that the community can handle and in a way that will lead to a whole-community approach to cybersecurity. In essence, it will lead to a "culture of security" being established within the community.

This book is designed for two audiences. The first, and most obvious, are communities and community leaders. The book is designed to help describe the basics of the CCSMM and to help communities launch their cybersecurity programs in a manner that will lead to a viable and sustainable program.

The second audience are students in cybersecurity programs at either the graduate or undergraduate levels. Few cybersecurity programs in the country address the topic from the viewpoint of communities but this is where a tremendous impact could occur and could lead to a national culture of security that would see a positive impact at all levels. A vision for this book is to help the nation embark on a journey that will see every American accept a level of cybersecurity responsibility appropriate for their home and their place of employment. If every citizen accepted that they have a responsibility to ensure their own cybersecurity, how much better off would the nation be?

Acknowledgment

The authors would like to thank The University of Texas at San Antonio (UTSA) and the Center for Infrastructure Assurance and Security (CIAS) for the flexibility and freedom to work on projects that we have found to be exciting and rewarding. We fully recognize that the CIAS is not the normal center found at an institution of higher education and we appreciate the opportunity to be part of a program that allows us to address cybersecurity issues that are impacting the nation today.

Along with UTSA and the CIAS, the authors would like to express their gratitude to IGI-Global for agreeing to publish this work. This is certainly not a typical textbook and we greatly appreciate IGI-Global taking a chance on us.

We also recognize and acknowledge the number of individuals who have played a part in the CIAS with the development of the Community Cyber Security Maturity Model (CCSMM). We especially want to thank Mr. Dwayne Williams and Mr. Larry Thompson who played a critical role in working with us as a team in developing the original design of the model. We also want to thank Larry and the strong team of security professionals he built and led that helped to flesh out the model as it evolved over several years. The model would not be what it is today without the tremendous effort of the members of the CIAS and we are grateful for everybody who has played a part in its development.

Finally, the authors would like to thank their respective spouses, Mr. Larry Sjelin and Mrs. Charlan White for their own continued support of us each individually. The strong support of a spouse is so very helpful in working through the many challenges that accompany working on a project such as this. We could not have accomplished what we have without your support.

Introduction

Much of the national effort to secure the nation's computer systems and networks has been focused on systems used by the federal government as well as the various critical infrastructures. These infrastructures, as defined by the Department of Homeland Security (DHS) are those systems and networks that are so vital to the nation that their destruction or disruption would have a debilitating impact on the nation's security and safety. (DHS 2019a) The sectors defined as part of the nation's critical infrastructures have changed slightly over the past few years but as of 2019, they include the following:

- Chemical Sector
- Commercial Facilities Sector
- Communications Sector
- Critical Manufacturing Sector
- Dams Sector
- Defense Industrial Base Sector
- Emergency Services Sector
- Energy Sector
- Financial Services Sector
- Food and Agriculture Sector
- Government Facilities Sector
- Healthcare and Public Health Sector
- Information Technology Sector
- Nuclear Reactors, Materials, and Waste Sector
- Transportation Systems Sector
- Water and Wastewater Systems Sector (DHS 2019a)

The Government Facilities Sector (n.d) includes not just the federal government but state, local, and tribal governments as well (DHS 2019b) and, presumably, territorial though not specifically listed on the DHS website.

While acknowledging that state, local, tribal, and territorial (SLTT, n.d.) governments are critical, the challenge for DHS in overseeing the security of systems used in the federal government and in the other sectors is massive enough that little time has been spent on SLTT security. The Government Facilities Sector Specific Plan (DHS 2015) includes a table that describes the responsible sector based on the predominant use of a specific facility (see Table 1).

Table 1. Facility predominant use by sector (DHS, 2015)

Predominant Use	Responsible Sector
Offices and Office building complexes	Commercial Facilities
Retail stores within government facilities, government agencies within commercial facilities.	Commercial Facilities
Housing or community service facilities provided for public use	Commercial Facilities
Food service establishments within government facilities	Agriculture and Food
Health clinics and medical units within government facilities	Healthcare and Public Health
Transportation-related government facilities*	Transportation Systems
Nuclear reactors, materials, and waste located in government facilities**	Nuclear Reactors, Materials, and Waste
Police, fire, and emergency services stations	Emergency Services
Emergency operations, command, dispatch, and control centers	Emergency Services
Public works facilities associated with:	
Water or wastewater treatment	Water
Power or Natural Gas	Energy
Telephone or Internet service	Communications, Information Technology
Highway or road service or maintenance	Transportation Systems

* Except for space exploration and any that are part of military installations.

** Except for all U.S. Department of Energy (DOE) facilities involved with storage or use of special nuclear material and all U.S. Department of Defense (DoD) nuclear facilities and materials associated with defense programs.

While Table 1.1 appears to be all-encompassing, and for the most part it does include what the government is concerned with, the problem is that the plans for the individual sectors do not provide the detail needed by SLTTs to actually take the steps necessary to secure all of the sectors in their individual area of responsibility. This is especially true for the private sector where the government is not, and arguably should not be, responsible for the actual securing of systems. While it is easy to say that it is the responsibility of an individual business to secure its own assets, this ignores the impact that businesses have on the overall state, community, tribe, or territory. The government should not be responsible for securing private businesses, but is there something they can and should do to help with security in the private sector? What steps, and in what order, should a state, community, tribe, or territory take once it becomes aware of its reliance on computer systems and networks? What assets can SLTTs rely on in the event of a large-scale cybersecurity event and what do they need to be prepared to accomplish on their own?

This chapter will introduce the events that led to the recognition of the need for a model designed for SLTTs to help them prepare for a cyber event within their individual jurisdictions. The model developed for this purpose and that will be used throughout this text is the Community Cyber Security Maturity Model (CCSMM).

BACKGROUND

In 1998, the White House released Presidential Decision Directive/NSC-63, commonly referred to as PDD-63. This directive had the subject line of "Critical Infrastructure Protection" and stated that the U.S. was becoming "increasingly reliant upon certain critical infrastructures and upon cyber-based information systems. (White House 1998) It went on to explain that because of our military strength, future enemies "may seek to harm us in non-traditional ways" and that "non-traditional attacks on our infrastructure and information systems may be capable of significantly harming both our military power and our economy." (White House 1998) PDD-63 then went on to explain the President's intent which was to "assure the continuity and viability of critical infrastructures" by taking "all necessary measures to swiftly eliminate any significant vulnerability to both physical and cyber-attacks on our critical infrastructures, including especially our cyber systems." (White House 1998)

The directive went on to discuss the need for a public/private partnership to address the issue of cyber-attacks on the critical infrastructures and proposed a plan for the Federal Government to organize for the defense of the critical infrastructures. The document included a number of different tasks that were to be performed by government agencies and created positions to help with implementation of a coordinated federal approach to addressing potential attacks. Most significantly for purposes of this text and the issue it addresses was the call for the creation by the various critical infrastructure owners and operators of private sector Information Sharing and Analysis Centers (ISACs). An ISAC was to "serve as the mechanism for gathering, analyzing, appropriately sanitizing and disseminating private sector information to both industry and the NIPC [National Infrastructure Protection Center]." As a result of this directive, the various critical infrastructure sectors formed individual ISACs over the next few years, with assistance from the Federal Government. Not all of them were formed at the same time, and the capability of any individual ISAC varies depending on the maturity of its established programs. There is no single template that identifies the "correct" format for an ISAC with each one determining what its structure would be and what services it would offer as a result of the desires and needs of its members.

Information sharing took another step forward in February 2013 when President Obama signed Executive Order 13636 *Improving Critical Infrastructure Cybersecurity*. An issue at this time was that federal agencies, such as the CIA and FBI, might have knowledge of a pending or ongoing cyber-attack on an organization but the mechanisms weren't in place to quickly and easily share that information with the organization or within the same sector. EO 13636 expressed the intent of the President to facilitate this sharing. The EO stated "It is the policy of the United States Government to increase the volume, timeliness, and quality of cyber threat information shared with U.S. private sector entities so that these entities may better protect and defend themselves against cyber threats." (White House, 2013) The EO directed the Attorney General, the Secretary of Homeland Security, and the Director of National Intelligence to each issue instructions to their individual organizations to "ensure the timely production of unclassified reports of cyber threats to the U.S. homeland that identify a specific targeted entity." (White House, 2013) While the implementation was not immediate and it took some time to iron out the exact way this would work in each agency, it at least meant that the government recognized the need to share information with the critical infrastructures so they could better protect themselves.

Another giant step forward in information sharing occurred two years later. In February 2015, President Obama issued another executive order addressing cybersecurity information sharing. Executive Order 13691 *Promoting Private Sector Cybersecurity Information Sharing* addressed another issue with the information sharing ecosystem at the time. Up until this point, information sharing had essentially only addressed cyber-attacks on the various critical infrastructures. EO 13691 essentially expanded the types of organizations that could be part of the information sharing landscape by creating Information Sharing and Analysis Organizations (ISAOs). The EO directed the Secretary of Homeland Security to select an entity to become the ISAO Standards Organization (ISAO SO) that would oversee the creation of

... voluntary standards or guidelines for the creation and functioning of ISAOs ... The standards shall further the goal of creating robust information sharing related to cybersecurity risks and incidents with ISAOs and among ISAOs to create deeper and broader networks of information. (White House, 2015)

The EO went on to further define what documents the ISAO SO should oversee the creation of:

These standards shall address, but not be limited to, contractual agreements, business processes, operating procedures, technical means, and privacy protections, such as minimization, for ISAO operation and ISAO member participation. (White House, 2015)

After issuing a call for proposals and then evaluating the submissions, DHS selected a team that included the Center for Infrastructure Assurance and Security (CIAS) at The University of Texas at San Antonio (UTSA), LMI (formerly known as the Logistics Management Institute), and the Retail Cyber Intelligence Sharing Center (R-CISC) to be the ISAO SO team. This new entity then created a process utilizing groups of volunteer information sharing subject matter experts to create a series of documents to help establish and operate ISAOs which, according to EO 13691, could be:

... organized on the basis of sector, sub-sector, region, or any other affinity, including in response to particular emerging threats or vulnerabilities. ISAO membership may be drawn from the public or private sectors, or consist of a combination of public and private sector organizations. ISAOs may be formed as for-profit or nonprofit entities. (White House, 2015)

Essentially this meant that any group of individuals with a desire to share information on cybersecurity could create an ISAO and become part of the information sharing ecosystem. Generally an ISAO needs to have some common characteristic that unites the members but that characteristic could be geographic in nature (such as a city or state), sector related (such as an ISAO for law offices), or event related (such as an ISAO created for a special sporting event such as the Olympics). The ISAO could also be extremely formal and include specialized services such as a 24/7 Security Operations

Center (SOC) or it could be very informal and only meet on an occasional basis. An extreme example of an informal ISAO might be an ISAO created to bring together Mariachi Bands – maybe something like the South Texas Mariachi Band ISAO. This example has been used in numerous briefings on the ISAO movement and is always met with smiles and some laughter – but it is a perfect example of a very informal ISAO. To understand why this is the case consider a few points:

- Do mariachi bands have a website? (*frequently, yes*)
- Do mariachi bands collect credit card information and store that on a computer? (*yes*)
- Would members of the mariachi bands benefit by periodically coming together and discussing cybersecurity as it relates to their organizations? (*yes, for example to discuss a topic such as ransomware or phishing*)

At this point, Mariachi bands do not require a 24/7 SOC and the type of information they might share, and the methods they could use (such as utilizing a simple email list of members) would be very limited when compared to some of the more robust ISACs in operation. What they would have created, however, is nonetheless an information sharing organization. How much better off would the nation be if all groups of affiliated individuals, whether geographically-, sector- or event-based, came together to discuss cybersecurity as it relates to them? This describes the vision of the growing information sharing ecosystem and illustrates the goal of the ISAO SO in building that ecosystem.

Information sharing is just one aspect of cybersecurity and makes up just one component of an overall cybersecurity program. The evolution that has occurred in the information sharing community, however, does serve to also indicate the priorities of the federal government when it comes to protecting the nation from cyber-attacks. The initial efforts in information sharing were within the federal government and between government entities and the various critical infrastructures. While one of the ISACs, the Multi-State ISAC, was focused on information sharing with states, and later cities as well, this one entity cannot accomplish all that needs to be accomplished for all states and communities. The focus of the initial legislation leading to the formation of the ISACs, and the efforts of the ISACs themselves along with the National Council of ISACs whose members were the ISACS, was on the critical infrastructures. This was a reasonable way to begin as the critical infrastructures, by definition, were the key infrastructures that the nation depends on for the country to function on a daily basis. An attack on any of these infrastructures, and especially an attack on two or more of them at the same time, would have a severe impact on the nation. Thus, it was not an unreasonable approach for the government to take as it began efforts to place more emphasis on cybersecurity. After 15 years, however, while cyber-attacks on the various critical infrastructures were still occurring, there was a significant number of attacks on organizations that were not part of the federal government nor on one of the critical infrastructures. This directly led to the executive order that called for the creation of ISAOs as well.

For the information sharing ecosystem, Executive Order 13691 was a giant step toward the recognition by the government that there were other entities that could also benefit from being part of a program to share cybersecurity information. While DHS played a significant role in the initial efforts to establish the Standards Organization for the ISAOs, with the change of the presidential administration, and after changes within the Department of Homeland Security, the interest in and support of the ISAO effort significantly diminished and the ISAOs were left to themselves to grow and become part of the ecosystem. While there was significant support from the government for the creation of the ISACs, they took well over a decade to really take shape A few individual ISACs were well on their way within that time period, but many were still only emerging. Without the support of the federal government, especially from DHS, it would be interesting to ask what shape the ISACs would be in today? Though the potential number of ISAOs will eventually dwarf by several orders of magnitude the number of ISACs, the federal government simply did not see the benefit, or need, to support them as they did the ISACs. The emphasis was still on the critical infrastructures and other entities were simply not as important or a priority. The government offered no plan to help grow the information ecosystem beyond the ISACs – it was left up to the ISAOs without support from the government.

Another example of the lack of support and the lack of any coordinated plan to help state, local, tribal, and territorial governments as well as the organizations that reside within their jurisdictions can be found in the stated priorities of DHS and the help it does offer to SLTTs. In the *U.S. Department of Homeland Security Cybersecurity Strategy* released May 15, 2018, DHS lists its objectives and intent in seven goals found in five pillars. These are:

- Pillar I – Risk Identification
  - ○ Goal 1: Assess Evolving Cybersecurity Risks. We will understand the evolving national cybersecurity risk posture to inform and prioritize risk management activities.
- Pillar II – Vulnerability Reduction
  - ○ Goal 2: Protect Federal Government Information Systems. We will reduce vulnerabilities of federal agencies to ensure they achieve an adequate level of cybersecurity.
  - ○ Goal 3: Protect Critical Infrastructure. We will partner with key stakeholders to ensure that national cybersecurity risks are adequately managed.
- Pillar III – Threat Reduction
  - ○ Goal 4: Prevent and Disrupt Criminal Use of Cyberspace. We will reduce cyber threats by countering transnational criminal organizations and sophisticated cyber criminals.
- Pillar IV – Consequence Mitigation
  - ○ Goal 5: Respond Effectively to Cyber Incidents. We will minimize consequences from potentially significant cyber incidents through coordinated community-wide response efforts.
- Pillar V – Enable Cybersecurity Outcomes
  - ○ Goal 6: Strengthen the Security and Reliability of the Cyber Ecosystem. We will support policies and activities that enable improved global cybersecurity risk management.
  - ○ Goal 7: Improve Management of DHS Cybersecurity Activities. We will execute our departmental cybersecurity efforts in an integrated and prioritized way.(DHS, 2018b)

Notice that as before, there is a stated interest in primarily addressing cybersecurity issues within the federal government and the critical infrastructures. States and communities are not mentioned as part of any of these goals. The term "community" as used in Goal 5 does not specifically refer to cities or local governments though in the section on Pillar IV Consequence Management there are passing references to issues that would involve state and local entities. The terms "tribal" and "territorial" appear only three times in the document, twice in reference to law enforcement and once in relationship to research and development efforts within DHS. Nowhere in the document is a strategy or a model proposed or mentioned that would be aimed at helping states, communities, tribes, and territories to establish viable and sustainable cybersecurity programs. There are some references to assistance that DHS offers such entities and it is useful to examine what these are.

The DHS Cybersecurity and Infrastructure Security Agency (CISA) web site on *Resources for State, Local, Tribal, and Territorial (SLTT) Governments* provides a list of items that CISA offers to SLTTs. It is important to immediately note that, as the title for the page declares, these are aimed at SLTT governments. (DHS, 2019c) The site provides best practice case studies and an SLTT Toolkit that can be downloaded. It also provides links to a variety of other resources grouped by where they would fall in an overall security program (i.e. Identify, Protect, Detect, and Respond). It also provides links to geographically specific resources listed by state, counties (it lists 3) and cities (it lists 2). To have a better understanding of the types of resources CISA offers and where they may still be lacking, it is useful to see what the list includes:

- Resources to Identify
  - Cyber Resilience Review (CRR)
  - Continuous Diagnostics and Mitigation (CDM)
  - Cybersecurity Evaluation Tool (CSET) and On-Site Cybersecurity Consulting
  - National Cyber Awareness System (NCAS)
  - Industrial Control Systems Computer Emergency Readiness Team (Industrial Control Systems Security) Recommended Practices
  - Cyber security Advisors (CSAs)
  - Protective Security Advisors (PSAs)
  - Federal Virtual Training Environment (FedVTE)
- Resources to Protect
  - SLTT Cybersecurity Engagement Program
  - Multi-State Information Sharing & Analysis Center (MS-ISAC)
  - Industrial Control Systems Security Training
  - Industrial Control Systems Security Recommended Practices
  - National Cyber Awareness System (NCAS)
  - Cyber Security Advisors (CSAs)
  - Protective Security Advisors (PSAs)
  - Stop.Think.Connect. Campaign
  - National Initiative for Cybersecurity Education (NICE)
  - National Initiative for Cybersecurity Careers and Studies (NICCS) Website
  - The National Cybersecurity Workforce Framework

- ○ Network Security Deployment (NSD)
- ○ Cybersecurity Service Offering Reference Aids
- ○ Process Control System Security Guidance for the Water Sector
- ○ NIST Cybersecurity Framework Explained
- ○ Federal Virtual Training Environment (FedVTE)
- ○ Enhanced Cybersecurity Services (ECS)
- Resources to Detect
  - ○ Continuous Diagnostics and Mitigation (CDM)
  - ○ Multi-State Information Sharing and Analysis Center (MS-ISAC)
  - ○ Network Security Deployment (NSD)
  - ○ Federal Virtual Training Environment (FedVTE)
  - ○ Enhanced Cybersecurity Services (ECS)
- Resources to Respond
  - ○ Multi-State Information Sharing and Analysis Center (MS-ISAC)
  - ○ Cyber Information Sharing and Collaboration Program (CISCP)
  - ○ Cyber Security Advisors (CSAs)
  - ○ Protective Security Advisors (PSAs)
  - ○ Cyber Incident Response and Analysis
  - ○ Cybersecurity Service Offering Reference Aids
  - ○ Enhanced Cybersecurity Services (ECS) (DHS, 2019c)

Taking a quick glance, it would appear that there are a plethora of ways CISA is ready to assist SLTTs. While there are indeed quite a few items in the list, several are appropriately repeated in multiple resource categories such as FedVTE, ECS, and MS-ISAC. Another issue with this list is exemplified in two of the resources, the Cyber Security Advisors (CSAs) and the Protective Security Advisors (PSAs). The description of what each of these can provide is as follows:

Cyber Security Advisors (CSAs)

CSAs are regionally located DHS personnel who direct coordination, outreach, and regional support to protect cyber components essential to the sustainability, preparedness, and protection of the Nation's critical infrastructure and SLTT governments. CSAs offer immediate and sustained assistance to prepare and protect SLTT and private entities. CSAs bolster the cybersecurity preparedness, risk mitigation, and incident response capabilities of these entities and bring them into closer coordination with the Federal government. CSAs represent a front-line approach and promote resilience of key cyber infrastructures throughout the U.S. and its territories.

Protective Security Advisors (PSAs)

PSAs are trained critical infrastructure protection and vulnerability mitigation subject matter experts. Regional Directors are Supervisory PSAs, responsible for the activities of eight or more PSAs and geospatial analysts, who ensure all Office of Infrastructure Protection critical infrastructure protection programs and services are delivered to Federal and SLTT stakeholders and private sector owners and operators. The PSA program focuses on physical site security and resiliency assessments, planning and engagement, incident management assistance, and vulnerability and consequence information sharing. (DHS, 2019c)

It is important to recognize the effort by DHS to address cybersecurity for SLTTs but there are two issues with the positions described and many of the offerings listed previously. The first is the sheer number of SLTTs versus the available resources that can be provided by CISA. For example, the number of incorporated cities in the United States in 2018 was 19,495. (Statista, 2019) If you include unincorporated cities that number rises to 35,000 according to the U.S. Geological Survey. There are simply not enough resources in CISA to be able to assist all incorporated communities in the country not to mention the unincorporated ones. Even if assistance was limited to only cities with more than 50,000 residents, CISA could not assist all of them. This also doesn't include assistance to counties, territories, or tribal areas. It should probably be mentioned that it is actually not reasonable to believe that CISA should be responsible for all communities in the nation – the funding for such an effort and the size of the organization that would be needed would not be accepted by the taxpayers in the nation.

The other issue is that the assistance is primarily focused on SLTT government entities and their critical infrastructures. As was already discussed, the vast majority of organizations within this country are not either part of a government at some level or a critical infrastructure. Even if public-private partnerships are considered, these are primarily with larger corporations and not small and medium sized businesses. Additionally, the focus of this book is not on the individual organizations within a community but rather the community as a whole. Again it should be mentioned that it is not reasonable to expect CISA to be responsible for securing all private organizations either because of the needed size of an organization to do so. What is needed is not individual efforts to help specific organizations at the SLTT levels but rather a program to help the SLTTs develop their own cybersecurity programs so that they can in turn help the organizations that fall within their jurisdiction.

CYBER INCIDENTS AT THE STATE AND COMMUNITY LEVELS

It should be no surprise to anybody who pays attention to the media that the number of cyber incidents and attacks has been increasing. Ransomware is a frequent attack vector impacting individuals and organizations. Ransomware is a type of malicious software that generally encrypts the data on a computer system and then sends a message to the owner/administrator stating that they can have the key to decrypt their data for a fee. If the data has not been backed up recently, the owner/organization faces the loss of this data which can often be considered critical or extremely valuable. Of significance is the fact that this is true for not just the federal government and industry but communities and individuals as well. Prior to about 2017, the majority of ransomware attacks reported in the media described an attack on an individual who had their personal data stored which was stored on their computer encrypted. Often this might include files considered very important to the individual such as family photos. Ransoms were in the neighborhood of a few hundred dollars and often people paid these ransoms so they could regain access to their photos or other important documents. Over a short period of time, as criminals perfected their approach to ransomware attacks, there was a distinct shift to other soft targets which in this case meant focusing on organizations such as cities and counties or specific offices within these local governments. Instead of demanding ransom amounts in the hundreds of dollars, ransoms in the tens or hundreds of thousands of dollars were demanded. Sometimes the organizations paid. Sometimes they didn't but even if they didn't, the impact to a community could be easily even greater than the ransom demanded. For example:

In March of 2018, several agencies in Atlanta were forced to convert to paper as ransomware encrypted their computer systems. Ultimately, this malicious cyber event will cost the city over $17 million to recover data, upgrade, and improve its systems and processes. (Cohen, 2019)

This incident was well publicized because of its extent and the cost to the city to respond to it. The fact that the cost to a community to pay the ransom is often so much less than what the cost to otherwise recover from the attack has prompted some to concede to the demands. Unfortunately, the attack on Atlanta was not the only incident of a city being targeted by cyber-attackers. Other communities, both large and small, have also been the victim of cyber-attacks including Baltimore MD, Riviera Beach FL, San Diego CA, Newark NJ, Albany NY, and Greenland, NH. Counties and states have also been the target of attacks including Fisher County, TX and Genesee County, MI as well as the state of Colorado. (Collier, 2019, Levin, 2019)

A related issue that shows why there needs to be a community (or state) approach to preparing for cyber-attacks is the concept of cascading effects. A cyber-attack on one organization within a community could easily impact others within the community and all organizations need to know what other sectors they are dependent on and what they have to do if they lose access to the resource. To illustrate, an attack on one of the critical infrastructures in a community will impact more than just that infrastructure – it will impact many parts of the community. What would the impact on a community be if power or telecommunications were lost? What about city services or emergency services? This extends beyond the traditional critical infrastructures, however. What would the impact be of having all schools within a city suddenly be shut down? How would parents/guardians handle this and what would be the impact on the organizations that the parents/guardians worked at? How prepared are all organizations within a community for significant attacks on some sector of the community and how well is the community when considered as a whole prepared? Attacks on individual businesses, even small and medium-sized businesses can have an impact on a community. Consider, for example, how many organizations within your community have your credit card information. What about local doctor or dental offices? They have access to sensitive health information about citizens within the community, yet these small, local offices often do not have extensive cybersecurity measures in place. It behooves the community to take measures to ensure that all entities within its boundaries have adequately addressed cybersecurity as even breaches at small organizations can adversely impact a possibly large portion of their citizens.

The Department of Homeland Security (DHS) produces an annual report entitled the National Preparedness Report. This report is a requirement for the department as specified by the *Post-Katrina Emergency Management Reform Act*. The report is designed to help in the evaluation of the "progress and challenges that individuals and communities, private and nonprofit sectors, faith-based organizations, and all levels of government have faced in preparedness." (DHS, 2018a) In the 2018 report, three key findings related to cybersecurity were identified:

- Evolving cyber threats continue to outpace the development of protective practices; at the same time, technology users often fail to implement precautionary measures to safeguard their cyber systems.
- Insufficient information sharing between the public and private sectors has hindered the Nation's effectiveness in defending against cyber threats.
- The Federal Government faces persistent challenges in the recruitment and retention of cybersecurity personnel, though it has taken steps to improve cybersecurity training for the nation. (DHS, 2018a)

These key findings related to cybersecurity are very interesting, especially when compared with the Core Capability Proficiency Ratings which are based on self-assessments by states and territories. Cybersecurity has consistently been at the bottom of the list of core capability mission areas in terms of the states' assessment of their own level of preparedness to handle a cybersecurity event. The assessment is insightful and points to areas needing improvement. The report explains that:

Most disasters in the Nation do not receive federal disaster declarations and are wholly led and managed by local and state emergency managers. In FY 2017, states and local jurisdictions relied on their own resources to respond to over 25,000 incidents that did not reach the level of a major disaster declaration. (DHS, 2018a)

When considering the response to disasters, cybersecurity events are similar to the natural events referred to above. The majority of the cyber events we are interested in are not a result of natural disasters but rather specific attacks launched by individuals. Preparing for them and responding once they occur, however, involve many of the same elements no matter what type of event it is or what caused it.

One key difference between cyber events and other emergency response events is in the approach needed to prepare for them. The federal government has led efforts to combat cyber incidents for years with states and communities either relying on a federal response to any event no matter what level it was aimed at or not realizing cyber-attacks on states and cities was even an issue.

The reality is that not only are states and communities targets as discussed earlier, but what is needed to prepare for them is a coordinated approach at all levels and not disparate programs with no linkage between them. Consider the following statement from a report in 2018:

Today's cyber threat environment features a proliferation of cybercrime and attacks from nation-state, nonstate, and nation-state-sponsored actors on both public and private sector systems, along with global "contagions" that can affect large swaths of digital infrastructure simultaneously. To address these challenges to America's security, we need to have a national cybersecurity program that is effective at all levels: national, state, local, and across various private sector industries. The federal nature of our government, and the resultant division in its structure and authorities, demand that state governments take an active and proactive role in responding to threats to their citizens and the organizations located in their jurisdiction. (Cohen and Nussbaum, 2018)

The following year, another report was released that extended the statement to include not just states but communities as well.

Cities and other local governments are the core service providers for citizens and businesses. Ensuring the security of municipal systems is essential to ensuring basic safety, quality of life, and economic prosperity. Increasing digitization means some city services are now managed and/or delivered using technology. In the past, cities have established relationships with public and private sector partners to prepare for and respond to catastrophic events such as natural disasters or terrorist attacks, both of which can threaten the viability of normal operations and the security of the community.

At this juncture, however, efforts to build similar partnerships to respond to cyberattacks are still early stage in most jurisdictions, leaving cities around the country significantly less than well protected. (Cohen, 2019)

The need for states and communities to be prepared to respond to cyber incidents is not something that was discovered in the last few years. Efforts have been underway to help states and local jurisdictions for almost two decades. One method used to make state and local leaders aware of cyber issues and how the loss of a cyber infrastructure could impact their jurisdictions was the creation and delivery of a number of cybersecurity exercise conducted between 2002 and 2008 by the Center for Infrastructure Assurance and Security (CIAS).

STATE AND COMMUNITY CYBERSECURITY EXERCISES

The first community cybersecurity exercise was conducted in San Antonio, TX in 2002. Called *Dark Screen*, the event was a tabletop exercise involving over 200 individuals from around the community representing several different sectors. The exercise was designed to bring the community together to learn how a cyber-attack could impact multiple parts of the community and that the best way to address such an attack was a cooperative whole-community approach. An important aspect of the design of the event was that it was not aimed at Information Technology (IT) or cybersecurity professionals but rather at the community leadership both public and private. The event was sector-based with each table representing a different sector such as the various utilities, city government, industry, media, federal and state agencies, and the military. San Antonio has a large military presence and of importance to this exercise was the fact that the Air Force's computer security office is located in San Antonio. One goal was to demonstrate how a cyber-attack on the city could impact the ability of the various military installations to accomplish their missions. The success of this directly led to follow-on funding from the Department of Defense (DoD) to conduct additional, similar exercises in other cities.

A major objective of the *Dark Screen* exercise was to have the community view the response to a cyber event from a whole-community perspective as opposed to a sector or individual organization perspective. How does an attack on one sector, for example, impact other sectors and how can the community respond to such an attack? Facilitators at each table guided the discussions at their table to focus on this whole-community approach and how each table, representing a specific sector, could work with the other sectors to respond to a cyber-attack. The initial exercise was followed by a period of time to allow the various organizations to make adjustments to their programs. This was then followed by a second exercise, this time a combination of a functional exercise and a tabletop. During this second exercise, events were simulated or actually conducted with observers watching to see how individuals responded. The leadership was again involved in a tabletop exercise with inputs from their organizations being provided. The second exercise was conducted partly over several days so that some events occurred in advance to simulate how reconnaissance activities might precede an actual attack and to test the community's ability and preparedness to share relevant cyber event information across sectors.

The final report from the *Dark Screen* exercise highlighted a number of issues with a major focus on the need for the community to be sharing information before and during a cyber event, especially because of the interdependencies between sectors. Specific findings included the following:

- Overall, there was a low level of awareness regarding information infrastructure interdependencies and vulnerabilities. The participants displayed little understanding of interdependencies between their organization and other organizations. The participants were also, for the most part, unaware of the vulnerabilities and capabilities of other organizations and how those might affect them.

- There was no process or mechanism to coordinate interorganizational responses to a cyber security incident. Most participants assumed that their organization's security procedures would be adequate for preventing, detecting and responding to cyber incidents. As a result of the tabletop exercise, however, they realized their assumption had been based on viewing their organization as a stand-alone entity. It did not take into account the interrelated and interdependent nature of the information infrastructure.

- The communications channels for disseminating information before and during a cyber security incident were ill defined. Although some participants were part of small, informal information exchange networks, these networks were based on personal relationships. There was a lack of understanding concerning what capabilities and information each organization had access to and how to share it. After the exercise, one participant summed up the general feeling: "Exchanging business cards before an event occurs is much better than exchanging them during one." (Goles, 2005)

Following the Dark Screen exercise in San Antonio, a similar exercise was conducted in Corpus Christi, TX to determine whether the format and type of event could be utilized in other communities of varying size. The second exercise was also successful resulting in similar findings for the community. The next step was a series of exercises, funded by the DoD, in communities in which there was a significant DoD presence. Tabletop exercises patterned after the Dark Screen exercise were conducted in five cities around the country.

Each one was considered a success by the participants who learned how the community could be affected by a cyber-attack and how such an attack could adversely affect the ability of the military installation in the community to conduct its designated mission. Having each be a success was not difficult as the first time anybody participates in a cybersecurity exercise, they are going to learn something and come away with a better understanding of the reliance on the various critical infrastructures by the community.

Following the series of DoD exercises, the CIAS did an analysis of the exercise program it had been implementing, made some modifications, and then received funding from the Department of Homeland Security to (DHS) continue to conduct exercises across the country. Under DHS guidance, a series of exercises were conducted in DHS selected states with each chosen state participating in a set of three exercises – four exercises in two communities (two in each) in the state and a state exercise with concurrent exercises in the communities to examine the state's ability to address a major cyber event that impacted more than one community. Seven states were selected to participate in the program with similar results to the exercises conducted previously with DoD funding. With similar results being seen in the states and communities where the exercises were conducted, the CIAS was able to develop guidance that can be used by states and communities to develop viable and sustainable cybersecurity programs.

LESSONS LEARNED: THE COMMUNITY CYBER SECURITY MATURITY MODEL

The community cybersecurity exercises were a success with participants leaving the events with a better understanding of the way a cyber event could impact a community or state. A number of participating community and state leaders realized for the first time how dependent they were on key cyber infrastructures and how the loss of them could have a severe impact on their state or community. They realized that steps were needed in order to better protect their cyber assets. Unfortunately, as the CIAS personnel who conducted the exercises soon learned, there was a significant issue that was not being addressed. While the leaders realized that they needed to do something to establish cybersecurity programs to protect their state and communities, the problem was in understanding what exactly needed to be done and what steps needed to be taken before others should be attempted? There were plenty of vendors willing to sell products and services, but what was really needed, and in what order should items or services be procured? Without an understanding of what they should be doing the exercises only served to raise the level of awareness but didn't lead to the key concrete actions required to secure states and communities.

After realizing this major issue with the exercise program, the CIAS took steps to develop guidance that could be used by states and communities in developing their cybersecurity programs. Based on its extensive experience working with states and communities, the CIAS developed the Community Cyber Security Maturity Model (CCSMM) to address the issue. Frequently when using the term community in relationship to cybersecurity issues, it is assumed to mean a group of individuals with a common interest or that share a common characteristic. In the case of the CCSMM the term community is used to refer to a group of individuals that live in the same area – such as a city or town. The model is designed to provide three things:

1. **A Yardstick:** The model allows states, communities, and organizations to determine where they are in the maturity of their cybersecurity programs.
2. **A Roadmap:** So that these same entities will know what they need to do in order to improve their programs and become more secure, the model describes what needs to be done and provides order to the development of a cybersecurity program. A key aspect of this is the recognition that initial efforts may have to be accomplished with little or no budget as entities often had not previously planned for any cybersecurity products or services.
3. **A Common Point of Reference:** Individuals from different parts of the country need a common lexicon that will help facilitate sharing of ideas. Without the common point of reference, cybersecurity programs could be developed in such drastically different ways that talking to an official in another community might not help but might actually confuse an individual just starting their own program.

The CCSMM is a large model with many components. What it does, in addition to the three goals already mentioned, is it incorporates and addresses elements from other frameworks and models so individuals can plan a way to implement them as well. For example, much has been written in the last few years about the National Institute of Standards and Technology's (NIST) Cyber Security Framework (CSF). (NIST, 2018) The CSF contains a tremendous amount of very useful information but for organizations that have no real understanding of cybersecurity to begin with, trying to incorporate the CSF can be a frustrating endeavor. The CCSMM leads organizations, communities, and states through a process where they can address the various parts of the CSF in an organized manner that will make sense to them and that they will find less frustrating. This is also true of other current popular topics in cybersecurity such as Information Sharing and the creation of Information Sharing and Analysis Organizations (ISAO). Many individuals and organizations wonder whether they should establish an ISAO or join an existing one but if they are not ready for it, they will not see the benefits of participating in an ISAO that was available to them. This is again another example of where the CCSMM will help establish a logical roadmap for participating in information sharing efforts. Without a viable cybersecurity program, participating in an ISAO and information sharing efforts will have limited impact and will likely die after a brief period of interest. A cybersecurity program is needed in order to sustain and provide a focus for the information sharing efforts of an organization, community, or state. The CCSMM provides the structure from which to build a cybersecurity program and identifies places where the appropriate parts of the CSF can and should be implemented. It should be mentioned, however, that interest in information sharing and in establishing an ISAO can be used as a catalyst to begin generating a program for an organization, community or state. The two easily go together.

SUMMARY

States and communities have increasingly become targets of cybersecurity attacks. Unfortunately, for the vast majority of States and Communities (as well as Tribes and Territories – collectively referred to as SLTTs) and in many instances organizations, a working cybersecurity program is nonexistent. The current state of affairs within communities and states has been shown both to be lacking in cybersecurity preparedness. This is attested to through both the presence of numerous articles in the media describing successful cyber-attacks on states and communities as well as assessments by the states that showed how well prepared, they are. Efforts at the national level have simply not focused enough on states and communities but have up to this point concentrated on the defense of the federal government and the various critical infrastructures. While the Cybersecurity and Infrastructure Security Agency (CISA) within DHS has established some resources to aid SLTTs, the sheer number of communities, counties, and states means that the vast majority will receive little support. Additionally, little to no guidance is provided on how to establish a "whole-community" approach to cybersecurity yet this is the best way to reach the majority of the country who are not part of a government entity or part of one of the critical infrastructures.

A series of cybersecurity exercises, starting with the Dark Screen exercise in San Antonio, TX, were conducted around the nation and resulted in lessons on what is needed in SLTTs. This then led to the development of the Community Cyber Security Maturity Model (CCSMM). This model is designed to provide

1. **A Yardstick,**
2. **A Roadmap,** and
3. **A Common Point of Reference**

for SLTTs trying to develop their own cybersecurity program. The model also incorporates other guidance, especially the NIST Cyber Security Framework, and shows how and when various elements should be added to a program.

The rest of this book will describe the various parts of the CCSMM in detail and what they entail. It offers sufficient detail for security professionals in SLTTs or organizations to utilize the CCSMM to develop a plan for implementing their own cybersecurity program. It should be noted up front, however, that individual SLTTs and organizations are different and two organizations implementing the CCSMM may very well create very different programs. This book and the CCSMM will generally tell the reader WHAT needs to be accomplished but specifics on HOW to implement individual components will be left to cybersecurity professionals to tailor the model and the program to the goals, objectives, and environment of their own organization or SLTT.

REFERENCES

Cohen, N. (2019). *Cyber incident response and resiliency in cities.* Retrieved February 26, 2020, from https://d1y8sb8igg2f8e.cloudfront.net/documents/Cyber_Incident_Response_and_Resiliency_in_Cities_2019-02-21.pdf

Cohen, N., & Nussbaum, B. (2018). *Cybersecurity for the states: Lessons from across America.* Retrieved from https://d1y8sb8igg2f8e.cloudfront.net/documents/Cybersecurity_for_the_States_Lessons_from_Across_America_FINAL_3.pdf

Collier, K. (2019). *Crippling ransomware attacks targeting US cities on the rise*. Retrieved from CNN website: https://www.cnn.com/2019/05/10/politics/ransomware-attacks-us-cities/index.html

Critical infrastructures sectors. (n.d.). Retrieved from US Department of Homeland Security CISA Cyber + Infrastructure website: https://www.dhs.gov/cisa/critical-infrastructure-sectors

Federal Register. (Ed.). (2013). *Executive Order 13636 - Improving critical infrastructure cybersecurity*. Retrieved from Govinfo.gov website: https://www.govinfo.gov/content/pkg/FR-2013-02-19/pdf/2013-03915.pdf

Goles, T., White, G., & Dietrich, G. (2005). Dark Screen: An Exercise in Cyber Security. *MIS Quarterly Executive*, *4*(2).

Government facilities sector. (n.d.). Retrieved from US Department of Homeland Security CISA Cyber + Infrastructure website: https://www.dhs.gov/cisa/government-facilities-sector

Levin, S. (2019). *'All we know is money!': US cities struggle to fight hackers*. Retrieved from The Guardian website: https://www.theguardian.com/cities/2019/jun/03/ransomware-attacks-hackers-cities-baltimore

NIST, National Institute of Standards and Technology. (2018). *Framework for improving critical infrastructure cybersecurity* (Version 1.1). Retrieved from https://nvlpubs.nist.gov/nistpubs/CSWP/NIST.CSWP.04162018.pdf

SLTT. (n.d.). *Resources for state, local, tribal, and territorial (SLTT) governments*. Retrieved from US Department of Homeland Security CISA Cyber + Infrastructure website: https://www.us-cert.gov/resources/sltt

Statista. (n.d.). *Number of cities, towns and villages (incorporated places) in the United States in 2018, by population size*. Retrieved from Statista website: https://www.statista.com/statistics/241695/number-of-us-cities-towns-villages-by-population-size/

The White House. (1998). *Presidential decision directive/NSC-63*. Retrieved from https://fas.org/irp/offdocs/pdd/pdd-63.htm

The White House. (2015). *Executive order - promoting private sector cybersecurity information sharing*. Retrieved from The White House President Barack Obama website: https://www.dhs.gov/sites/default/files/publications/2015-03714.pdf

U.S. Department of Homeland Security (DHS). (2015). *Government Facilities Sector-Specific Plan*. Retrieved from https://www.dhs.gov/sites/default/files/publications/nipp-ssp-government-facilities-2015-508.pdf

U.S. Department of Homeland Security (DHS). (2018). *2018 National Preparedness Report*. Retrieved from https://www.fema.gov/media-library-data/1541781185823-2ae55a276f604e04b68e2748adc95c68/2018NPRRprt20181108v508.pdf

U.S. Department of Homeland Security (DHS). (2018). *U.S. department of homeland security cybersecurity strategy*. Retrieved from https://www.dhs.gov/sites/default/files/publications/DHS-Cybersecurity-Strategy_1.pdf

Chapter 1
The Community Cybersecurity Maturity Model (CCSMM)

ABSTRACT

Lessons learned from the community cyber security exercises showed common threads each community needed to focus on in order to improve the community's cyber security posture. These similarities were grouped into four areas of improvement called dimensions. The dimensions are awareness, information sharing, policies, and planning. The methods in which communities can implement improvement are called implementation mechanisms. These mechanisms are common approaches used every day such as establishing metrics, implementing technologies, creating processes and procedures, and conducting training and assessments.

INTRODUCTION

Threats to communities have been traditionally thought of in terms of natural disasters. There have been a number of U.S. cities that have been severely damaged or completely destroyed by natural disaster. Galveston, Texas was hit by a category 4 hurricane in 1900, "destroying nearly 4000 homes, all bridges to the mainland, telegraph lines, most ships in the wharf and even rail lines as far as 6 miles inland" (Crezo, 2012). In 1906, San Francisco, California experienced an earthquake followed by fires. "The initial tremors destroyed the city's water mains, leaving firefighters with no means of combating the growing blaze, which burned for several days and consumed

DOI: 10.4018/978-1-7998-4471-6.ch001

much of the city" (History.com, 2018). The St. Louis Tornado Disaster in 1927, "killed 79 people and caused $1.8 billion dollars in damage (adjusted)" (Crezo, 2012). More recent disasters that should be noted here are Hurricane Katrina in 2005 that flooded 80% of New Orleans after the levees failed, and Superstorm Sandy affecting New Jersey and New York in 2012. Sandy knocked out subway service in New York City and destroyed multi-million-dollar homes at the Jersey Shore. (Harrington, 2018).

These early natural disasters led to the creation of the Federal Emergency Management Agency (FEMA) in 1979. "The Federal Emergency Management Agency coordinates the federal government's role in preparing for, preventing, mitigating the effects of, responding to, and recovering from all domestic disasters, whether natural or man-made, including acts of terror" (Fema.gov).

Since FEMA's inception, it has assumed a variety of roles, but it continues to maintain its original mission and over the years has produced many guides to assist communities to prepare for disasters. In 2012, FEMA published a guide called "Threat and Hazard Identification and Risk Assessment Guide: Comprehensive Preparedness Guide (CPG) 201, First Edition". In this guide a table of threats and hazards was provided for jurisdictions to identify the risks most likely to impact their community. Identifying the threats will assist the community to focus preparedness efforts and resources. The risks are categorized into three specific areas:

- Natural – resulting from acts of nature
- Technological – involves accidents or the failures of systems and structures
- Human-caused – caused by the intentional actions of an adversary

Notice in Figure 1, the list of threats has expanded beyond natural disasters. This table represents the recognition that communities potentially face many threats that once were not considered. Cyber incidents are also listed in this table under the human-caused threats. This is significant because it shows the federal government has recognized cyber incidents as a threat a community should prepare for and build capabilities to prevent, protect, mitigate, respond to and recover from.

In May of 2018, the 3rd Edition of the Comprehensive Preparedness Guide (CPG) 201 was published, and the list of example threats expanded and changed the cyber references to "cyber-attack against data" and "cyber-attack against infrastructure" as seen in Table 2. These examples suggest the recognition

Figure 1.

Natural	Technological	Human-caused
Resulting from acts of nature	Involves accidents or the failures of systems and structures	Caused by the intentional actions of an adversary
<ul><li>Avalanche</li><li>Disease outbreak</li><li>Drought</li><li>Earthquake</li><li>Epidemic</li><li>Flood</li><li>Hurricane</li><li>Landslide</li><li>Tornado</li><li>Tsunami</li><li>Volcanic eruption</li><li>Wildfire</li><li>Winter storm</li></ul>	<ul><li>Airplane crash</li><li>Dam/levee failure</li><li>Hazardous materials release</li><li>Power failure</li><li>Radiological release</li><li>Train derailment</li><li>Urban conflagration</li></ul>	<ul><li>Civil disturbance</li><li>Cyber incidents</li><li>Sabotage</li><li>School violence</li><li>Terrorist acts</li></ul>

of the cyber threat to a community can potentially impact systems that store data and any systems that are used to support the infrastructure.

Once a community has identified the threats and hazards it faces, preparedness efforts can be planned, processes and procedures can be developed and implemented, and capabilities the community plans to achieve to manage

Figure 2.

Natural	Technological	Human-caused
Avalanche	Dam failure	Active shooter incident
Drought	Hazardous materials release	Armed assault
Earthquake	Industrial accident	Biological attack
Epidemic	Levee failure	Chemical attack
Flood	Mine accident	Cyber-attack against data
Hurricane/Typhoon	Pipeline explosion	Cyber-attack against infrastructure
Space weather	Radiological release	Explosives attack
Tornado	Train derailment	Improvised nuclear attack
Tsunami	Transportation accident	Nuclear terrorism attack
Volcanic eruption	Urban conflagration	Radiological attack
Winter storm	Utility disruption	

the threats can be put in place. Exercises are then used to test the plans to see how well they work and are also used to assess existing capabilities needed to respond to an incident. There are different types of exercises that can be used to assess the community plans, processes, and capabilities. They are:

- **Walkthroughs, Workshops, or Orientation Seminars:** Used to provide information regarding the response, continuity, communications plans and roles and responsibilities.
- **Tabletop Exercises**: Facilitated discussion used to describe roles and response capabilities through scenarios provided.
- **Functional Exercises**: Used to simulate an emergency situation allowing personnel to perform their duties. This type of exercise tests capabilities of the team, processes and shows the availability of resources needed.
- **Full-scale Exercises**: Takes place on location using personnel and equipment that would be needed to respond to an incident, and local businesses often participate. This type of exercise is the most realistic ("Exercises," n.d.).

Exercises help the community to recognize weaknesses they may have in terms of capability to address an incident, resources that may be needed and availability of that resource and the procedures that may be missing or should be changed before an incident occurs.

This chapter describes the creation of the Community Cyber Security Maturity Model (CCSMM). The model was designed and created as a result of the lessons learned from many community and state cybersecurity tabletop exercises that were conducted from 2002 through 2008. Tabletop exercises were used because this method provides a platform to achieve maximum participation and low-cost execution. The use of tabletop exercises allows the participants to gain an awareness of the cyber threat, its potential impacts on the community, and allows the participants to recognize the gaps the community may have in their preparedness. The intent of the CCSMM is to provide a framework that can be used to develop a cybersecurity program for a community.

BACKGROUND

The Center for Infrastructure Assurance and Security (CIAS), a cybersecurity research center, at the University of Texas at San Antonio (UTSA) was established in 2001. During this time, there was very little, if any, cybersecurity research nor outreach initiatives being conducted at the university. The CIAS was the first center established to address cybersecurity initiatives. Through the CIAS, cybersecurity research was encouraged in the College of Computer Science, College of Business, and the College of Engineering. The first cybersecurity community outreach initiative accomplished by the CIAS was a tabletop exercise known as Darkscreen.

The Darkscreen tabletop exercise was the initial community cybersecurity exercise led by the CIAS. The exercise was the first of its kind, that we know of, and was conducted in San Antonio, Texas in fall of 2002. The exercise scenario focused on fairly simple cybersecurity events. There were no physical attack events as part of this exercise. This is a significant point. The CIAS researchers believed that developing a cybersecurity exercise that excluded physical events would force the participants to focus on how they would handle a cybersecurity event. The idea was that if physical was integrated into an exercise before participants were comfortable with cybersecurity events, they would focus all their attention on the event that was understood, and they knew how to respond to. By developing an exercise that only contained cyber events, the participants would be able to focus their efforts on each cyber incident and have facilitated discussions about what each incident could potentially do to the organization, what response might be appropriate, and when to share information about a cyber incident.

There were a number of considerations that needed to be addressed in the design of this first exercise. First, the exercise needed to show participants that cybersecurity preparedness includes understanding what is needed before the incident occurred, during the incident and after the incident. This drove the development of three modules. The first module was the pre-event scenario, the second module focused on the cyber event and the third module contained post event and wrap-up events. The next consideration in the design of the exercise centered around how to organize the scenarios. The exercise needed to allow participants in the same or similar organizations to discuss how a cyber incident could impact their organization and sector. This led to the development of the exercise scenarios to be organized by sector. Each sector was provided with an exercise guide that contained unique cybersecurity injects. The purpose for this was to allow each sector to work through cyber incidents that were realistic for their sector. Conversations could then be sector specific which was important in discussing capabilities and response processes that existed in the sector and identifying policy, capabilities and resources that did not exist. Logistically, each sector that participated in the event had a designated table, shown in Figure 3, where the sector participants were grouped together allowing them to discuss their actions.

Figure 3.

The table arrangements were as follows:

Table 1: City of San Antonio – Emergency Operations Center
Table 2: City of San Antonio – Information Technology
Table 3: City of San Antonio – Other Agencies
Table 4: Bexar County – Emergency Operations Center
Table 5: Bexar County – Other Organizations
Table 6: Air Intelligence Agency

Table 7: San Antonio Military Bases
Table 8: Texas State (Texas Guard, Department of Information Resources, Attorney General's office)
Table 9: Federal Agencies
Table 10: Industry
Table 11: Media
Table 12: Critical Infrastructures

Each sector table had a designated reporter to capture the key points that came from the discussions that occurred from the injects. The content captured was then synthesized and used in a final report. Each sector table also had a facilitator to explain concepts, provide additional information when requested, and guide the conversations, as needed, to ensure the goals of the overall exercise were met. The facilitator's job also included keeping the participant discussions on topic and within the time period allotted for each inject.

The final report summarized the findings from each sector and then provided recommendations for improvement. There were many lessons learned that were taken from this exercise and implemented into the community exercises that were conducted afterward.

COMMUNITY CYBER SECURITY EXERCISES

Implementing cybersecurity practices and capabilities within an organization can be a difficult task, especially when limited resources are available. State and local organizations have these difficulties as well, but the significant difference is what a cyber incident can impact. An organization must protect their assets, intellectual property, trade secrets and data from an actor who may want to steal, misuse, delete or deny the organization use of their data and assets. A state, jurisdiction, county, or other community must protect data, assets and services for not only the agencies, but for the citizens who live in those communities. The worst-case scenario for an organization that faces a cyber-attack may be the organization cannot recover and goes out of business. The worst-case scenario for a community is the loss of civilian safety or loss of life. This is a strong statement and to date there has not been a cybersecurity incident that has directly caused death or injury to citizens. The idea here, is to recognize that an organization and community may have different priorities but both experience cyber incidents and should be prepared to address them. Many aspects of cybersecurity practices are similar at the organizational level, communities at the state and local levels will have many cybersecurity considerations that have potentially never been considered. Community Cyber Security Exercises can increase awareness of cyber incidents and attacks that could impact the business operations and emergency services a community provides.

Community Cyber Security Exercises, as mentioned in chapter one, were conducted across the nation starting in 2002. The exercises were designed to present various cybersecurity scenarios that would assist a community, and especially the leadership and key stakeholders of the community, to recognize what a cyber incident was and to understand the potential impacts a cyber incident could have on the entire community. It was believed that once an overall awareness was shared this would allow the community to implement cybersecurity practices that would improve their cybersecurity posture and enable them to address the cybersecurity gaps and insufficiencies they had regarding their cyber capabilities.

The challenge in the early 2000's, revolved around the idea that cyber was considered a technical concern and not really something an organization, community or state leader would need to focus on. That challenge still exists today, but it is not as significant as it was then. The problem to solve was to identify a way to introduce the leadership into an environment where they could learn about the cyber landscape and the issues they faced. Cybersecurity training, at that time, was not effective because the leadership would send their technical talent to the training rather than go themselves. Another issue was there was very little cybersecurity awareness training specifically designed for executives and decision makers. Another obstacle to overcome was the amount of time a leader could secure on their calendar. The CIAS needed to find a way to deliver compelling content in a very short amount of time. Ultimately, conducting a cybersecurity exercise was the approach taken. Jurisdictions and states have historically used exercises to find gaps in their overall preparedness and incident response capabilities. A tabletop exercise could be designed to be executed in a few hours, it could deliver meaningful real-world scenarios, and would have high visibility with leaders in the community. So, with these considerations in mind, the first cybersecurity exercise specifically designed for communities was created and named "Darkscreen" and later these exercises became known as Community Cyber Security Exercises.

The exercises were always successful, primarily because cyber concepts were so new, and participants of the exercises always learned something. At the end of the exercise, the participants understood how services such as critical infrastructures and emergency services could be delayed and or disrupted which could drastically impact the whole community. They also understood the need to develop a cybersecurity program that would cultivate partnerships among various stakeholders across the community and integrate cybersecurity processes into their preparedness and response capabilities. Once the exercise was completed, the CIAS researchers provided the community with an after-action report (AAR). The report listed the organizations that attended the exercise, summarized the objectives and scenarios presented, and included a list of all the events used in the exercise. The AAR then provided the community with observations, an analysis and recommendations associated with each of the capability-based objectives. As an example, each of the Community Cyber Security Exercises focused on a planning capability. The following example is taken from an actual AAR. The name of the community and state have been excluded.

CAPABILITY 1: PLANNING

Capability Summary: *This capability is the foundation on which all other capabilities are developed and enhanced. Specifically, all hazards planning is a mechanism to:*

- *Identify hazards and evaluate their impacts*
- *Prioritize emergency preparedness efforts based on hazard identification and evaluation*
- *Identify functions performed and describe how those functions are integrated*
- *Describe how emergencies are managed across all hazards and all functions*
- *Describe a resource allocation and prioritization system*
- *Integrate plans within the jurisdiction, among jurisdictions, and between levels of government.*

No specific event was designed to address this capability as such. Instead, the general tone of all events was such that the importance of this capability was emphasized regularly. In particular, the integration of the detection and response functions across city/county/state entities was a major thread that ran throughout the exercise events.

Observation 1.1: This is an area for improvement. Though the State has already taken steps to establish a state office to address cyber security issues, this is needed at the community-level as was seen during the community exercise that was conducted.

Analysis: It is imperative that if a community is going to establish a viable cyber security program, that a state program should exist as well. Communities need a plan for how to implement cyber security programs and it is important at the state level that individual community programs are somewhat consistent or are at least compatible with what the state has set up.

Recommendation: State Involvement: The state should (potentially utilizing the cyber security group approved by the state legislature) lead the effort to establish guidelines for communities to develop their cyber security programs. A potential help in this regard is the use of the Community Cyber Security Maturity Model which can help provide a roadmap for the types of training and activities that the state should be promoting.

Observation 1.2: This is an area for improvement. A common theme among the tables at the exercise was the realization that there was either a lack of policies covering cyber incidents or that the policies that were present were either not well publicized or were inadequate.

Analysis: The bedrock of a viable security program is the collection of policies that the technology and the processes and procedures rest upon. These policies are utilized to develop the procedures that individuals are to follow in the event of an incident. While participants had ideas on what to do to respond to various incidents that were portrayed in the exercise, it was frequently the case that no established procedures were in place to address the event. When there was a procedure, participants were often unsure of the procedure or did not know that it existed at all.

Recommendations: Development of policies for handling cyber incidents: There are three recommendations in this area. One is specific to an event used within the exercise. The other two are more generalized recommendations that cut across several of the events.

1. Annex to existing response plans: A cyber security annex should be developed to go along with existing emergency management/civil defense response plans to cover both the state and community levels. At a minimum the documents should include reporting procedures for suspected cyber security relevant events. This includes not just actual incidents (e.g. intrusions, attempted intrusions, denial of service attacks, etc.) but events that might be the precursor to actual attacks. The annex

should also include the processes that will be followed when a security relevant event is reported and should outline the interface between the community, State, and Federal agencies (to include the military installations within the community) in the event of a cyber incident.

2. Process to follow in the event of an email bomb threat: A simple policy that was found to be almost universally lacking, and which is a rather simple one to start with which could then serve as an example for other cyber security policies, is a policy for employees to follow should they receive an email bomb threat. It is recommended that city government develop a policy for this type of incident and then share it, utilizing the information sharing mechanisms being developed for the community, with other organizations within the community.

3. Policy life cycle: As policies are developed, it is recommended that they include an identified review cycle to ensure the continued applicability and relevancy of the policy. It should be noted that policies have a life cycle, just as hardware and software does. In an environment which changes as fast as computer systems and networks, and with the constant revelation of new vulnerabilities and threats, it is imperative that policies are reviewed on a regular basis.

After some time had passed, the CIAS researchers went back to each community to find out exactly what they had implemented to improve their cybersecurity posture. What was discovered was that, while the community leaders still knew cyber was something that they needed to be concerned with, after a year they had almost universally not done anything to improve their cyber security posture. The issue appeared to be that although the leadership understood something needed to be done, the question was what they should start with. There were and still are numerous products and services available but which, if any, should be the first thing to purchase. Additionally, where would they obtain the money to pay for the service or product since budgets had already been established which did not include funds for such a purchase? These were the issues the leadership faced, in essence, where should they begin? This led to the creation of the Community Cyber Security Maturity Model.

THE DEVELOPMENT OF THE CCSMM

The CIAS researchers had discussion with some of the communities searching for explanations as to why none of the communities had been able to achieve the recommendations left with the community to improve their cybersecurity practices. They found that each of the communities:

- understood that a cyber event could impact the business operations of the community
- recognized that a cybersecurity incident could have cascading events that could impact a much larger geographic area
- understood that a cyber-attack could impact or redirect emergency response activities
- understood that public and private partnerships needed to be established for richer situational awareness and for incident response capabilities
- understood a cyber security program needed to be put in place

Even though the communities understood all of these things, they had not implemented controls that would minimize the impact of a cyber-attack. There were vendors who were willing to provide services and technology to address some cyber security issues, but the communities didn't know what to purchase. Ultimately, the community leaders didn't know how to begin building and implementing a program community-wide to address the cyber threat. The biggest questions from these communities were:

- What do we need first?
- What steps should be taken?
- Who should be involved?
- Where do we get the money for this?

The researchers quickly realized that what was lacking was a coordinated plan to help communities (and by extension, states and organizations) get started on developing a viable and sustainable cybersecurity program.

The Community Cyber Security Maturity Model (CCSMM) was developed to be the coordinated plan that would provide communities or local jurisdictions with a framework to identify what is needed to build a cyber security program focused on "whole community" preparedness and response at the local level addressing a cyber incident or attack. Essentially, the CCSMM is a guide that allows communities to establish a cybersecurity baseline at the local level. Once established, the baseline can then be used to identify cyber-attacks that impact an organization, an entire sector, or cross-sector organizations and agencies in a specific geographic area. It can also be used to communicate with other individuals and communities about capabilities and improvement. The strategies identified in the framework go beyond protecting systems and networks within local government agencies. The CCSMM can assist communities to identify what needs to be done in building a viable and sustainable cyber security program, what is needed to prepare to detect a cyber-attack, develop plans to respond during an attack, and determine what to do after an attack has occurred. The remainder of this chapter will describe and explain the various aspects of the Community Cyber Security Maturity Model.

THE DIMENSIONS

The model addresses specific areas of improvement that a community needs to consider when faced with a cyber threat. These areas were identified after analyzing the after-action reports from each of the community exercises. The result of the analysis was there were many similarities in the recommendations identified in each of the reports and ultimately, they could be grouped into four specific areas. The four areas are awareness, information sharing, policies and planning. These areas of improvement are called dimensions. The term dimension was selected for its definition of "an aspect or feature of a situation, problem, or thing" ("Dictionary," n.d.). While these dimensions will focus on specific areas of improvement, they are essentially intertwined, and there will be many instances where they will overlap.

AWARENESS

The awareness dimension was selected because several of the recommendations from the exercises were provided to ensure members of the community understood the overall cyber threats they face. The following are examples of several of the recommendations that fell into the awareness category:

Note that one of the recommendations above suggests ensuring media representatives are aware of cyber issues. This is deliberately recommended primarily because media can assist with public awareness and provide a positive reinforcement of concepts. However, if media are not on the same

Table 1. Recommendations

Find or develop, then implement and share cyber security training and awareness programs
All personnel who have access to a computer system and network should receive basic security training on topics such as password security, phishing and social engineering, and malware. Low- or no-cost training options should be explored.
Identify community leaders who should be aware of cyber issues. Some possibilities may include the city manager, mayor, police, fire, medical, financial, business leaders, critical infrastructure providers, education, and media representatives
Explore methods of improving community leaders' awareness of cyber issues, such as presentations by cyber security organizations, awareness courses, cyber security exercises, leadership meetings with cyber security discussion topics, and the creation of a cyber security council
Research and implement low- or no-cost awareness programs both within and across organizations such as posting flyers, issuing email reminders, holding lunch seminars, and recognition or awards programs

page as the community leadership, reported information regarding cyber incidents can have a negative effect by causing confusion.

Awareness is "the quality or state of being aware: knowledge and understanding that something is happening or exists" (Merriam-Webster, 2019). Through working with the communities, it was found that most people understand that cyber threats exist, however not as many understand the extent of the threat, the current attack trends, how a cyber incident can impact a community, what the vulnerabilities are that should be addressed, and what the cascading effects may be if a community was under a cyber-attack. The cascading impacts, mentioned, are the chain of events that are caused by the initial attack and often have unforeseen consequences with adverse effects. The awareness dimension was created to assess the cybersecurity awareness levels of various groups of the community. Fundamental questions were developed to assess the awareness levels about cyber security issues within the community.

The fundamental questions are:

- Is the leadership in your community aware of current cyber security trends?
- If a critical service or resource is disabled from a cyber-attack throughout the community, is leadership aware of what the potential cascading effects might be?
- How is this awareness level maintained?
- What programs exist to increase cyber awareness throughout the community (for individuals, organizations, and sectors)?

These questions focus, first, on the awareness levels of the leadership. This was done intentionally because it was found, working in the communities, that if the leaders of the community understood the impact of a cyber incident and had a solid understanding of the cyber threat there was a much better chance that they would become invested in the overall cybersecurity improvement program. Therefore, key elements of a successful awareness program are to introduce leaders of the cyber trends, attacks and impacts and then to find a way to maintain their awareness of current cybersecurity issues. Once the leadership, as a group, has developed an awareness of the cyber threat then additional groups in the community should be addressed.

INFORMATION SHARING

The information sharing dimension was selected because there was often confusion, conflicting opinions, or it was unknown what someone should do with information on a cyber incident and where the information should be reported. In addition, it was observed that if one sector had shared information with another then the second sector might have been able to prevent the incident from occurring. Recommendations around sharing information on a cyber incident included the following:

The information sharing dimension is used to address what organizations should do with cyber-related information both internally and externally. If an organization is willing to share certain types of cyber-related information, who specifically will they share it with both inside and outside of their organization, and in what time frame should they share it? A related, and equally important question is how the information will be shared. This, in particular, is one aspect of this dimension that will change significantly as the organization matures in their security processes.

The dynamic of sharing information about cyber incidents or attacks is a difficult one. There is a hesitancy to share cyber-related information because there is a fear that sharing information might harm the organization. With this in mind, how do organizations overcome these challenges? If everyone shared all information regarding their cyber infrastructures, would this generate an information overload situation where organizations have more information than can be effectively managed? How will organizations separate the meaningful information that is actionable from the disparate and fragmented information that may not be useful to them in the current context?

Table 2. Recommendations

Develop a coordinated community information-sharing initiative or working group, utilizing already established programs and organizations wherever possible, to examine interdependencies and develop or improve information sharing processes
Create contact lists to use in the event that a cyber incident occurs, and be sure to update them regularly
Identify local cyber security experts and create a cyber incident response team for the community and encourage organizations within the community to establish their own, if they haven't already
Consider cooperative recurrent training programs across the community to establish relationships across sectors while also providing new and updated information throughout the community
Establish clear thresholds for when and how to share information about cyber security incidents based on what is normal for the organization or community
Develop processes to accomplish bidirectional information sharing that effectively accommodate receiving information as well as transmitting it, and ensure that these processes take into account external reporting requirements and laws
Expand connections to neighboring communities to facilitate information sharing
Coordinate breakfasts, luncheons, and/or conferences for community members with discussion topics related to cyber security
Encourage community members to join, and, if they don't already exist, establish local chapters of security organizations such as ISSA, ISACA, ASIS and InfraGard.
Community organizations should determine the value of information used by their organization and prioritize that information based on that analysis.

Fundamental questions to assess the level of information sharing in a community include:

- What mechanisms are in place within the community to share information about cyber-related security events?
- What mechanisms are in place to do an analysis of the cyber security information? Is there a mechanism to validate or verify the information?
- What triage and analysis are performed between cyber and physical security information that can create meaningful information?
- What distribution methods are in place and who should receive cyber-related information?

POLICY

Policies establish, at a high-level, the guidelines the community would like implemented. They establish expectations and limitations. The selection of the policy dimension was intended to ensure the cybersecurity principles needed would be reflected. It was found that if policies did not specifically focus on cybersecurity, the policy was not executed by various people consistently, nor were they interpreted by different people the same way. Recommendations surrounding policy implementation included the following:

Table 3. Recommendations

Review and/or create policies to address specific cyber events that might be experienced
Work with the state to develop state processes, procedures, and guidelines for communities to address cyber security incidents
Specify policy life cycles to ensure the continued applicability and relevancy of the policy.
Review existing policies to identify barriers to cyber security goals and determine if the barriers are real or perceived, and if and how they can be worked around
Ensure that policies are simple and easy to understand to promote individual ownership of cyber security
Ensure that each policy is compliant with any and all applicable laws

This dimension addresses the need to integrate cyber elements into the policies or guiding principles and includes all guiding regulations, laws, rules, and documents that govern the daily operation of the community. The policies should reflect the cyber-related approaches a community intends to use during normal business operations, and before, during and after a cyber incident. Every policy must be looked at to see if cyber issues have been addressed specifically. For example, city government may have a policy to operate with secure and resilient business practices. The processes and procedures supporting this policy should be analyzed to ensure all new technologies used on city networks have been identified and incorporated. In addition, the city government may decide to add a minimum cyber security health standard for all vendors or partners who use the city network. Social media is a new cyber related tool used to provide information to the general public. These policies should be analyzed to ensure social media practices have been included. Additionally, other cyber-specific policies may need to be developed to cover cyber issues not addressed in other established policies?

The fundamental questions to assess cyber integration into community policies include:

- What policies are in place in various organizations within the community to address cyber security?
- Have community-wide policies been examined to see if they specifically address relevant cyber implications as applicable?

17

- Have supporting processes and procedures been examined to see if they specifically address cyber issues as appropriate?
- What testing/exercise/practice is conducted to evaluate the procedures and supporting policies that have been developed? Are they adequate?
- Who in the community should know about cyber additions to policies? Have they been trained?
- How often are policies updated to address current and emerging cyber threats?
- Is the time between policy updates sufficient to ensure new threats are addressed in a timely manner?

Evaluating policies throughout the community will be a progressive process. The organizations that should have their policies assessed first are the critical infrastructures and local government, including law enforcement. Next should be the largest organizations in the community. Eventually, over time all organizations to the smallest business should be included.

PLANNING

The planning dimension was selected to ensure cybersecurity elements are included in the plans the community develops and utilizes to address incidents that could adversely impact it. Communities have established plans to address many different hazards, however many did not include cyber incidents that could impact the operations of the community. The recommendations for planning included:

Table 4. Recommendations

Create an advisory group on cyber issues for the community
Involve key organizational stakeholders, such as executive-level management, legal departments, and communications groups, as early as possible in planning processes
Provide opportunities for community leadership and executives to obtain additional education and training on security issues and techniques
Create or continue exercise programs that address cyber and cyber/physical issues, vulnerabilities, and response options
Implement cyber security improvement plans, and integrate these into existing improvement plans
Utilize readily available templates for policies and procedures from free online sources such as the SANS Institute and National Institute of Standards and Technology
Research no/low-cost government and non-profit training resources, such as DHS, various universities, NIST, and the CIAS

The planning dimension is focused on the need to incorporate cyber into all continuity, emergency and disaster recovery plans addressing how to prepare, mitigate, respond to and recover from incidents. This dimension needs to identify how cyber can impact the whole community and identify the cascading effects a cyber incident may cause. Each plan should be analyzed to identify cyber resources and actions needed and include them in the overall strategy to achieve objectives. An example would be to ensure cyber incident response teams have been established to act in the event a cyber-attack on the community occurs. Plans can include Continuity of Operations Plans (COOP), Disaster Recovery Plans (DRP), Emergency Operation Plans (EOP), and so on.

The fundamental questions used to evaluate how cybersecurity has been incorporated into community plans include:

- To what extent is cyber considered in the community's disaster planning process?
- What incident response steps have been implemented and tested?
- Do plans include consideration of both cyber-only events as well as how cyber issues can impact other emergency situations?
- Is cyber considered in the community's disaster planning process?
- What incident response steps have been implemented?
- How is a cyber incident impacting the entire community detected?
- If a cyber incident impacted the community for an extended period of time, is there a plan on how to request assistance and with whom?
- Is there a community cyber incident team established in your community?
- Do plans include consideration of both cyber-only events as well as how cyber issues can impact other emergency situations?

THE IMPLEMENTATION MECHANISMS

Once the areas of improvement were determined, the next stage of development for the CCSMM was to identify how improvement would occur and what activities would be needed to improve in each dimension. Some of the questions considered were:

- How will awareness be increased and who will need to understand cybersecurity principles?

- How will information sharing practices be established?
- What will be needed to add cyber policies in a meaningful way?
- How will cyber be incorporated into continuity plans?

After considerable discussion, there were several points that were agreed upon. First, there needed to be a way to determine improvement. A community would need to be able to assess their current cybersecurity posture and they also needed to know what should be measured. Improved cybersecurity practices and information sharing would at some point would need to be supplemented with technology. New practices and technologies would require a shared understanding and potentially new skillsets. Finally, there needed to be a way to test the new implementations to ensure they worked as expected. Based on these points, the activities and tools added to the CCSMM to assist the communities to improve their cybersecurity posture were metrics, technology, training, processes and procedures, and assessments. In the model, they are called implementation mechanisms.

Metrics

Metrics were selected as an implementation mechanism primarily because communities needed to answer the questions:

- What should the community be measuring to improve its security posture?
- How does the community know if it has been successful improving its capability to prevent or defend against cyber-attacks?
- How does a community know what to measure in their program?
- How does the community measure increased awareness on cybersecurity issues?

Metrics are the measurement criteria that allow individuals, organizations, or the community to determine where they started and will allow them to assess if an increase of cyber preparedness within each dimension was achieved. Improvement areas that can be measured to determine an increase of preparedness can be:

- **Cybersecurity Awareness:** determine the level of awareness of community leaders and citizens.

Figure 4.

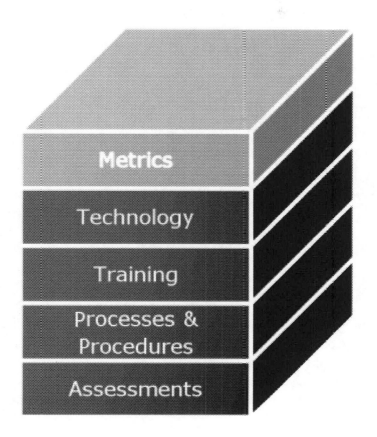

- **Cybersecurity Capabilities:** determ_ne what capabilities the community started with; the time it takes to realize a cyber incident has occurred; or the time it takes to respond to a cyber incident.
- **Information Sharing:** determine if infcrmation sharing is occurring across the community. Is two-way sharing occurring? In other words, is the information shared being acted upon?
- **Policies:** determine the percentage of policies that address cybersecurity specifically. Determine the percentage of organizations in the community that have certain polic_es.
- **Plans:** determine the percentage of plans that address cybersecurity specifically. Determine the percentage of organizations in the community that have certain plans.

Metrics can also be used to provide the ability to gauge whether a community is under attack. To determine if a community is under attack, first a baseline must be established. A baseline is created based on historical data that is gathered indicating what normal activity is within the community. The metrics collected, can then be aggregated for the community to provide an overall picture of hostile cyber activity within the community. These metrics have been used for several years at the organizational level. Similarly, information from communities can be aggregated at the state and federal levels to provide a picture of activity within the state and nation respectively.

Technology

Technology was selected as an implementation mechanism because it is an essential part of any discussion on advancing the security posture of a community. The questions that need to be addressed are:

- What technology currently exists to monitor cybersecurity activity associated with the community?
- What is needed to increase security controls in the community?
- What technology will be needed to accomplish the measurements outlined in the metrics?
- What technology will be used to collect data for information sharing across the community?
- What technology will be used to fuse, analyze, and correlate information?
- What technology will be needed to securely distribute information across the community?

It is also necessary to define the types of technology that will be needed at each stage of preparedness. Technology can assist to identify, prevent, detect, respond to and recover from cyber incidents. Some examples of these technologies may be:

- **Identify:** determine monitoring technologies that may be used to watch traffic and track anomalous behaviors and assist with the volume of cyber activity.
- **Prevent**: determine technologies that may be used to block attacks.
- **Detect**: identify technologies that provide aggregated alerts on anomalous behaviors and can analyze the activity to identify potential

Figure 5.

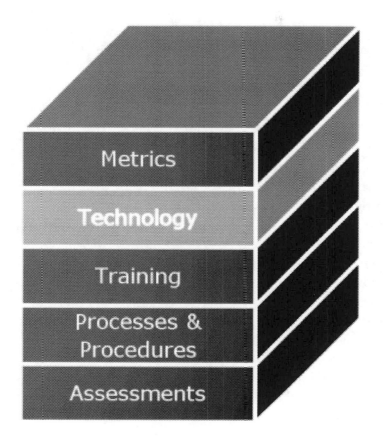

indications of intrusive activity. Determine technologies that can securely distribute information about cyber incidents.

- **Respond:** determine tools needed for incident analysis to include forensic gathering and analysis.
- **Recover:** select tools and technologies that can assist in recovering data, systems, and other measures to get the community back to normal operations.

Understanding what technologies are available and what will work best for the community will be a key factor. As communities mature in their cyber programs and identify what technologies are required, new technologies will be needed to increase the capability of the community.

Training

The most common method used to increase or improve a needed skill, knowledge or behavior is through training. This is reason training was selected as an implementation mechanism. The questions related to training activities were:

- How can the community increase its knowledge in regard to cyber related issues?
- How can behaviors change to become more security focused?
- How can new activities that are implemented in the community be distributed?
- Are the all the skillsets needed to improve the community's cybersecurity posture addressed? If not, how will the community increase the skillsets needed?
- If new technologies are introduced to improve cybersecurity, what methods are available to ensure the community can implement and operate them?
- As new or existing policies and plans are revised or created to address cyber related issues, how will the new practices be distributed and how will we ensure the knowledge required is achieved?

Training is essentially an organized activity conducted to improve the performance and increase skills, knowledge, attitudes, and behaviors in regard to a specific topic. Any knowledge, skills or expected actions addressing the cyber threat must to be taught to the intended audience at the appropriate level to address their needs. Training methods are used in every aspect of the model:

- **Awareness:** determine who in the community needs to be trained on cyber-related issues and to what extent.
- **Information Sharing:** train the community on what information should be shared; with whom the information should be shared; when it should be shared; and how it should be shared.
- **Policies:** determine the principles, rules and guidelines the community should adopt regarding cybersecurity and incorporate these concepts in all training conducted to the community.

Figure 6.

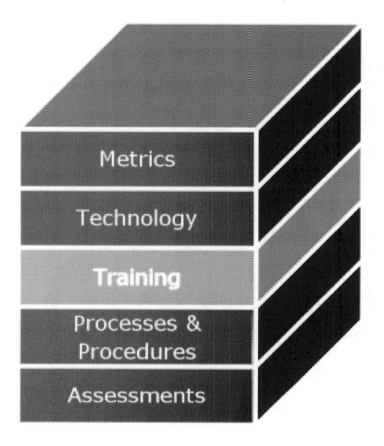

- **Plans:** integrate cyber principles into community continuity and incident response plans and then train community stakeholders to ensure awareness and understanding is achieved.
- **Metrics:** training will be used to ensure metrics are being gathered, analyzed, and distributed as needed.
- **Technology:** audit all technologies used for cyber preparedness and train key individuals on how the technology works, who to contact if it is not working, and how to address maintenance, updates and replacements.
- **Processes and Procedures:** training will be used to introduce new processes and procedures and to address proper implementations and understanding.

- **Assessments:** training will be used to ensure exercises, vulnerability assessments, penetration tests and other testing mechanisms are being conducted correctly and as needed.

It is important to note that training is not a one-time effort. Training should be considered part of the improvement plan for the community and should be conducted routinely as new information and practices are developed and implemented.

The methods of training will vary depending on what needs to be addressed and in what time frame. Training needs to be done in a way that addresses different groups of people and their roles specifically. Cyber awareness training, as an example, has not been successful when it is approached generically as an annual training for everyone. Training should be used to target particular people and what their role is, specifically as it relates to cyber security. Therefore, technical training should not be given to non-technical people (i.e. individuals who do not have a need to understand the technical aspects of a system).

Processes and Procedures

The natural implementation mechanism to support policies that are created regarding cyber preparedness are processes and procedures. There were many questions surrounding processes and procedures such as:

- What do people know about cyber-related issues and how should they handle them?
- What kinds of technologies are used to identify, prevent, detect, respond to and recover from a cyber-related issue and where will it be documented?
- Does the community have step by step processes and procedures on how to accomplish each?
- What processes and procedures are in place now and do they address all cyber-related aspects?
- Who addresses cyber incidents in the community?
- What is the process for integrating new cybersecurity principles into community operations and plans?
- How and when is the information provided?
- How often should the community review and update cyber-related processes?

Figure 7.

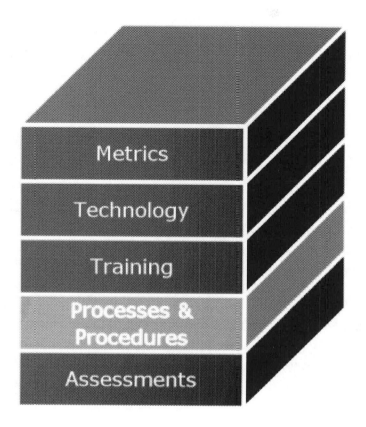

Processes and procedures are the series of tasks and methods required to specifically address the step-by-step growth in the community's capability. They should reflect exactly how a community wants to handle cyber related issues. How, for example, can a community detect if the community is under a coordinated cyber-attack impacting cross sector organizations. Is there a process to communicate isolated or seemingly disparate events? Is there a process to report abnormal incidents? Who addresses cyber incidents in the community? Is it law enforcement? A fusion center? Are there step by step processes that assist in identifying possible cyber incidents? Who is analyzing the information to see if this is a coordinated attack? How and when is the information provided? All of this should be incorporated into a Policy with accompanying step by step directions on how it will be accomplished.

Consider using the dimensions to determine what is needed to improve awareness across the community; information sharing collection, analysis, triage and dissemination should be addressed both inside and outside of the community; how the community will identify and implement policies for the community; and how plans will be documented, adopted and tested. A successful cybersecurity program must include people, processes and technology. If any one of these is forgotten or not addressed the program will likely fail. At a minimum, communities should have processes and procedures addressing these areas:

- **People:** determine what processes and procedures will ensure the individuals in the community know what is required from them, what roles they play, and ensure everyone who needs this information knows how to find the requirements.
- **Processes:** determine how cybersecurity preparedness activities will be carried out and document them. This will include how new activities are identified, incorporated, executed, trained, tested and updated.
- **Technology:** determine what is needed, how it will be procured, implemented, and maintained. Considerations for who will be responsible for installation, operations, and who will need to be trained to manage the technology will also need to be addressed.

Determining what policies are needed and which need to be established first can be a challenging task. The National Institute of Standards and Technology has produced the *Framework for Improving Critical Infrastructure Cybersecurity which was updated in 2018* (NIST, 2018). The framework provides a risk-based approach to managing cybersecurity risk and provides a tiered approach for organizations to advance in their own security programs in identified in 5 core functions. While designed to address security for critical infrastructures, the basic elements outlined in the framework can help states and communities to establish policies, processes, procedures, and guidelines that can be used in developing their cyber security programs. The tiered nature of the framework blends seamlessly into the CCSMM. More detailed information in regard to the NIST Cybersecurity Framework will be provided in later chapters.

Assessments

The final implementation mechanism selected was Assessments. The purpose for this mechanism is to test and exercise every activity, process, procedure and capability to ensure they work as intended. The questions in regard to assessments were:

- What testing mechanism is needed to evaluate whether the community has met their goals?
- How will policies and procedures be evaluated to ensure they address cybersecurity?
- How can information sharing activities between organizations of the community be exercised?
- Do our community emergency response plans and continuity plans have gaps that need to be addressed?
- How can we test our cybersecurity capabilities?

Assessments can be technical in nature, as an example, they can be used to identify computer and network security deficiencies. Assessments can also be non-technical and can be used to determine if personnel know specific procedures to follow in a given situation. Non-technical assessments can be as simple as asking various people in the community if they know where to report a cybersecurity incident to within the community.

Below are some examples of areas that can be tested:

- **Effectiveness of Training:** determine the effectiveness of the cyber training that has been conducted
- **Increased Capabilities:** determine what new cybersecurity capabilities are in the community. Drills can also be conducted to determine individual performance of a specific capability.
- **Information Sharing:** determine the value of the information being shared. Determine if it is actionable, relevant, and timely.
- **Policies:** determine the effectiveness of cybersecurity policies that have been implemented.
- **Plans:** determine the operational impacts of cyber-attacks and if recovery procedures are executed as planned.

Assessments of how cyber prepared we are can be accomplished in many ways. They can be conducted through exercises and drills, statistics,

Figure 8.

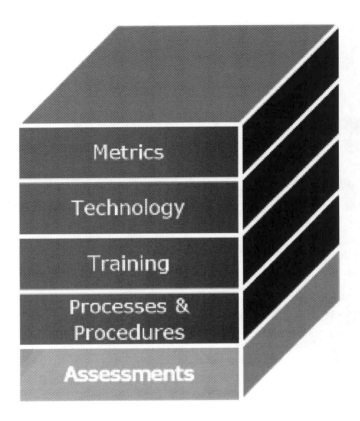

penetration testing or vulnerability assessments. At each level of maturity, assessments will assist to ensure the community has identified all gaps and has incorporated updates as cyber issues change in the future.

CONCLUSION

Community Cyber Security Exercises, conducted across the nation, resulted in the realization that there was a need for a coordinated plan for communities to follow to assist them to build a cybersecurity program. Based on the lessons learned from these exercises, the Community Cybersecurity Maturity Model was established to be the framework needed to develop a viable and sustainable community cybersecurity program. The model addresses four areas for improvement. Those areas are awareness, information sharing, policies, and plans. Cybersecurity controls and measures can be incorporated into the program using the implementation mechanisms such as metrics, technology, process and procedures, training and assessments.

REFERENCES

About the Agency. (n.d.). Retrieved from FEMA website: https://www.fema.gov/about-agency

Awareness. (n.d.). Retrieved from Merriam-Webster website: https://www.merriam-webster.com/dictionary/awareness

Crezo, A. (2012). *5 U.S. cities that were destroyed - and completely rebuilt.* Retrieved from Mental Floss website: http://mentalfloss.com/article/12982/5-us-cities-were-destroyed%E2%80%94and-completely-rebuilt

Dictionary. (n.d.). Retrieved from Google.com website: https://www.google.com/search?q=what+does+dimension+mean

Exercises. (2016). Retrieved from Ready website: https://www.ready.gov/business/testing/exercises

Harrington, J. (2018). *What are the worst floods in American history? A rundown of the top 30.* Retrieved from USA Today website: https://www.usatoday.com/story/money/economy/2018/07/24/worst-floods-in-american-history/37070093/

History.com (Ed.). (2018). *San Francisco earthquake of 1906.* Retrieved from History.com website: https://www.history.com/topics/natural-disasters-and-environment/1906-san-francisco-earthquake

Types of Training. (2019). Retrieved from Business Jargons website: https://businessjargons.com/types-of-training.html

Chapter 2
The Two–Dimensional CCSMM

ABSTRACT

The community cyber security maturity model (CCSMM) defines four dimensions and five implementation mechanisms in describing the relative maturity of an organization or an SLTT's cybersecurity program. These are used in defining levels of maturity and the cybersecurity characteristics of an organization or SLTT at each level. In order to progress from one level to the next, a variety of activities should take place, and these are defined in terms of five different mechanisms. In between two levels are a variety of activities that should take place to help the entity to advance from one level to the next. These groups of activities describe four phases, each of which takes place between two levels. Thus, Phase 1 defines the activities that should occur for an entity to advance from Level 1 to Level 2.

INTRODUCTION

The Community Cyber Security Maturity Model (CCSMM) was developed as a result of the lessons learned in conducting state and community cybersecurity exercises around the nation. Exercises are an awareness tool to help people understand the issues related to a specific disaster situation. They are also a proven method to test to see if the mechanisms, processes and procedures an organization has put in place are sufficient to address a variety of different disaster scenarios. With cybersecurity, the issue was first one of awareness – state and community leaders were mostly unaware of the potential impact of a cybersecurity event and needed to be made aware that cybersecurity is

DOI: 10.4018/978-1-7998-4471-6.ch002

an important issue for them. Community leaders needed to understand that without cybersecurity, their community could be negatively impacted in a variety of ways that could cause severe consequences for their citizens. The belief at the time was that by making leaders aware they needed to pay attention to cybersecurity they would then follow up with development of the needed processes, procedures, and technology. The reality proved to be different.

When the team that conducted an exercise returned to the state or community to see how well they were doing after about a year, they discovered that while the leaders were still aware that cybersecurity was something they needed to address, they had most often not taken any real steps in forming a strategy to implement a cybersecurity program. There were plenty of vendors willing to sell products and services but which of these were the most important and which needed to be accomplished first before the others? The exercise team had made the incorrect assumption that participants in the exercise would know what to do and that simply did not prove to be the case. They therefore took a step back and created guidance that could be provided to states and communities that would provide a path for them to follow – keeping in mind that most participants did not at the time have a budget to purchase cybersecurity products or services. The resulting plan that was created was the CCSMM.

BACKGROUND

A critical factor in developing the CCSMM was that cybersecurity is not a binary issue. A state or community does not either have security or it doesn't. There are many levels of security preparedness and not every entity needs the same level of security preparedness – it should be based on the actual threats to the state, community, tribe, territory, or organization. This implies there are different levels of security that can be implemented so one of the first tasks in developing a program would be to understand the different levels, understand what is currently implemented, and know what the ultimate goal is. In other words, what security level is needed or desired by the community? The CCSMM was thus created to provide three things:

1.   A "yardstick" so that SLTTs could determine where they currently are in the maturity of their cybersecurity program. What level are they currently at? How prepared is the community as a whole, or individual

organizations within the community, to prevent, detect, and respond to and recover from a cyber-attack? At first the critical infrastructures in the community and the local government entities will be the primary components the model will focus on but as the community matures, it will increasingly take on a whole-community approach. There are several dimensions that will be described and a community may not be at the same level for all dimensions at the same time. In fact, it is will not be uncommon for a community to be at several different levels among the dimensions as it progresses. To be considered at a specific level overall, however, the community has to exhibit the characteristics in all of the dimensions at that level.

2. A "roadmap" to describe a path to advance from one level to the next. This would describe the various activities that need to take place in order to advance. After determining what level the community currently is at, a decision needs to be made concerning what level they aspire to. Not all communities are the same and not all communities will need to attain the highest level of security represented in the model. The level of threat to a community will be heavily dependent on what organizations reside in the community. For example, is there a military installation or a large component of the federal or state government? Is there a significant national monument or historical site that serves as a symbol for the nation? Is there a significant industry or manufacturing installation present in the community? All of these will impact the likelihood of an attack on the community as well as the potential threat actor (i.e. who might want to launch an attack on the community or organizations within the community – a nation-state, a criminal organization, a terrorist group, or curious individuals). The roadmap will help the community and organizations within the community to determine what they need to do on their path to their desired level.

3. A "common point of reference" so that individuals in different communities across the country could talk about their individual programs and relate them to each other. If all are working from the same model it makes it easier to discuss common issues, problems and solutions. If there is no common point of reference then it is harder for individuals to compare their program and thus to benefit from the experiences each has had in attempting to secure their own community. It is counterproductive for communities to all try to build their own programs without benefiting from the experiences of others. Communities should not all have to make the same mistakes in order to learn what they can do – they should be

34

able to benefit from others who have been down the same path before them but for this to work the paths need to be roughly similar.

With these three goals in mind, one of the first tasks that needed to be defined was the different levels of the model. The levels SLTTs would be striving for. Each of these levels would then describe the characteristics of an SLTT at that level which would provide a description for what the SLTT was striving to obtain. It would also aid in the creation of the steps that would need to be taken to reach that level and provide a basis for different communities to share their experiences.

DEFINING THE LEVELS

There are a number of different maturity models that have been created for a variety of different environments. In 2014 the Department of Energy (DOE) published Version 1.1 of the Cybersecurity Capability Maturity Model (C2M2). Among other things, it offered a very good definition of what a maturity model is:

A maturity model is a set of characteristics, attributes, indicators, or patterns that represent capability and progression in a particular discipline. Model content typically exemplifies best practices and may incorporate standards or other codes of practice of the discipline. A maturity model thus provides a benchmark against which an organization can evaluate the current level of capability of its practices, processes, and methods and set goals and priorities for improvement. Also, when a model is widely used in a particular industry (and assessment results are shared), organizations can benchmark their performance against other organizations. An industry can determine how well it is performing overall by examining the capability of its member organizations. To measure progression, maturity models typically have "levels" along a scale—C2M2 uses a scale of maturity indicator levels (MILs) 0–3, which are described in Section 3.2. [of DOE 2014] A set of attributes defines each level. If an organization demonstrates these attributes, it has achieved both that level and the capabilities that the level represents. Having measurable transition states between the levels enables an organization to use the scale to:

- *Define its current state*
- *Determine its future, more mature state*
- *Identify the capabilities it must attain to reach that future state.* (DOE 2014)

The model proposed by the DOE utilized four Maturity Indicator Levels (MIL) to describe the different levels of maturity that an organization could be at. Level MIL 0 basically represented an organization that did not perform any of the practices defined for higher levels. The practices are grouped into ten domains as follows:

- Risk Management
- Asset, Change, and Configuration Management
- Identity and Access Management
- Threat and Vulnerability Management
- Situational Awareness
- Information Sharing and Communications
- Event and Incident Response, Continuity of Operations
- Supply Chain and External Dependencies Management
- Workforce Management
- Cybersecurity Program Management

In 2015 the Software Engineering Institute (SEI) at Carnegie Mellon University (CMU) published the *Cybersecurity Capability Maturity Model for Information Technology Services (C2M2 for IT Services), Version 1.0*. This document was largely taken from the DOE C2M2 as it described in its Acknowledgements section. (SEI, 2015) In 2019 the Department of Defense announced the creation of a Cybersecurity Maturity Model Certification (CMMC) program to be implemented in 2020. The program was developed in conjunction with the Johns Hopkins University Applied Physics Laboratory and the SEI at CMU. (MeriTalk, 2019) It leaned heavily on the requirements specified in the NIST SP 800-171 publication (Edwards and Hays, 2019) and has a mapping of the Controlled Unclassified Information (CUI) security requirements in the NIST SP 800-53 publication *Security and Privacy Controls for Federal information Systems and Organizations*. (NIST 2015)

There are five notional CMMC levels which describe the maturity of the organization's security processes. These five levels are:

Level 1: Processes are ad hoc

Level 2: Processes are documented
Level 3: Processes are guided by policy
Level 4: Practices are periodically evaluated for effectiveness
Level 5: Processes are tailored and improvement data is shared

All of the more recent documents attest to the desire to help organizations develop strong security programs. The CCSMM, which was originally developed in 2008 and first discussed in 2009 (White, 2009), is obviously not based on these later documents but shares many of the same components and is also a five-level model. Since these other security related maturity models came after the creation of the CCSMM, it was actually influenced more by the original Capability Maturity Model (CMM) for software engineering which was published by the SEI at CMU in 1987. Since then there have been several other publications describing it, some with slight wording variations. It was designed to help an organization mature their software development processes to help them become more efficient and ultimately produce better and more reliable software. The CMM has five levels:

Level 1: Initial
Level 2: Repeatable
Level 3: Defined
Level 4: Managed
Level 5: Optimizing

Each level, with the exception of Level 1, has a number of Key Process Areas (KPA) that describe the basic requirements that should be met by the organizations software processes. Level 1 had no KPAs assigned to it. The levels provide a path for organizations to follow as they seek to improve their software development processes.

These are not the only maturity models in existence and new ones are periodically being developed. What is important to understand about the CCSMM is that it was initially designed to not address specific security requirements as a model such as the NIST Cybersecurity Framework does, but instead it addresses the type of requirements that are needed for a cybersecurity program. As such it allows for the specific requirements that might be required of an organization in a given sector while another organization in a different sector might have a different specific requirement. For example, the CCSMM might talk about the need for security assessments to be performed on a periodic basis. For an organization in a sector such as the Financial Services

Sector this might translate to a specific type of external assessment being accomplished annually while a different organization in a different sector, say a retail shoe store, may find it adequate to accomplish an external assessment every other year. The point from the perspective of the overall CCSMM model is that entities are conducting appropriate assessments when they should be.

Like the CMM, the CCSMM also has five levels. Initially it was designed to help communities to improve the maturity of their cybersecurity processes or program. Later, it was expanded to cover more than just communities and this will be covered in the next chapter. Just like the CMM, the CCSMM provides a path for communities to follow in order to improve the maturity of their cybersecurity program. The five levels of the CCSMM are shown in Figure 1.

Figure 1. The Five Levels of the CCSMM and the Characteristics Found in Each level

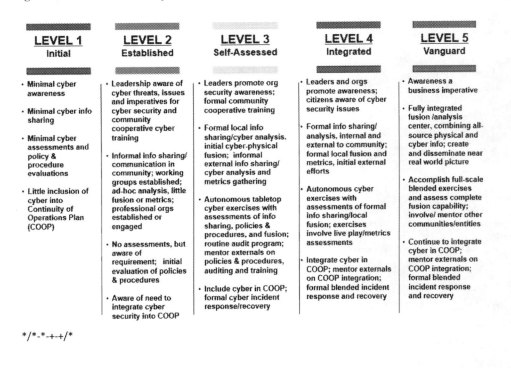

LEVEL 1 Initial	**LEVEL 2** Established	**LEVEL 3** Self-Assessed	**LEVEL 4** Integrated	**LEVEL 5** Vanguard
• Minimal cyber awareness • Minimal cyber info sharing • Minimal cyber assessments and policy & procedure evaluations • Little inclusion of cyber into Continuity of Operations Plan (COOP)	• Leadership aware of cyber threats, issues and imperatives for cyber security and community cooperative cyber training • Informal info sharing/ communication in community; working groups established; ad-hoc analysis, little fusion or metrics; professional orgs established or engaged • No assessments, but aware of requirement; initial evaluation of policies & procedures • Aware of need to integrate cyber security into COOP	• Leaders promote org security awareness; formal community cooperative training • Formal local info sharing/cyber analysis. initial cyber-physical fusion; informal external info sharing/ cyber analysis and metrics gathering • Autonomous tabletop cyber exercises with assessments of info sharing, policies & procedures, and fusion; routine audit program; mentor externals on policies & procedures, auditing and training • Include cyber in COOP; formal cyber incident response/recovery	• Leaders and orgs promote awareness; citizens aware of cyber security issues • Formal info sharing/ analysis, internal and external to community; formal local fusion and metrics, initial external efforts • Autonomous cyber exercises with assessments of formal info sharing/local fusion; exercises involve live play/metrics assessments • Integrate cyber in COOP; mentor externals on COOP integration; formal blended incident response and recovery	• Awareness a business imperative • Fully integrated fusion /analysis center, combining all-source physical and cyber info; create and disseminate near real world picture • Accomplish full-scale blended exercises and assess complete fusion capability; involve/ mentor other communities/entities • Continue to integrate cyber in COOP; mentor externals on COOP integration; formal blended incident response and recovery

/-*-+-+/*

CCSMM Level 1: Initial

Using the CCSMM as a framework for community cybersecurity, a Level 1 community may not have in place the processes that are needed at the higher levels. They may not even have an overall program to address cybersecurity. Communities at Level 1 may have implemented certain processes or programs but have not implemented enough to qualify for Level 2.

Figure 1 also provides a short description of the characteristics that communities should display for the four dimensions of the model. For example, at Level 1 the community and its leaders have minimal awareness of cybersecurity and the potential impact the loss of security could have on the community. They most likely do not understand the dependence the community has on cyber infrastructures. The community has either no organized cybersecurity information sharing program, or at best has a minimal one that only a few organizations are a member of. The processes that may be in place within the community are not assessed or tested on a regular basis and there is most likely no cyber part of the community's Continuity of Operations Plan (COOP). It is interesting to note, but probably not surprising, that none of the communities that the CIAS conducted community exercises for were past Level 1 in the maturity of their programs.

CCSMM Level 2: Established

At Level 2: Established your community has established a basic program and has elements and processes for all four of the dimensions in place. Awareness programs (such as user cybersecurity training and training aimed specifically at community leaders) have been implemented and leaders know of the importance of cybersecurity to the community and to their individual organizations. They are also aware of the need for user training as they understand that cybersecurity is not just the responsibility of IT or security staff but is a function that all are collectively responsible for.

The community will also have established at least an informal cybersecurity information sharing program. This does not mean that a Security Operations Center (SOC) has been created with staffing around the clock, but it does mean that methods have been implemented that allow for communicating information on cybersecurity issues to organizations around the community. The community may still not be conducting assessments or other activities to test the processes, policies, and procedures but the need for these is understood and organizations may be conducting their own at this point. The community has also implemented cyber into its COOP and has created a cyber incident response plan. The community may not have conducted any exercises but plans should be in the process of development to do so in the future.

CCSMM Level 3: Self-Assessed

Communities at Level 3: Self-Assessed have progressed far enough that they have an established, stable cybersecurity program. They understand enough about cybersecurity and what needs to be accomplished that they are capable of conducting their own assessments to determine how well the community is doing. This is not to say that there can't be improvements and additional components added to their program, but by this point they should have at least a minimal viable and sustainable program that is the goal of the CCSMM program. When participating communities reach Level 3, they should be much more aware of gaps in their current security posture. They should be establishing baselines, sharing information on a regular basis, and refining processes and procedures. They understand that performance in these areas is to be monitored and measured often. Leadership must continue to promote security awareness at all levels and training initiatives should be well underway. In the exercise realm, those at Level 3 should be conducting events at least once per year that include a cyber component and preferably have at least one exercise that is primarily cyber focused. The exercises may at first be conducted with participation from just the critical infrastructures and local government entities but should progress to a whole-community approach that will include involvement from industry. The community should incorporate the key concepts from previous levels as often as possible in the exercises. This includes information sharing, policies and procedures, and continuity of operations. Cyber incident response and recovery should be formalized by this point and will be a major focus of the exercises that are conducted. At Level 3: Self-Assessed the community will also have an understanding of the impact that individuals and organizations in the community (as well as the state and other communities) have on the community itself.

CCSMM Level 4: Integrated

At Level 4: Integrated cybersecurity is integrated across the community wherever it should be considered. Citizens and organizations have a role in community cybersecurity and the citizens as a whole understand this. The community needs to be communicating with the state as well (assuming there is a state program, otherwise they may need to communicate directly with other communities or organizations such as the Multi-State ISAC). The message that up to this point has been largely contained within organizations should be spread to everyone within the community. Assessments of process, procedures, policies, and technology are conducted on a regular basis. There should be at least annual cyber exercises but also exercises in which cyber is blended with attacks that affect both physical and cyber assets or functions. Emergency management organizations should have a solid grasp on cybersecurity concepts and integration into normal operations is crucial. Community-centric incident response plans must directly address cyber incidents, and regular assessment of procedures associated with those plans should be conducted. The real thrust of Level 4: Integrated is that the community should be integrating its efforts with all members and organizations within the community as well as working with the state and other communities. Cybersecurity is considered an integral concern for the community and for organizations within the community.

CCSMM Level 5: Vanguard

Attaining Level 5: Vanguard means your community is maintaining a fully-vigilant cybersecurity posture. Exercise capabilities are well-rounded and include cyber and non-cyber events. Communities and the organizations within them must continue to evaluate current policies, procedures, and plans for additional integration and refinement. This is especially true where incident response is concerned due to the highly volatile nature of the threat landscape. Cybersecurity programs include the entire population of a community at this point, and a complete sense of cybersecurity awareness is found among citizens. Exercises are routinely conducted with other communities and organizations at the local level and with the state. Exercises should also be full-scale events that are as realistic as possible, with live-fire events that incorporate as many elements to test as is appropriate. Exercises have moved beyond simple tabletop events (though these may still also be conducted) and now should include functional exercises.

At this level, information sharing is at its most advanced, where fusion and dissemination of data received from various sources occurs at an acceptable pace. Information gathered is considered "all-source", meaning it is received from all sectors within the community and is processed in near real-time. The result is what is known as "near ground truth", or what is happening at this moment in time.

It is expected that at Level 5: Vanguard, communities are actively involved in mentorship of other SLTTs for the purposes of increased cybersecurity and information sharing. Even if there aren't any additional capabilities expected after Level 5, communities should routinely re-evaluate their cybersecurity posture in accordance with the metrics for each of the CCSMM levels. This helps keep everything on track and avoids complacency among stakeholders.

There is a lot more to each of the levels described above which will be addressed later in this book. For now, however, the basic differences between the levels, and the specific focus of each level should be understood. A comparison of the descriptions of each level in the previous paragraphs or in Figure 1 will yield a number of different activities that must be accomplished as the community progresses. The specific levels are connected by the events that take place to progress between levels for each dimension. These occur in what are referred to in the model as Phases. Phase 1 contains activities that will occur between Level 1 and Level 2, Phase 2 will connect Levels 2 and 3, and so forth.

THE PHASES

To advance from one level of the model to the next will take time as several activities will need to be performed, processes instituted, and programs developed. The term Phase is used to define the period of time between levels, and the activities performed during that period of time. There are four phases for the five levels of the CCSMM.

If the CCSMM's levels are milestones, then the phases of the model are the roadmap to achievement. Each phase must be followed in order to arrive at the next destination, and it's imperative that every phase requirement be met in order to ensure preparedness for subsequent phases. In that vein, the CCSMM's phases have been constructed with a set of requirements that are organized into five categories.

Metrics help communities and their citizens determine what to measure so the current security posture can be fully understood. **Technology** obviously will play a role as well so ascertaining when is the right time to purchase and deploy new technology (both hardware and software) to address a characteristic at the next level is something organizations and communities must often consider. The question of who needs what **training** should be asked as part of the program and each phase introduces new training for additional users. **Processes and procedures** are foundational to cybersecurity readiness and looking to upcoming level requirements means that each phase will address what is already documented versus what still needs to be created. Finally, **assessments** are instrumental in evaluating success and participants must decide how to best plan and conduct both as part of their CCSMM strategy. With these five categories of requirements in mind, the phases can be discussed and will be examined in more detail in later chapters.

Phase 1: Initial to Established

Phase 1 is really just about initiating the conversation on a variety of cybersecurity topics. There is little expectation in terms of having a lot of processes and procedures in place, and minimal information sharing is expected beyond inter-departmental discussions. As organizations, communities, and states progress through Phase 1, increased awareness at high and middle level management will occur, information sharing becomes a major discussion point, and topics such as cybersecurity training and exercises are introduced.

By the end of this phase, participants must have at least a defined cybersecurity awareness program, informal but regular information sharing working groups, some level of cybersecurity training and education, assessment and planning finished, and should have conducted at least one cybersecurity exercise or be planning one. In this case the exercise will be for awareness purposes and will most likely be a tabletop exercise. In later levels, once procedures are established, the exercise can be used to evaluate the effectiveness of established processes, procedures, and programs. It should be noted that when the model was developed it was understood that most, if not all, communities that are at Level 1 will likely not have a large budget for implementing the activities in Phase 1. Budgets are generally set at least a year if not more in advance. When the community first starts on its path to cybersecurity preparedness members of the community will be learning about the things they need to do and can at that time better budget for it. This means that for the most part, activities in Phase 1 should be at no- or low-cost to the community and its organizations. As the community advances in its level of maturity there will be time for a cybersecurity budget to be introduced so that later phases will have the funding that will be required to accomplish all that will need to be done to establish a long-term, viable and sustainable program.

Phase 2: Established to Self-Assessed

Phase 2 takes the lessons learned from implementing Phase 1 and adds additional focus on information sharing and exercises. Organizational and community leadership should be actively involved in promoting cybersecurity awareness at all levels (e.g. user, supervisor, and executive levels), showing support as often as required. If interest in cybersecurity issues is not shown by the leaders of an organization the employees will also not be interested. On the other hand, if a CEO, mayor, or head of a government department routinely asks about the cybersecurity status of the organization then it will have a positive impact on the next level of leadership which will translate to an increased interest down through all levels of the organization.

By the end of Phase 2, information sharing working groups should be well-established, meeting regularly with formal agendas and discussion topics. Whenever possible, such working groups should include a mix of public and private organizations. This helps keep conversations relevant to the entire community and leads to the whole-community focus that is desired.

Technology assessments should be conducted by this point, with the questions answered concerning what is needed and where. Basic implementation of "low hanging fruit" is strongly suggested but not necessarily required. What is meant by this is that simple, inexpensive security processes or technology (especially well documented and reviewed public domain software) that will improve some aspect of cybersecurity should be considered to advance the status of an organization or the community.

Where needed, to go along with the increased awareness of the importance of cybersecurity for all individuals in an organization, training and education should be in place to provide each group with the knowledge and skills they will need to be more secure. This could include, for example, organization-sponsored training seminars conducted by internal staff or formal training classes by a vendor. The point here is to ensure some level of training is occurring on a periodic but scheduled basis. There may also be the possibility of sharing cybersecurity training programs between organizations in the community. There may exist an organization that has developed an effective user cybersecurity training program that they may be willing to share with others in the community. Taking a look at the cybersecurity problem from a whole-community perspective makes it more likely that such sharing might take place.

Finally, exercises must incorporate incident response and recovery from a cybersecurity event. If the community's emergency management organization has annual drills or exercises, some of these should have a strong cyber element to them and in fact an annual cyber-only exercise should be planned. What communities will often find when they introduce a cyber element to a more traditional community exercise (such as a natural disaster, chemical accident, or terrorist attack), the exercise participants will gravitate toward the aspects they are comfortable with and may ignore the parts they are not as familiar with. A cyber aspect to one of these other exercises is only going to be valuable if it is considered along with all of the other issues that need to be addressed. Too often communities may find that an answer such as "we would just go back to doing it with paper and pencil like we did years ago" will be the answer and the cyber event will be swept aside. What folks who have actually experienced an event in which cyber assets were lost have seen is that going back to the old ways is not always easy and may not even be possible. Forms that used to exist and the training and processes needed to use them instead of the newer cyber processes may no longer be available and individuals, especially those who were not around in "the old days" will not know what to do. Including cyber components/events in other exercises helps introduce the broader exercise programs that are part of Phase 3 and beyond but having a cyber-only event will allow for the participants to focus on cyber issues exclusively and will not allow them to sweep cyber aside to concentrate on more familiar emergency responses.

Phase 3: Self-Assessed to Integrated

When a community arrives at Level 3 it has advanced far enough in the CCSMM to have developed a sustainable cybersecurity program. Communities, and organizations within them, that are moving from Level 3 to Level 4 should expect a lot more emphasis on measuring success in areas such as awareness, information sharing, and processes and assessments (such as exercise planning). Phase 3 involves greatly expanding cybersecurity awareness to move beyond

Information sharing continues to be a key initiative in this phase. Communities will need to increasingly be making strides towards establishing a formal fusion center that operates on an around-the-clock basis. Fusion Centers are entities often at a state level but also may be established in larger communities which accept reports of various "observations" from around the community and "fuse" them together to determine those that may be related and that may indicate a bigger issue may be brewing. On the cybersecurity side, there are also companies that can provide assistance with the current state of cyber threats and could be a valuable addition to the community program or to individual organizations. Fusion centers are often associated with the law enforcement and intelligence communities and employ individuals with a background in one or both of these fields. Fusion centers are similar to ISAOs but have a broader focus in that they look at all hazards that occur within a community. The "organizational boundaries and into the local community at an even greater level. Citizens should be notified of preventative security measures that can be made in their daily lives, and information pertaining to cybersecurity incidents that might have an impact on them should be disseminated in a standardized manner. An annual cybersecurity day that may first be introduced at a lower level for the community should now feature an increased number of things that citizens can/should do. Public service announcements on local TV, cable, and radio stations could feature short messages on cybersecurity and short training and awareness programs could be featured on community channels on a variety of cybersecurity topics, some now even at a technical level.

fusing" of information is not an easy mission but is one that has been discussed in greater detail over the past few decades. A well-known example might be the bombing of the federal building in Oklahoma City in 1995. The individuals who detonated the bomb had in the months leading up to the attack purchased large (but not uncommon) amounts of ammonium nitrate (which can be used in bomb making but is also commonly used as a fertilizer), nitromethane and Tovex. They had attempted to purchase the nitromethane under the pretense that they needed it for fuel for motorcycle racing. The amount they wanted was unusual and the first individual they approached to make the purchase refused to sell it to them and, in fact, reported the request to the FBI. They also stole 500 blasting caps from a quarry. They then acquired seventeen bags of ANFO (ammonium nitrate/fuel oil) for use in the bomb. These items were not purchased or stolen from one community but occurred over several states. They also rented storage space and then a truck to transport the bomb. The job of a fusion center would be to note the purchase of items that could be used in bomb making, especially under suspicious circumstances as reported by the one individual to the FBI. All of these seemingly disparate events when put together provide a different possible picture of what is occurring than what might be assumed by looking at the individual events separately. This is the goal of a Fusion Center – to put the pieces together in order to prevent an attack from occurring. The difficulty in accomplishing this, however, is also evident in this same example as it occurred over more than one community and state, the individuals used an alias, and individually all of these are common transactions. To accomplish similar activity for the cyber domain, public and private partnerships should be established at this level, and clear lines of communication should be defined and developed. From a process, planning, and exercise perspective, the fusion center participants will increasingly have a very active role in identifying needed processes to be able to spot crossovers between cyber and other domains, creating plans for addressing cybersecurity incidents, and exercising those plans on a regular basis.

Assessments will increase in frequency and in detail as Level 4 is attained. The topic of assessments is receiving increased attention in the cybersecurity field. For several years, some organizations in industry have required that their vendors who access their information or connect to their networks have specific types of assessments performed before they will accept them as vendors. The topic is frequently also discussed in relationship to cyber insurance policies and branches of the federal government have also increasingly been laying requirements on any industry that wants to do business with them. It is important to explain the role of the community in assessments and what they are expected to do. Individual organizations within the community may require assessments be conducted by their vendors but this is not a community requirement but an individual organization requirement. The community will not be involved in assessment of individual organizations and their security policies except as it pertains to the whole-community cybersecurity effort. The community can, however, provide recommendations for individual organizations, especially small businesses, as to what they might want to examine in their own programs. This is another area where organizations may be willing to share what they use with others in the community and increasingly free resources can be found on the Internet to help organizations conduct assessments – especially against things like the requirements found in the NIST Cyber Security Framework. DHS/CISA also offers some forms of assessments for local governments and infrastructures.

Exercises, which are a major part of a community's assessment effort, will transition from tabletop events to more functional exercises in real or near-real time. In other words, for a functional (or partially functional) cybersecurity exercise or physical exercise with cyber elements the actual sequence of events an attacker might take will be conducted to a certain level to determine if individuals and organizations know what they should do. This level of exercise requires a lot more coordination to conduct and should incorporate as many stakeholders as possible. The key here is simulating a real event as much as possible without having to alter real-time system operations or impacting operational networks. Not impacting operational networks is a critical factor – while you want to "touch" operational networks potentially, the exercise should not unduly impact ongoing operations. When possible, exercise planners should seek input and participation from external organizations and neighboring communities for a true picture of how a cyber event may affect the region.

Phase 4: Integrated to Vanguard

In the fourth and last phase of CCSMM implementation, all of the pieces will be combined into a comprehensive program. The result will be a community that contains full cybersecurity awareness at all levels, including public and private organizations within the community as well as local citizens. Similar to a physical crime or event, a citizen is equipped with tools for reporting cyber incidents to proper authorities for further investigation, follow-up and response. Residents will be taught how to protect themselves, their data, and their devices using low or no-cost methods. Programs that simulate in the cyber arena non-cyber programs such as Crime Stoppers and Neighborhood Watches have already been proposed and implemented at some level in some communities. "Neighborhood Cyber Watches" and "Cybercrime Stoppers" will actually begin to be introduced at a lower level but at Level 5 this aspect should be well incorporated and understood in the community. A broad "culture of cybersecurity", though started at an earlier level, should be resident throughout the community.

Information sharing will be solidified during this phase, with full, bi-directional sharing and fusion of data. As organizations and individuals begin to share information, they are generally hesitant to share their own information although they are interested in receiving information. As they become more comfortable with the information sharing program they will gradually enter into a two-way sharing effort where they will not only receive information but will also be willing to share information about things that they see and that have occurred in their own organization. In addition to gathering data from multiple sources in various sectors, the fusion center and/or the community ISAO will regularly disseminate relevant information to stakeholders. Participation in the fusion center and/or community ISAO will expand to include all major community functions, including law enforcement, emergency services, various government functions, the private sector, education, etc. The fusion center and/or community ISAO will be either supported by local government funding or will be fully self-sufficient (in the case of the ISAO model). They will be integrated into emergency response activities when needed.

Technology decisions for security will be made consistently and include the needs of the community as part of the decision-making process. Any minor improvements should have been accomplished by this point, and major projects will be initiated or scheduled to be started. Sharing of best practices in terms of tools and processes to use them will be prevalent in the community.

Training and education will include the needs of the local community and will accomplish both awareness and specialized training for professionals. This effort will expand to include K-12 schools and higher education institutions providing a robust pipeline of security savvy individuals, and the community should provide assistance where possible.

Cyber incident response and recovery will become formal, with key partnerships established and well-documented. Mutual aid agreements between organizations or surrounding communities may be necessary and will be established. A mutual aid agreement is simply a document that lays out how two or more communities will agree to assist each other should one or more of them become involved in a cybersecurity event that is having a negative impact. It may include things such as an agreement to allow the attacked community to utilize the computing resources of the supporting community while they are recovering from the event. Leadership will provide support and assistance where needed. Plans that are derived as part of the CCSMM implementation will be reviewed at least annually, and a team should be established for the purpose of approving and implementing changes.

Finally, assessment, test, and exercise activities will evolve to a more advanced and comprehensive level. All of these should now include interaction with the state and other communities. Wherever possible, all exercises, no matter what the focus, will consider including cybersecurity elements. This includes natural disaster drills, anti-terrorism exercises, and medical emergency events. Participation in such activities will evolve to become well-rounded, meaning all sectors within the community will be represented. The CCSMM does not prescribe the type of exercise for this phase and leaves that decision up to planners. However, it is strongly suggested that at least one full-scale, community-wide cyber/physical exercise be planned and conducted every year. This is really the only way to ensure that everyone knows their role during an emergency that directly or indirectly impacts cyber assets within the community.

Also remember that Level 5 is the "Vanguard" level. Efforts in this phase should begin to incorporate elements from outside of the community. Other communities should be invited to participate in cybersecurity indicators of compromise information sharing, training, sharing of best practices, and exercises. In reality, a community will not simply jump into becoming a vanguard during this phase, elements will have been introduced at lower levels, but during this phase it becomes ingrained into the planning process.

LESSONS LEARNED: THE COMMUNITY CYBER SECURITY MATURITY MODEL

Without a model, such as the Community Cyber Security Maturity Model, to follow, cities can easily flounder in their attempt to establish a sustainable security program. An initial rise in cybersecurity awareness and a desire to do something to improve cybersecurity can quickly take a back seat to other issues that occur in the community. Even with the model, establishing a community-wide program is not an easy task. It will take time and it is easy for initial interest in it to dissipate as organizations face their day-to-day concerns and requirements. This is especially true in communities where the leadership changes on a regular basis. Elected officials have a number of concerns and cybersecurity is usually not one of the campaign points that they push. What has been shown to be a key factor in a community's ability to sustain the development of the program until it is mature enough to sustain itself is the need for a champion in the community.

It is not critical what sector the champion comes from, but it is essential that the champion remains in the community for a period of time sufficient for the community to establish the community program. In the past, champions have been individuals such as a city employee such as the city's CISO or CIO, a leader from an industry/business in the community such as a member of the local Chamber of Commerce, or an individual from an organization with sufficient support from leadership to spend time in coordinating meetings and encouraging individuals and various sectors across the community. At first the entire community may not be represented but there are a few organizations that are particularly important to have represented as early in the process of establishing a program as possible. This includes local government, the different utilities, community emergency management, law enforcement, and representatives from significant industry within the community.

It has also been shown to be helpful to have political coverage as well. A representative from Congress for the community can often pull together people in a meeting when interest may begin to dwindle due to other priorities within the community. Another item that can help is to quickly establish a Cybersecurity Day or a Culture of Security Day for the community. These events should include parts for government, industry and citizens so the level of cybersecurity in the community is raised and motivation to continue with establishing the program will be periodically rekindled.

From the beginning of the program, participants should understand that establishing a cybersecurity program will not occur overnight, nor is it something that can be done once and forgotten. It will be an ongoing effort that constantly will need to be updated as new technology is developed. Just like the police department, fire department, or emergency services, the need to maintain a high level of preparation and training in cybersecurity is essential as the "problem" is not going to go away.

CONCLUSION

Attacks on states and communities have increased and have become almost commonplace. In order to better handle intrusions and to hopefully prevent them in the first place, an organized cybersecurity program needs to be established within organizations in a community and with the community from a whole-community perspective. Awareness is often the first step taken to establish such a program but only raising the awareness of cybersecurity as an issue to be addressed is not sufficient to maintain long-term support for cybersecurity. Awareness alone is also not enough to ensure an organized approach to developing a sustainable program.

The Community Cyber Security Maturity Model (CCSMM) provides a way for a community to determine where they are in the maturity of their program, a plan to decide what they need to do in order to progress in maturing their program, and a common lexicon to be able to discuss programs between communities in different areas of the country. Discussing and being able to compare programs provides a way for all communities to share ideas on how to implement various aspects of the model and thus for all communities to work together in creating a more secure nation.

A community will need to first evaluate where they are at in terms of the maturity of their cybersecurity program. Then they must decide at what level they believe they will need to be in order to address the threats to their community. Not all communities have to be at the same level and not all communities need to attain the highest level of the model.

The 2-dimensional model contains five levels – Initial, Established, Self-assessed, Integrated, and Vanguard. Communities all start at the Initial level which is where they start planning for their program. When communities first recognize the importance of cybersecurity they generally do not have any budget set aside for it as budgets are established a year or more in advance. Efforts at the Initial level therefore are limited to as much as possible no- and low-cost items.

The second level is Established. As the name implies, programs at this level have been formally established and efforts to have a viable and sustainable cybersecurity program within the community are well underway. At the third level, Self-Assessed, communities have advanced far enough that their program should be sustainable and is mature enough that they are able to assess and understand their needs. Organizations within the community should be able to, and should actually be conducting efforts, to help each other. The fourth level is Integrated. At this level the community and organizations don't see cybersecurity as a separate component to their other operations but recognize that cybersecurity is cross-cutting and impacts every aspect of the community. Thus, cybersecurity needs to be considered by everyone. Finally, the fifth level is Vanguard and communities at this level are considered to be models for others to follow. A Vanguard community will be reaching out to the state and to other communities to help them with their own programs.

The CCSMM model is designed around four dimensions. At each level the characteristics for a community at that level in each of the dimensions is described. The dimensions are Awareness, Information Sharing, Policy and Planning. These will be discussed in more detail in subsequent chapters. In between each of the levels is a Phase which consists of the activities that must occur to advance the community from one level to the next. With five levels, there are four advancement phases.

Finally, it should be emphasized that it is often easy to confuse activities for individual organizations within a community and the overall whole-community cybersecurity program. While the community should be encouraging individual organizations to advance their own level of cybersecurity maturity, the community (as in the local government) is not responsible for the security of all organizations within its geographic boundaries. The CCSMM program is designed to help the whole-community to advance its level of security preparedness. It will include encouraging some organizations (such as the critical infrastructures and local government entities) to adopt certain cybersecurity practices but these are done only in relationship to how they impact the entire community. There are other models (including other parts of the CCSMM) that are designed to help individual organizations and these are discussed briefly in later chapters.

REFERENCES

Cybersecurity capability maturity model (C2M2). (2014, February). Retrieved February 27, 2020, from Energy.gov website: https://www.energy.gov/sites/prod/files/2014/03/f13/C2M2-v1-1_cor.pdf

DoD to streamline cyber acquisition with new certification model. (2019). Retrieved from MeriTalk website: https://www.meritalk.com/articles/dod-to-streamline-cyber-acquisition-with-new-certification-model/

Edwards, S., & Hays, S. (2019). *What is the cybersecurity maturity model certification (CMMC)?* Retrieved from SUMMIT7 website: https://info.summit7systems.com/blog/cmmc

White, G. (2011). The community cyber security maturity model. *IEEE Conference on Technologies for Homeland Security*, 173-178.

White, G. (2012). A Grassroots Cyber Security Program to Protect the Nation. *45th Hawaii International Conference on System Science.* 10.1109/HICSS.2012.60

White, G., & Granado, N. (2009). Developing a Community Cyber Security Incident Response Capability. *42nd Hawaii International Conference on System Science.*

ADDITIONAL READING

Curtis, P., Mehravari, N., & Stevens, J. (2015). *Cybersecurity capability maturity model for information technology services (C2M2 for IT services), version 1.0* (Technical Report No. CMU/SEI-2015-TR-009). Retrieved from Software Engineering Institute Carnegie Mellon University website: https://apps.dtic.mil/dtic/tr/fulltext/u2/1026943.pdf

Ross, R., Viscuso, P., Guissanie, G., Dempsey, K., & Riddle, M. (2015). NIST Special Publication: Vol. 800-171 Rev. 1. Protecting controlled unclassified information in nonfederal information systems and organizations. Retrieved from National Institute of Standards and Technology website: https://nvlpubs.nist.gov/nistpubs/SpecialPublications/NIST.SP.800-171.pdf

Chapter 3

The Three–Dimensional Model for a Community

ABSTRACT

The community cyber security maturity model (CCSMM) was designed and developed to provide communities with an action plan to build a viable and sustainable cybersecurity program focused on improving their overall cybersecurity capability. Not long after the initial development of the model, it was realized that there are intertwined relationships that needed to be addressed. This drove the creation of the three-dimensional model broadening the scope to include individuals, organizations, communities, states, and the nation. This chapter will provide an overview of the development and importance of the 3-D model and will describe the scope areas that were included.

INTRODUCTION

The 2-Dimensional model was the initial step to creating a roadmap for communities to follow when developing their cybersecurity program. The established characteristics help to define a community's cybersecurity posture at each level. As a reminder, the characteristics are organized by awareness, information sharing, policy, and planning dimensions. They also establish the three building blocks; a yardstick, a roadmap, and a common point of reference as previously discussed. It wasn't long after the characteristics were developed, that the CIAS researchers were discussing how cybersecurity

DOI: 10.4018/978-1-7998-4471-6.ch003

guidelines affecting individuals in the community could be integrated into the CCSMM or how cybersecurity concepts for states should be integrated. This led to the realization that the model didn't have enough depth to address these other areas. After many discussions, it was determined that the model needed to be 3-Dimensional (3-D). The model needed to be able to incorporate what individuals would need to do to improve their cybersecurity posture. It also needed to address organizations, states and ultimately the nation. There are two major considerations supporting this:

1) Everyone should have a role in cybersecurity
2) Effective cybersecurity is a collaborative effort

These concepts became the "The Whole Community Approach" theme for the Department of Homeland Security's cybersecurity initiatives many years later.

THE 3-DIMENSIONAL MODEL

The purpose of the 3-D Model is to broaden the capability of the framework allowing it to be flexible and scalable to address all aspects of a cybersecurity program. Consider the idea that individuals make up organizations; individuals and organizations make up communities; individuals, organizations and communities make up a state, tribe or territory; and the states, tribes and territories make up the nation. The change from a 2-D model to the 3-D model was a pivotal point in the creation of the Community Cyber Security Maturity Model. This shift created a model that can provide the improvement progression for everyone in the nation because the model can now support a roadmap for individuals, organizations, communities, states and the nation. In addition, it can integrate other frameworks such as the National Institute of Standards and Technology's (NIST) Cyber Security Framework (CSF) (NIST, 2018) outlining the security controls necessary for an organization. It can also support the National Initiative for Cybersecurity Education (NICE) Cybersecurity Workforce Framework (NICE Framework) (NIST, 2017) a resource that categorizes and describes cybersecurity work and the cybersecurity workforce. Communities should be able to advance their cybersecurity posture naturally, but a defined program that provides step by step guidance is the assistance that is realistically needed.

Once the 3-D Model was accepted, all the major concepts needed to be brought together. A visual was developed that could show the primary concepts in an easy and understandable fashion. The visual depiction of the 3-D Community Cyber Security Model is a cube as shown in Figure 1. The cube contains blocks representing the dimensions, the levels of improvement, and the scope areas. Across the top there are 5 blocks that identify the progression levels of cybersecurity maturity. The lowest level of maturity is Level 1 – Initial, and the most mature is Level 5 - Vanguard. Each level is a different color making the distinction of levels easier to see. The 4 vertical blocks represent the dimensions. The dimensions are the focus areas where cybersecurity is being improved. The blocks are 5 deep. Each of these blocks represents the scope areas. The scope areas are individual, organization, community, state and nation. These represent who is improving their cybersecurity posture.

The 3-D Model shown in Figure 1 shows the relationships of preparedness for the scope areas. As an example, the composition of a community includes individuals and organizations. The community's maturity level is influenced by the maturity of the individuals and organizations in that community. This dynamic shows how they are integrated together, and this directly affects the ability of the community's cybersecurity preparedness to address cyber threats. In fact, these relationships drive home the point that everyone has a role in cybersecurity.

The last major concept that needed to be reflected in the 3-D Model is how the implementation mechanisms are used to transition from Level 1 to Level 2 and so on. This visual depiction is represented in Figure 2.

Each block in the cube individually represents the characteristics for the level and the **phase** activities to transition to the next level. Each phase is associated with a specific **scope area.** To transition from one **level** to the next, for a specific **dimension**, the **implementation mechanisms** listed in the block are utilized to provide the activities needed to transition.

To use Figure 2 as an example: the separated block represents an organization that is currently at Level 1 and working on improving their cybersecurity awareness. The activities they need to complete in order to improve their awareness are metrics, technology, training, processes and procedures and assessments.

Figure 1.

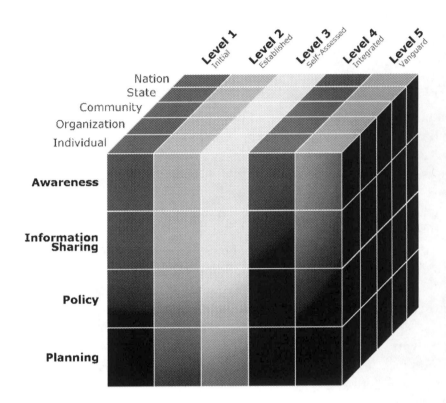

THE SCOPE AREAS

The CCSMM identifies specific scope areas that have a role in cybersecurity preparedness. The scope is defined as the range or the extent of the area that is involved in maturing their cybersecurity posture. As mentioned previously, the scope areas are individuals, organizations, communities, states, and the nation. Each of these scope areas can determine their own maturity level which ultimately affects each of the other areas.

It is important to reinforce the idea that everyone needs to have some level of understanding of cybersecurity. Technology touches every aspect of our modern lives. What once seemed to be science fiction, is reality today. Consider the technology and number of devices that connect to the internet found in homes, vehicles, and the extensive capabilities of smart phones. In addition,

Figure 2.

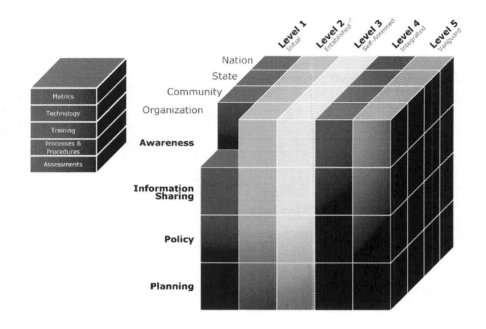

there aren't many jobs left that don't integrate technology to some degree. How secure individuals are at home can now impact the organization they work for. Working from home with a compromised computer and connecting to your organization's network; or moving information from home to work with a USB containing malware; or posting valuable business information on social media, are all significant risks to the business. This principle also exists between organizations in the community, the communities and the state and so on. This is the reason it is critical for the CCSMM to recognize each scope area.

Individual

The individual scope includes everyone who uses technology in some form. Improving an individual's cybersecurity preparedness, will start with the internet connected devices they use personally and are responsible for securing themselves, such as smartphones and their home wireless technologies. It should also include their computing habits while online.

Using the dimensions as a guide, individuals need to understand the following:

- **Awareness:** Individuals need to understand the threats they face using technologies, and if their device or online account is compromised, how this can impact them. They need to identify all the devices and data that is important to them and then learn how to protect them. They need to understand how to protect their privacy and why this is important. They also need to understand the importance of computer ethics especially as it pertains to downloading software, music or other licensed digital products.
- **Information Sharing:** What should be done when one sees malicious activity, experiences a cybercrime or incident? Individuals need to know who to report these activities to, when and how to report them.
- **Policy:** The individual needs to know what are good cybersecure practices they should be using while using their computers, laptops or other devices. They also need to understand good and bad practices while using email, social networking sites or purchasing online.
- **Plans:** What does the individual do if they are compromised? Here is where the individual should understand how to do backups, why they are important. They should also have some understanding of what to do if they have been compromised.

At each level of maturity, the activities of improvement will become more complex.

This scope area can support other frameworks and program initiatives that address cybersecurity at home, cybersecurity for the youth such as cyber bullying, cybersecurity gaming, cybersecurity competitions and cybersecurity educational activities. Cybersecurity initiatives such as the Culture of Cybersecurity shown in Figure 3. The Culture of Cybersecurity was created by the Center for Infrastructure Assurance and Security at the University of Texas at San Antonio. This and other programs should be considered to improve cybersecurity awareness for everyone. More information about programs such as this will be covered in more detail in the chapter for Awareness Programs.

Organization

The areas covered by the organization scope includes small businesses, government agencies, non-profit organizations, mid-size companies and large corporations. Essentially, the organization is any business activity in a community. An organization's cybersecurity preparedness should include the individuals or employees, its customers, partners, and supply chain. Its

Figure 3.

preparedness capabilities should also include the organizations assets including information, computers, and networks.

Using the dimensions as a guide, organizations need to understand the following:

- **Awareness:** Organizations need to understand the threats they face. As an example, threats could be introduced to the organization through malicious or criminal attacks, system failures and glitches, human error, or exploited through social engineering tactics. Each threat should be identified.

Organizations need to know how the identified threats can impact the business. Attacks such as destructive malware, stolen credit card details, or mobile ransomware, to name a few, have shown attacks can impact not only the business operation, but can impact customers, employees, or supply chain partners by making information unavailable that is critically needed. Cyber incidents can also impact how secure the information is or modify the information making it untrustworthy. Organizations must safeguard all areas of the business including their reputation.

Organizations need to know how to detect malicious activities on their networks.

Organizations need to know how to protect their information and systems; understand how physical security plays a role in their cybersecurity program; and will need to address what level of cybersecurity awareness each employee, partner or supply chain associate needs to protect the organization.

- **Information Sharing:** Organizations should consider information sharing both inside their organization and outside. Employees should know who within the organization to report suspicious activity to. They should also address how to escalate cyber incident information to levels of management for their situational awareness and in more critical situations, to make decisions for the business. In addition, it should be determined what types of cyber incidents will be reported outside the organization, to whom and what threshold must be reached to trigger external reporting. It's a good practice to consult legal counsel to ensure compliance, privacy and other regulatory requirements have been considered. Establishing relationships and building trust with organizations and agencies before an incident will make the whole process easier because it is already known who to contact, what to expect and what to ask for. When the organization is in an emergency situation, not knowing what to do and who to contact will add stress to the situation and will add time to the response.
- **Policy:** Organizations need to document the cybersecure practices everyone associated with the organization should be using. Some examples are internet use, accessing social networking sites, connecting to the organization remotely, and technology disposal. How often policies should be reviewed and updated should also be implemented.
- **Plans:** Organizations should have at a minimum a plan to backup organizational information. Once established, organizations should

implement plans for cybersecurity incident response, continuity, and disaster recovery plans.

At each level of maturity, the activities of improvement will become more complex.

Frameworks to improve organizational cybersecurity can be incorporated in this scope area for example, the National Institute of Standards and Technology's (NIST) Cyber Security Framework (CSF) (NIST, 2018) outlining the security controls necessary for an organization can be utilized in the policy dimension. The Department of Defense's new verification mechanism of cybersecurity controls called the Cybersecurity Maturity Model Certification (CMMC) can also be incorporated. To categorize and describe positions needed within the organization, the National Initiative for Cybersecurity Education (NICE) Cybersecurity Workforce Framework (NICE Framework) (NIST, 2017) can be used.

Communities

The area covered by the community scope is a defined geographical area. A community includes small, mid-size and large businesses, local government, emergency services, non-profit organizations, critical infrastructure, and the citizens living in that geographical area. The community will determine the area covered by the community scope that will be included in their cybersecurity preparedness; for example, a community may determine their cybersecurity program will include the surrounding cities and counties that are on the outskirts of the metropolitan area. Alternatively, the smaller cities or counties will have their own cybersecurity program but may look to the larger community as a mentor.

Using the dimensions as a guide, communities need to address the following:

- **Awareness:** Communities need to understand the threats they face and how these threats can impact the business operations, and critical services (essential functions) they provide. They will also need to determine what the potential cascading effects may be and how community services, organizations and citizens may be impacted. In the case of a cyber incident disrupting a critical service such as power, the community needs to recognize that additional communities, states or regions may be impacted. This could affect who the community could get assistance from.

Examples of ransomware attacks the past couple of years have shown how attacks such as this can disrupt local governments and public services with devastating financial impacts and potentially life-threatening consequences.

Communities need to identify what information and systems they will need to protect. They should also understand how physical security plays a role in their cybersecurity program; and will need to address who in the community needs what type of cybersecurity awareness.

- **Information Sharing:** Communities will need to consider information sharing both inside their community and outside; and will need to understand what cyber threat indicators are needed to recognize the community is under a cyber-attack.

Communities need to address how to escalate cyber incident information to state and national agencies. In addition, the types of cyber incidents that will be reported outside the community needs to be determined, who it should be reported to, and what threshold must be reached to trigger that reporting. Building relationships and establishing trust with these organizations and agencies before an incident will assist to ensure the information shared is timely, relevant and actionable.

- **Policy:** Communities will need to integrate cybersecurity concepts into established community policies. These policies will address at minimum, standard operating practices, communication methods, and establish the authorization hierarchy for the community. As an example, communities who augment their communications methods with the use of social media channels should ensure these policies include good cybersecurity behaviors with privacy and security considerations. Communities need to identify roles, and the authorization hierarchy to address cybersecurity practices for the community. As an example, who makes the final decision to take a server that supports a critical service "off-line".
- **Plans:** Communities should have at a minimum a continuity of operations plan (COOP) or an emergency management plan to address disasters that may impact the community. These plans should be reviewed to ensure cybersecurity elements have been incorporated. Additional plans that should be in place as the community matures, is a cybersecurity incident response plan such as a Cyber Incident Response Annex, and a disaster recovery plan, also called a disruption plan.

A very important consideration that must be addressed in the community plans is what will be done at the local level. All incidents occur at the local level and even if the incident must be escalated to the state or federal level for assistance, there could be a significant amount of time before assistance is onsite. The community should have a plan for what will be done, at a minimum, 72 hours after assistance has been requested. Recognize the time it takes to recover and get back to normal may be considerably longer. Communications with the media and citizens must be considered. Alternate operations methods for essential functions must be considered. There have been many examples of communities having to revert to paper and pencil for critical functions. How many people on staff will know what to do in this case? Does training exist to ensure this backup capability can be achieved?

The community scope area is where Fusion Centers, Security Operations Centers, and Community Information Sharing and Analysis Organizations (ISAOs) will be integrated into the community cybersecurity program. Professional organizations such as ISACA, ISSA, and InfraGard chapters should be established and integrated into the program to improve both cybersecurity and information sharing capabilities throughout the community. Initiatives such as cybersecurity workforce development may be established at local community colleges or universities.

States

The scope for a state includes its counties, cities, towns, critical infrastructures, state agencies, and citizens. While the scope area here only mentions the state, it is also intended to address tribes and territories. States, tribes, and territories are different in many ways, especially where planning for disasters is concerned; however, the cybersecurity practices that should be considered are very similar.

The cybersecurity preparedness of a state typically addresses the government agencies throughout the state and may include the critical infrastructures. Addressing the government agencies alone in a state is a tremendous task as there are likely hundreds of agencies in any given state. The issue, however, is all individuals, organizations and communties in the state can affect the states cybersecurity preparedness in both positive and negative ways. Simply put, if communities within the state are not prepared, they may need extensive incident response assistance and require significant resources. State cyber resources are most likely limited, which means a cyber-attack impacting multiple communities simultaneously may deplete all the resources available and in fact, there may not be enough resources to support multiple attacks. On the other hand, the private sector offers tremendous and valuable cybersecurity capabilities and skillsets. The state would benefit from public private partnerships such as this and may be able to supplement cybersecurity resources in the event a significant cyber incident occurs. This is also where the National Guard can be integrated to assist in responding to cyber-attacks and incidents.

Using the dimensions as a guide, states, tribes and territories need to understand the following:

- **Awareness:** States, tribes and territories need to understand the threats they face and how these threats can impact the business operations and critical services provided within the state. They will also need to determine what the potential cascading effects may be and how state and community services, organizations and citizens may be impacted.

States need to identify what critical services, information and systems will need to be protected. They should also understand how physical security plays a role in their cybersecurity program; and will need to address who in the state needs what type of cybersecurity awareness.

- **Information Sharing:** States will need to consider information sharing within the state and should also address how to escalate cyber incident information to national agencies. States need to understand what cyber threat indicators are needed to recognize the state is experiencing a cyber-attack.

In addition, it should be determined what types of cyber incidents will be reported, who it should be reported to, and what threshold must be reached to trigger that reporting. Building relationships and establishing trust with these agencies before an incident will assist to ensure the information shared is timely, relevant, and actionable.

- **Policy:** States will need to integrate cybersecurity concepts into established policies. These policies should address, at a minimum, the standard operating practices, communication methods, roles, and the authorization hierarchy to address cybersecurity practices for the state. This should include policies surrounding how communities in the state can request assistance regarding cyber preparedness and cyber incident response.

- **Plans:** States need to have, at a minimum, a continuity of operations plan (COOP) or an emergency operation plan to address "All Hazard" disasters that may impact the state. These plans should be reviewed to ensure cybersecurity elements have been incorporated. Additional plans that should be in place are a cybersecurity incident response plan such as a Cyber Incident Response Annex, and a disaster recovery plan, also called a disruption plan. This is where cyber incident response teams and the National Guard may play a role.

The state's plan should also address how, who, with what resources, and under what circumstances it will assist communities in the state to implement cybersecurity practices and respond to cyber-attacks or incidents.

The state scope area should also consider how the following organizations and agencies are integrated into the overall cybersecurity program for the state:

- Fusion Centers
- State Operations Centers
- Security Operations Centers
- Information Sharing and Analysis Organizations (ISAOs) to include community, regional, private sector
- Information Sharing and Analysis Centers (ISACs) associated with critical infrastructure

Nation

The scope for the nation includes states, tribes, territories, communities, critical infrastructures, federal agencies, and citizens. The role of the federal government is to ensure personal freedoms, economic vitality and to provide national security for the citizens of the United States. The federal government also has a role in cyber preparedness for the nation. "On November 2018, President Trump signed into law the Cybersecurity the Cybersecurity and Infrastructure Security Agency Act of 2018," which establishes the Cybersecurity and Infrastructure Security Agency (CISA), to "build the national capacity to defend against cyber-attacks and works with the federal government to provide cybersecurity tools, incident response services and assessment capabilities to safeguard the'.gov' networks that support the essential operations of partner departments and agencies.

For cybersecurity, CISA's main focus areas include:

- Combatting Cyber Crime and Cyber Incident Response
- Securing Federal Networks, Protecting Critical Infrastructure, and providing Cybersecurity Governance
- Promoting Information Sharing, Training and Exercises, and Cyber Safety information" (DHS, 2019).

Using the dimensions as a guide, the national scope area should address the following:

- **Awareness:** The federal government needs to understand the threats the nation faces and how these threats can impact critical services provided the federal government. They will also need to determine what the potential cascading effects may be and how services may be impacted.

The federal government needs to identify what critical services, information and systems will need to be protected. They should also understand how physical security plays a role in their cybersecurity strategy; and will need to address who in needs cybersecurity awareness and to what extent.

- **Information Sharing:** The federal government will need to consider information sharing within the nation. In addition, it should be determined what types of cyber incidents will be shared, who it should be shared with, and what constitutes a cyber incident that may impact the nation.
- **Policy:** The federal government will need to integrate cybersecurity concepts into established policies. These policies will address standard operating practices, communication strategies, and the protection of critical infrastructures.
- **Plans:** The federal government needs to have a continuity of operations strategy to address all hazard disasters, that includes cyber, that may impact the nation. They need to have a cybersecurity strategy that can be incorporated into all national policies. In addition, a national cyber incident response strategy needs to be in place. This dimension is where cyber incident response teams and the Department of Defense plays a role.

The federal government has established a significant number of programs to increase public-private partnerships to improve situational awareness of cyber threats and improve cybersecurity capabilities; developed strategies that are cybersecurity focused or include cybersecurity; established information sharing initiatives to increase cybersecurity capabilities; and created plans that states and communities can use as templates to improve their cybersecurity capabilities.

Some examples of initiatives, programs and partnerships that have been established by the federal government to improve the nation's cybersecurity posture are:

- **Protected Critical Infrastructure Information Program:** Formed as a result of the passage of the Critical Infrastructure Act in 2002, the PCII Program affords protections to information provided by the private sector to the federal government. These protections include exemption from the federal FOIA, state and local disclosure laws, regulatory action, and civil litigation. Although DHS manages the PCII program at the federal level, states are encouraged to maintain their own programs in order to provide access to PCII protected information for state and local authorities with a need to know.

- **ISAO SO** - The ISAO Standards Organization is a non-governmental organization established through Executive Order 13691 on October 1, 2015. The ISAO Standards Organization's mission is to improve the Nation's cybersecurity posture by identifying standards and guidelines for robust and effective information sharing related to cybersecurity risks, incidents, and best practices.

As per the Executive Order, the ISAO Standards Organization, led by the University of Texas at San Antonio has been continuously working with, and will continue to work with, existing information sharing organizations, owners and operators of critical infrastructure, relevant agencies, and other public and private sector stakeholders to identify a common set of voluntary standards or guidelines for the creation and functioning of ISAOs.

- **National Training and Education Division**: The National Training and Education Division (NTED) provides tailored training to enhance the capacity of state and local jurisdictions to prepare for, prevent, deter, respond to, and recover safely and effectively from potential manmade and natural catastrophic events, including terrorism.

- **Cyber Security Advisors (CSAs):** are regionally located DHS personnel who direct coordination, outreach, and regional support to protect cyber components essential to the sustainability, preparedness, and protection of U.S. critical infrastructure and state, local, territorial, and tribal (SLTT) governments. CSAs offer immediate and sustained assistance to prepare and protect SLTT and private entities. They bolster the cybersecurity preparedness, risk mitigation, and incident response capabilities of these entities and bring them into closer coordination with the federal government. CSAs represent a front-line approach and promote resilience of key cyber infrastructures throughout the United States and its territories.

- **National Continuity Programs:** The Federal Emergency Management Agency's National Continuity Programs (NCP) serves the public by coordinating the federal programs and activities that preserve our nation's essential functions across a wide range of potential threats and emergencies. On behalf of the White House, the Secretary of Homeland Security, and the FEMA Administrator, NCP guides and assists the planning and implementation of continuity programs that enable federal, state, tribal, territorial, and local governments to deliver critical services to survivors throughout all phases of a disaster. Continuity and sustainment of essential functions is a shared responsibility of the whole community. Development and maintenance of continuity capabilities helps build and sustain a more resilient nation equipped to sustain essential functions, deliver critical services, and supply core capabilities under all conditions.

- **The National Cybersecurity and Communications Integration Center's (NCCIC):** mission is to reduce the risk of systemic cybersecurity and communications challenges in our role as the Nation's flagship cyber defense, incident response, and operational integration center. Since 2009, the NCCIC has served as a national hub for cyber and communications information, technical expertise, and operational integration, and by operating our 24/7 situational awareness, analysis, and incident response center.

- **Critical Infrastructure Partnership Advisory Council (CIPAC):** Those who engage in these partnerships enhance their communication, planning, risk assessments, program implementation, incident response, recovery and operational activities.

- **The Regional Consortium Coordinating Council (RC3):** provides a framework that supports existing regional groups in their efforts to promote resilience activities in the public and private sectors. RC3 supports its member organizations with awareness, education, and mentorship on a wide variety of subjects, projects, and initiatives to advance critical infrastructure security and resilience, vulnerability reduction, and consequence mitigation.

- **National Risk Management Center**: is the Cybersecurity and Infrastructure Security Agency's (CISA) planning, analysis, and collaboration center working to identify and address the most significant risks to the Nation's critical infrastructure. Through the NRMC's collaborative efforts with the private sector, government agencies, and other key stakeholders, the CISA works to identify, analyze, prioritize, and manage high-consequence threats to critical infrastructure through a crosscutting risk management paradigm.
- **The National Cyber Incident Response Plan (NCIRP):** The NCIRP describes a national approach to dealing with cyber incidents; addresses the important role that the private sector, state and local governments, and multiple federal agencies play in responding to incidents and how the actions of all fit together for an integrated response. The NCIRP reflects and incorporates lessons learned from exercises, real world incidents and policy and statutory updates, such as the Presidential Policy Directive/PPD-41: *U.S. Cyber Incident Coordination*, and the National Cybersecurity Protection Act of 2014. The NCIRP also serves as the Cyber Annex to the Federal Interagency Operational Plan (FIOP) that built upon the National Planning Frameworks and the National Preparedness System.

CONCLUSION

The 3-Dimensional Model expanded the capability of the CCSMM framework allowing it to be flexible and scalable to address all aspects of a cybersecurity program. The 3-D Model provides the improvement progression for everyone in the nation. It is a roadmap to improve cybersecurity for individuals, organizations, communities, states and the nation, called scope areas. The scope areas can address cybersecurity by using the dimensions to improve their awareness of cyber threats and impacts, information sharing capabilities of cyber threat indicators, incorporate cyber into their policies and to understand what plans are needed for continuity, response and recovery.

The individual scope includes everyone who utilizes technology, no matter if it is a smart phone, smart television, laptop, tablet, iPad or some other device connected to the internet. This scope area will also include the youth of our country and should include safety topics such as cyber bullying. It should also include engaging initiatives such as cybersecurity gaming, cybersecurity competitions and other educational activities.

The scope for organizations includes small businesses, government agencies, non-profit organizations, mid-size companies and large corporations. An organization's cybersecurity preparedness will include all individuals associated with the organization. This could include individuals or employees, customers, partners, and those included in the supply chain. Organizational assets should be included in preparedness capabilities including information, computers, and networks.

The community scope is a defined geographical area, and includes small, mid-size and large businesses, local government, emergency services, non-profit organizations, critical infrastructure, and the citizens living in that geographical area. The community should define the area of scope included in its preparedness efforts. This could include smaller cities and counties surrounding the community. The larger community could, alternatively, become a mentor to adjoining smaller cities and counties.

The scope for a state, tribe or territory includes its counties, cities, towns, critical infrastructures, state agencies, and citizens. Cybersecurity preparedness for a state, tribe or territory most likely addresses government agencies and may also include critical infrastructures. In order to address other aspects that may impact the state, cybersecurity preparedness should also include individuals, organizations in the private-sector and communities in the state, tribe or territories. In addition, the role of Fusion Centers, State Operations Centers, ISAOs and ISACs should be considered in the overall cybersecurity program.

Finally, the scope for the nation includes states, tribes, territories, communities, critical infrastructures, federal agencies, and citizens. The federal government has a role in cyber preparedness for the nation and has established numerous initiatives, programs and partnerships to improve cybersecurity, information sharing and cybersecurity capabilities.

The next several chapters will expand the concepts of the dimensions and provide a mapping for the improving through the levels.

REFERENCES

About Us. (n.d.). Retrieved August 16, 2019, from ISAO Standards Organization website: https://www.isao.org/about/

CISA Cyber Infrastructure. (n.d.). *Protected critical infrastructure information (PCII) program.* Retrieved August 22, 2019, from U.S. Department of Homeland Security CISA Cyber Infrastructure website: https://www.cisa.gov/pcii-program

CMMC model v1.0. (n.d.). Retrieved February 25, 2020, from Office of the Under Secretary of Defense for Acquisition & Sustainment Cybersecurity Maturity Model Certification website: https://www.acq.osd.mil/cmmc/draft.html

County of Marin. (n.d.). www.marincounty.org/depts/ad/divisions/management-and-budget/ administrative-policies-and-procedures/administrative-regulation-no-1_25

Cyber Incident Annex. (n.d.). Retrieved August 13, 2019, from US Department of Homeland Security FEMA website: https://www.fema.gov/media-library/assets/documents/25556

Cybersecurity division mission and vision. (n.d.). Retrieved August 17, 2019, from US Department of Homeland Security CISA Cyber + Infrastructure website: https://www.dhs.gov/cisa/cybersecurity-division

DHS role in cyber incident response. (n.d.). Retrieved August 25, 2019, from US Department of Homeland Security CISA Cyber + Infrastructure website: https://www.cisa.gov/publication/dhs-role-cyber-incident-response

Information sharing and awareness. (n.d.). Retrieved August 22, 2019, from US Department of Homeland Security CISA Cyber + Infrastructure website: https://www.cisa.gov/information-sharing-and-awareness

National continuity programs. (n.d.). Retrieved August 2, 2019, from US Department of Homeland Security FEMA website: https://www.fema.gov/national-continuity-programs

National Institute of Standards and Technology. (2018, April). *Framework for improving critical infrastructure cybersecurity* (Publication No. Version 1.1). Retrieved from https://nvlpubs.nist.gov/nistpubs/CSWP/NIST.CSWP.04162018.pdf

NIST Special Publication 800-181. (2017). *National Initiative for Cybersecurity Education (NICE) Cybersecurity Workforce Framework (NICE Framework)*. Retrieved from https://nvlpubs.nist.gov/nistpubs/SpecialPublications/NIST. SP.800-181.pdf?trackDocs=NIST.SP.800-181.pdf

The national cyber incident response plan (NCIRP). (n.d.). Retrieved August 19, 2019, from US Department of Homeland Security CISA Cyber + Infrastructure website: https://www.us-cert.gov/ncirp

U.S. Department of Homeland Security. (n.d.). *Cybersecurity strategy*. Retrieved October 27, 2019, from https://www.dhs.gov/sites/default/files/ publications/DHS-Cybersecurity-Fact-Sheet.pdf

U.S. Department of Homeland Security. (n.d.). *Cybersecurity*. Retrieved August 24, 2019, from The Department of Homeland Security website: https://www.dhs.gov/topic/cybersecurity

Welcome to the national preparedness course catalog. (n.d.). Retrieved August 31, 2019, from National Training and Education Division | US Department of Homeland Security - FEMA website: https://www.firstrespondertraining. gov/frts/npcc

Chapter 4
Awareness

ABSTRACT

Awareness is a term used to describe an individual's knowledge of a topic. One would expect that awareness of the cybersecurity threat is well understood because of the continual reports of cyber incidents and attacks impacting individuals, organizations, and cyber-attacks on communities and states. The CIAS found it was true that people understood cyber incidents and attacks were happening. They also understood they needed to protect their assets and information, and they needed to be able to respond and recover from incidents that might occur. The significant gap was they did not understand all the impacts that could occur from a cyber incident, and they didn't understand the cascading impacts that could domino from a single attack. The lessons learned regarding awareness are incorporated into the awareness dimension of the CCSMM and include what each member of a community needs to know based on their role in the community.

INTRODUCTION

A security awareness program can be a valuable tool to ensure everyone understands the cyber threat and to reduce the amount of weaknesses that can be exploited by an attacker. Everyone needs to be aware of common threats, so that, at the very least, they do not become a victim of easier scams and phishing attempts. When addressing more sophisticated attacks, users can at least apply the knowledge acquired during training to mitigate the effects of the attack, gather the info necessary for security professionals to act and

DOI: 10.4018/978-1-7998-4471-6.ch004

know who to notify through the right channels. End users are an incredibly important aspect of a security program to reduce risks and to prevent cyber threats.

Security awareness programs often get scrutinized when determining their worth. The greatest argument against the awareness program is no matter how much training users receive; breaches that target end users are still occurring and continue to have a high success rate because people continue to be the weakest link in the cyber security chain. Often, it is also pointed out that there is a disconnect between the users' performance and ability to recognize threats in their behaviors and responses in a real-life environment. When designing a security awareness program and implementing a cybersecurity culture, the important aspect to focus on is not whether security awareness is worth it, but whether the program implemented is effective and really addresses the needs of the community.

Questions to think about include:

- Is the effort supported by leadership?
- Are awareness topics relevant to the individual based on their role in the community?
- Have we educated people on data breach prevention and response?
- Do people know who to contact if they discover a security threat?
- Do people know what constitutes a security threat?
- Do people understand the real value of data?
- Do we have regular training to keep the most current cyber threats known within the community?
- How do we know the awareness program is effective?

BACKGROUND

The community cybersecurity exercises, discussed in previous chapters, were used as a tool to not only assess the preparedness of the community in terms of how they would respond to a cybersecurity event, but it was also used as a mechanism to provide relevant awareness to the stakeholders in the community. Using the exercise as the catalyst, CIAS was able to introduce cybersecurity terminology, various types of cyber-attacks, show how each attack could impact a particular organization or sector, and the exercise injects were used to show the cascading effects a single cyber-attack could have on the greater community.

Injects used in the exercise included attacks such as:

- email bomb threats to the city
- defaced web pages
- malicious software that caused the loss of critical data
- malicious software that created bogus computerized transactions
- distributed denial of service attacks
- increased intrusion detection system alarms
- spam and phishing attacks
- misinformation attacks
- war driving
- war chalking
- cyber advisories
- physical events impacting cyber capabilities
- cyber-attacks causing physical effects

These attacks were used in the exercise against a variety of targets within the community, such as portions of the city government, the port authorities, utilities, the Coast Guard, and industry. The targets were tailored specifically to the community; therefore, if the community did not have the Coast Guard represented, a different sector would have been chosen. Academic institutions, not normally used in first responder situations, were utilized as launching points for some of the cyber-attacks. Lessons learned, from an awareness perspective, revolved around who in the community had the potential to see or act on suspicious activities that could lead to better situational awareness or early detection of the incident. Questions asked of the exercise participants provided insight into what was really understood regarding the cyber threat. It helped to determine if participants recognized the potential implications of the cyber incident. It also helped to determine if the participants knew who to report suspicious activity to, and what other actions were needed, if any.

Recommendations from the community exercises noted that awareness programs needed to be established in the community for the various stakeholders, and low and no cost solutions to provide quality cybersecurity training needed to be researched and implemented in a cooperative manner.

COMMUNITY AWARENESS

Creating a cybersecurity awareness program for a community is different from creating an awareness program for an organization. Awareness at the organizational level will be focused on supporting the mission and goals for the organization. The individuals that will be trained are primarily the workforce, partners, and possibly customers. The training will include the potential threats to the organization; and will address how to protect the systems and information that are collected and used for the business. In comparison, a community awareness program can be much bigger in scope and the awareness needs will be much more diverse. If the community awareness program is all inclusive, it will need to include everyone in a specific geographical area. The program would address small, mid-size, and large businesses, local government, emergency services, non-profit organizations, critical infrastructure, and the citizens. Everyone in the community has a role in cybersecurity and the program should address each at various levels. Overall, the community's awareness would need to include the cyber threats the community may face and would need to address how these threats can impact the business operations, and critical services (mission essential functions) they provide. Additionally, the awareness program would also need to help the community understand what the potential cascading effects may be and how community services, organizations and citizens may be impacted.

Community awareness starts with ensuring the leadership of the community have a good understanding of the cyber threats the community may face. This could be executives in industry, business owners, local government officials, elected officials, leadership in religious organizations throughout the community, leaders associated with schools, colleges, or universities. This is most certainly not an all-inclusive list, and ultimately a leader is defined as anyone who has influence in the community. Once those leaders are engaged, they can promote cybersecurity awareness within their organizations, then include more organizations, then the citizens, until everyone in the community is engaged in the program.

Culture of Cybersecurity

Cybersecurity ultimately needs to be a state of mind and integrated into everything. A culture of cybersecurity needs to be established. National campaigns such as Smokey Bear and McGruff the Crime Dog can be used as examples. Smokey Bear was created in 1944 and is the longest-running public service campaign. He is one of the most recognized mascots in modern history, and eight in 10 people recognize his message "Only You Can Prevent Forest Fires." McGruff the Crime Dog was introduced in 1979, to encourage Americans to help with crime prevention. McGruff's image and slogan "Take a Bite out of Crime" are still effective today, with more than 93% of children recognizing the crime dog ("Crime Prevention," n.d.). The CIAS has created a family of characters to help people of all ages to become more aware of cybersecurity principles that will help them navigate the digital world safely. The CyBear Family were introduced March 2019. To appeal to all ages and to address varying interests and needs with technology, an entire family was created. Each of the CyBear family members is named after a significant historical person who contributed to cybersecurity. A website providing activities for kids, tips for adults and links to free cybersecurity educational games is available at www.cultureofcybersecurity.com.

Figure 1.

A culture of security will take time. It requires everyone to share a set of values surrounding security behaviors, such as how they think about cybersecurity. The values will also help to set their expectations of what good cybersecurity practices are. A culture of cybersecurity will require more than awareness, it will require all the principles of the CCSMM to be implemented creating a mix of knowledge and application. Striving for a culture of security should be considered in the design of the community cybersecurity program. The awareness portion of the program should start immediately because it will take time to reach everyone in the community and to achieve a real level of cybersecurity understanding.

Implementation of a culture of security can be broken down into segments. Targeting specific portions of the community can make implementation much more focused and will make this a manageable initiative. Below are suggested groupings the community can consider. An important point here is to recognize that scope areas are often intertwined. Improving any dimension whether it is awareness, information sharing, policies or plans, there will likely include other areas of scope. For instance, the community will often need to consider the individuals and organizations in order to improve the overall awareness for the community. The same is true of the dimensions. An example here would include instances where awareness is needed for information sharing processes and plans for incident response.

- **Culture of Security for Leadership:** This will be one of the first initiatives needed. The leadership in the community will be a key factor to building a culture of security throughout the community. Leadership buy-in will make all the difference when it comes to planning for future initiatives, funding those initiatives, setting priorities, and keeping the movement active. It will be important to identify which leaders in the community should initially be involved and then how additional leaders in the community can be brought into the discussions and activities in building the program. A method for how to improve leadership cybersecurity awareness will be needed. Exploring ways that will fit into their busy schedules and the level of content that will help them to understand exactly what the cyber threat is today, how it may impact organizations in the community, how it may impact the community as a whole and what is needed to prepare for incidents will help leaders to make decisions, assign resources, and direct actions as needed. Defining how to maintain awareness for the leadership will also need to be considered. Monthly or quarterly briefings may work to support leadership awareness. As the number of leaders who are participating grows, a leadership forum may be created and those briefings to provide updates, trends and new threats can be presented to the group.
- **Culture of Security for K-12:** Building initiatives that include K-12 in the community will also need to be implemented early in the

development of the program. The youth are exposed to technology at very young ages. Even two-year old children are given a parent's phone to watch videos or to facetime a family member or friend of the family. By the time a child is in school they most likely have been exposed to technology or are using technology such as a gaming unit like PlayStation or Xbox that can be played online. Children who are using technology should be at a minimum introduced to the basics of how to stay safe online and cyber ethics may also be a good thing to teach. There are many existing programs that can be integrated into the community program. Additionally, there are Science Technology Engineering Mathematics (STEM) K-12 initiatives that include cybersecurity that students in this category can benefit from. Exposing students to STEM activities encourages them to become familiar and potentially become very interested in career paths such as cybersecurity. Cybersecurity puzzles, worksheets, games, competitions and internships can be used to increase cybersecurity awareness for K-12, and can also build technical competencies and hone their skills. Cyber Threat Defender (CTD) the collectible cybersecurity card game can be used in middle school and high school classrooms to introduce and reinforce cybersecurity topics in the classroom. The CyberPatriot program and Code Jam are additional cybersecurity resources that can be introduced to this group. Check to see if any of the schools in the community are participating in cybersecurity STEM programs such as these. If there are none, find out how to bring them into the community to start a culture of security for K-12.

- **Culture of Security for Higher Education:** This group will include two-year colleges, technical training institutions, and universities. If local colleges and universities do not have cybersecurity degree programs, the community may want to encourage them to be created and offered. This can be a lengthy process for a higher education institution as they will have accreditation requirements they must meet for new courses. Having degree programs offered will assist in creating workforce with cybersecurity knowledge and skills. Some two-year colleges and technical institutes offer courses to prepare students to obtain certifications such as CompTIA Network+, Security+, and A+. Students with the skills to receive these certifications are attractive to companies needing technically capable employees. The community can determine if there is a local college or university participating in the Collegiate Cyber Defense Competitions. If there are none, this is a tremendous program that assists the students to apply what they are learning and practice new skills. If there is a college or university involved in this program, the community can support this activity by encouraging students to participate and provide volunteers to mentor and coach the players.

- **Culture of Security for Workforce:** Employed citizens by local organizations may be receiving cybersecurity awareness training through their organizations. This is most often done as a compliance measure and may not address how a cyber incident can impact the greater community. A possible place where the community can play a role in the workforce awareness is by coordinating efforts throughout the community to assist organizations to have access to low-cost training and other resources that are being offered around the country that may not be known. A working group could be formed with members from the community representing the various groups such as the leadership, K-12, organizations including small business, critical infrastructure organizations, and the citizens. This working group can identify the types of awareness initiatives and training that are needed and can research free resources that can be distributed throughout the community. There are a number of DHS resources that can be obtained for free. Some examples are from the DHS program "STOP. THINK. CONNECT." This is a DHS campaign for national public awareness aimed at increasing the public's understanding regarding cyber threats. The campaign shares cyber tips and resources, videos on online security and how individuals can protect themselves. Another free resource is the FEMA training posted on firstrespondertraining.gov that has both online and instructor-led training available. The training found on this website has technical training to enhance skills and capabilities of technical personnel and has non-technical training for everyone regarding cybersecurity. The working group may be part of the cooperative cyber training program discussed later in this chapter.
- **Culture of Security for Public awareness:** Cybersecurity awareness that extends to the public will take time. The community may want to consider creating ways to engage the public early in the development of the culture of security program. The STOP. THINK. CONNECT. campaign sponsored by DHS was established in 2010 and even today there are people that have never heard of it. This is a testament to how important it is to have multiple ways to communicate and engage the public about cybersecurity. If the other areas of the culture of security

are segmented and approaches taken to specifically target each group, the end result will be that more people are being reached in a shorter period of time and are being exposed to cybersecurity issues that impact them directly and they can relate to making the concepts more relevant. The remainder of the public that would need to be targeted for cybersecurity awareness initiatives are stay at home parents, students who are home-schooled, people who are retired and the unemployed. This may not be a complete listing but will cover a large portion of the public that might not receive cybersecurity awareness in other ways. These portions of the public can be reached by distributing information and resources such as the Cybear activity sheets and tips to those who are at home or being home-schooled. Engaging professional groups that may include members who are retired and connecting with retired social groups is another way to reach this portion of the public. These groups sometimes look for speakers at luncheons or as part of their normal meetings. Cybersecurity presentations for these events can be an interesting and enlightening engagement.

- **Culture of Security for Small Businesses:** Small businesses are highly targeted by cyber criminals. The Verizon Data Breach Investigation Report (DBIR) shows that 43% of all data breaches targeted small businesses (2019 Data [Page #5]). Often times small businesses are unable to dedicate the cybersecurity resources needed to protect their networks and data. The community may find that it is beneficial to include small businesses in their program. Small businesses may have a large customer base within the community and any information loss could impact those in the community directly.

- **Culture of Security for Critical Infrastructure:** "It should be noted that critical infrastructure is more than just the power grid and includes the defense and healthcare sectors, critical manufacturing and food production, water and transportation" (Cobb, 2018). Critical infrastructure has been recognized since the late 1990's as an important aspect of any community that needs protecting but "most critical infrastructure in the United States is owned and managed by organizations in the private sector" ("Critical infrastructure," n.d.). Every year there are reports of critical infrastructure breaches due to Industrial Control System (ICS) network and Supervisory Control and Data Acquisition (SCADA) weaknesses, aging technology and lack of information sharing. As the community culture of security is developed, the community may want to identify all critical infrastructure organizations that do business in the jurisdiction. Then consider critical infrastructure that may be outside the jurisdiction that the community relies on.

Activities Used for Awareness

Increasing cybersecurity awareness within the community can be done in many ways. Organizations in the community can do many of these activities as collaborative efforts. These partnerships will not only build awareness but will also connect people to share information about cybersecurity and build trust among the community members.

- **Conferences and Seminars:** Partnerships can be established with local universities, community colleges, chamber of commerce or other organizations within the community, to hold cybersecurity conferences or seminars. The facility could possibly be provided by a college or university at a minimal cost. Speakers can be professionals within local organizations or from an ISSA or ISACA chapter. Another way to find speakers is to connect with organizations such as the FBI, who have outreach programs where they will speak to groups within the community. This is a low-cost way to provide cybersecurity awareness. A great timeframe for a cybersecurity conference or seminar would be during Cybersecurity Awareness Month in October.

An example of a community conference is a Community Cybersecurity Day. The community can hold a cybersecurity awareness day that focuses on different parts of the community and presents information that would be beneficial for local government, industry, critical infrastructure, small businesses, and the public. This can be organized in a conference-style with speakers discussing cybersecurity trends, challenges, and best practices for preventing, mitigating, responding, and recovering from incidents. The day can be arranged to have speakers discussing cybersecurity topics that will benefit large organizations, critical infrastructure and local government in the morning, small businesses in the afternoon and can be open to the public encouraging citizens to learn more about cybersecurity in the evening. A day such as this can be a low-cost method to engaging the community to learn more about cybersecurity. Speakers can be found in the community. The FBI often speaks at community events to increase cybersecurity awareness, InfraGard, ISSA and other organizations often have people who are willing to speak at local events about cybersecurity. There are organizations around the community who may be willing to provide space for the Cybersecurity Day for a nominal cost or may donate the space at no cost. A day such as this could prove very effective in making sure community organizations and citizens understand the threat to their community and can also provide an opportunity to let people know where they should report incidents to and what resources are in the community such as organizations or people who may be able to provide assistance in the event of a breach, cyber-attack or incident.

- **Games:** Cybersecurity games take important and serious concepts and create a fun delivery method to introduce these topics. Games are gaining popularity and are being used as STEM educational tools for K-12 students. Initiatives such as these are addressing the cybersecurity workforce shortage by introducing cybersecurity principles and future career possibilities to middle school through high school students that might not otherwise consider this as a career path.

Cyber Threat Defender (CTD), created by the CIAS, is an original product that has the potential to transform classroom conversations about cybersecurity by introducing terminology, concepts and careers in an approachable game-based format. More than 40,000 decks of CTD have been distributed both nationally and internationally. The game is being used in middle school and high school classrooms, STEM clubs, cyber patriot teams, coding camps and new implementations are occurring all the time.

Originally created for middle and high school students, this game is also being used by organizations to increase workforce awareness of cybersecurity.

- **Training:** Cyber security training is an effective tool in building a security culture. There are a variety of types of training available, from traditional instructor-led training conducted with PowerPoint presentations that could have hands-on activities to hone skills on a particular topic. Web-based training is available 24 hours a day and 7 days a week. This is a great option to reach a broad audience and provides training when it's convenient for the learner. Another type of training is to integrate training into simulators. Simulations are designed to mimic the processes, events, and circumstances a user may be confronted with. This is a great way to role-play or provide scenarios for the learner to go through.

Figure 2.

CIAS Game Development

Cyber Threat Defender is Changing the Way Cybersecurity is Taught and Learned in Schools Across the Nation

Security training needs to be strong, more effective, more comprehensive, more in-depth and should leave a sense of responsibility to those being trained. Cybersecurity training tends to be provided on an annual basis and as a compliance measure. INFOSEC reports on their website that random security training results in an approximate 10-15% reduction of the likelihood an attack will be successful, but with consistent training there is an estimated 40-50% reduction. Get away from the mindset that security training is to check off a box for compliance and make the community cybersecurity training fun and make it available often.

- **Train-the-trainer**: This model is used to train potential instructors or less experienced instructors on best practices to deliver established training materials or content. This can be a very useful way to broaden the cybersecurity reach throughout the community. By getting more instructors up to speed on cybersecurity awareness content, more people can be reached, and more people can become involved in cybersecurity activities. As an example, if there is one instructor teaching a cybersecurity course, they may be able to train 30 people at a time. If there are 5 people providing the same course across the community in various locations, the same content has been distributed to 150 people.

The train the trainer model is normally thought of in conjunction with a classroom style environment, while this format still works, the train-the-trainer model can be used in other capacities. Some examples of train-the-trainer activities are to train:

- K-12 teachers how to integrate cyber concepts into their classroom lesson plans such as the Cyber Threat Defender Card Game.
- mentors who are assisting CyberPatriot and Collegiate Cyber Defense Competition (CCDC) students to prepare for competitions. Mentors can be trained on various cybersecurity concepts such as perimeter security, flashing and patching, networking, operating systems and vulnerabilities, services and applications, various tools and malware reversing and analysis.
- high school, community college and technical college teachers on cybersecurity concepts to prepare students for entry-level certifications such as CompTIA's Network +, Security +, and A+.
- sponsors how to add cybersecurity into summer camps offered to K-12 students.
  - **Competitions:** Cyber security competitions are competitive events that provide an environment for students learning cybersecurity. Competitions can also be used for professionals desiring to hone their skills, and to practice their technical and decision-making skills to design, configure or protect a network. Competitions start at the middle school level and continue to cybersecurity professional levels. Competitions at the college levels often lead to internships, scholarships and job offers. There are many cybersecurity competitions offered throughout the country and vary in target audience and specialty. Some examples are:
    - **CyberPatriot** is a K-12 program sponsored by the Air Force Association. One of its initiatives is a cyber defense competition for middle school and high school students. "Through a series of online competition rounds, teams are given a set of virtual operating systems and are tasked with finding and fixing cybersecurity vulnerabilities while maintaining critical services. The top teams in the nation earn all-expenses-paid trips to Maryland for the National Finals Competition where they can earn national recognition and scholarship money" ("What Is Cyberpatriot?," n.d.).

- **National Collegiate Cyber Defense Competitions (NCCDC)** is the championship event for the top 10 winning teams of the regional collegiate cyber defense competitions conducted throughout the nation. Established in 2004 by the CIAS, the NCCDC is the largest college-level cyber defense competition in the United States ("National Collegiate," n.d.). The Collegiate Cyber Defense Competition system (CCDC) was the first competition system to focus on the operational aspects of managing and protecting an existing "commercial" network infrastructure. CCDC events provide an excellent opportunity for students to gain practical, hands-on experience in cyber security and information technology that allows them to expand their educations beyond the traditional classroom environment.
- **Code Jam** is Google's longest running global coding competition. "Code Jam, calls on programmers around the world to solve challenging, algorithmic puzzles against the clock. Contestants advance through four online-hosted rounds to compete at the annual Code Jam World Finals that is held at a different international Google office each year. Each round brings new challenges and in the end 25 contestants will have the ultimate chance to put their skills to the test, vying for cash prizes and the coveted championship title at the World Finals" ("Code Jam What's,"n.d.).

Code Jam also has a K-12 program called **Youth Code Jam** targeting kids from ages 7 to 17. This after-school program offers hands-on activities focused on computing programs and provides teacher development to bring computer science to every school and classroom ("Code Jam What's,"n.d.).

- **Internships:** Developing a cybersecurity internship program can benefit both students and organizations in the community. A summer internship program offers high school and college students the chance to discover what it's like to work in an organization whether it is a government agency or large or small business. Interns can learn and deliver innovative solutions to real business challenges. A community internship program would coordinate high school, community college and college students interested in cybersecurity and pair them with participating local organizations. These organizations may be looking to find future employees and may want to utilize an internship as a way to evaluate the intern's work ethic, ability to learn the organization's culture and processes and fit into the work environment. Internships can be paid or unpaid, either way interns are a low-cost way to introduce future talent to the cybersecurity career field. Internships not only help the students in the community but will also enhance the local workforce. A community internship program is a cost-effective public relations tool and can assist in expanding awareness of cybersecurity throughout the community.

- **Education and Degree Programs:** More universities and colleges are offering information security, information assurance and cybersecurity degrees. Degrees such as this can grow a capable workforce by developing future information security analysts, system administrators, cybersecurity consultants, penetration testers and will also expand talent for general Information Technology positions such as software developers, computer programmers, and information systems managers, to name a few. "The New York Times reports that a stunning statistic is reverberating in cybersecurity: Cybersecurity Ventures' prediction that there will be 3.5 million unfilled cybersecurity jobs globally by 2021, up from one million positions in 2014" (Morgan, n.d.).

- **Certifications:** Cybersecurity certifications are a credential that you earn to show specific skills or knowledge have been obtained. They are usually tied to an occupation, technology, or industry. Certifications are typically offered by a professional organization or a company that specializes in a field or technology and require an individual to pass a test to earn the certification. Certifications are often used by hiring employers to verify skills and capabilities of the applicants ("Earning a certification," n.d.). Some examples of cybersecurity certifications are as follows:

  - **Certified Information Systems Security Professional (CISSP):** the CISSP is an advanced-level credential offered by the International Information Systems Security Certification Consortium (ISC²). This certification requires a minimum of 5 years of experience in one or more of the 8 Common Bodies of Knowledge (CBK). The CBK domains are:
    - Security and Risk Management
    - Security Architecture and Engineering
    - Asset Security
    - Identity and Access Management

- ▪ Security Operations
- ▪ Security Assessment and Testing
- ▪ Software Development Security
- ▪ Communications and Network Security
- ○ **Certified Ethical Hacker (CEH):** CEH is an intermediate-level certification from EC-Council (International Council of E-Commerce Consultants). Individuals with this certification have expertise in hacking practices such as "scanning networks, system hacking, worms and viruses, Trojans, sniffers, social engineering, denial-of-service attacks, enumeration, foot printing and reconnaissance, session hijacking, SQL injection, hacking web servers, cryptography, wireless networks and web applications, honeypots, evading IDS, penetration testing, and firewalls" ("Top 7 Cybersecurity," n.d.).
- ○ **Certified Information Security Manager (CISM):** CISM is a high-level credential and it is aimed at the IT professionals responsible for developing, overseeing, and managing information security systems in different enterprise level applications. This certification requires a minimum of five-years' experience and have proven skills in program development and management, security risk management, incident management and response, and governance ("Top 7 Cybersecurity," n.d.).
- ○ **CompTIA Security+:** is a globally recognized, vendor neutral security credential. This is an entry-level certificate and requires individuals to have two-years' experience in network security. The certification is compliant with the ISO-17024 standard. Those who receive this certification are knowledgeable in areas such as cryptography, threat management, identity management, security risk identification and mitigation, security infrastructure, security systems, and network access control ("Top 7 Cybersecurity," n.d.).
- ○ **SANS GIAC Security Essentials (GSEC):** an entry-level credential offered by GIAC. Individuals with this certification have technical skills and knowledge in areas, such as access authentication, recognizing and mitigating general and wireless attacks, password management, fundamentals of cryptography, access controls, DNS, IPv6, ICMP, network mapping, public key infrastructure, network protocols, and Linux ("Top 7 Cybersecurity," n.d.).

- **Tabletop Exercises:** can provide an inexpensive (depending on the level of detail) way to build incident response skills and to identify potential discrepancies in plans, processes, and training programs. Tabletop exercises are designed to test a hypothetical situation and evaluate the community's ability to cooperate and work together, as well as test their readiness to respond to the incident presented. While exercises are traditionally used for testing established mechanisms and capabilities within the community, the CIAS found the tabletop exercise to be an invaluable tool for increasing awareness in regard to cybersecurity terminology, methods in which a cyber incident can occur and the potential impacts.

Effective Awareness Programs

Effective security awareness programs have these qualities:

- need to be fun
- supported by the leadership
- focused on changing the behavior of individuals
- interactive (encouraging feedback and ideas)
- diverse deployment methods (use newsletters, posters, email tips and other communications on a regular basis)
- individuals of the security awareness program need to be exposed to the same message repeatedly
- the awareness program needs to be sustainable, repeatable and long-term

The effectiveness of the security awareness program needs to be measured. Security is not a destination, it is a journey and the progress needs to be measured. Most security programs measure effectiveness by how many people complete training. This really only focuses on attendance. The metrics that should be collected are those that show a change in behavior.

Cooperative Cyber Training Program

Establishing a cooperative cyber training program is one way to introduce cybersecurity training for all community stakeholders, and an initiative such as this, can be started with resources already available in the community. The cooperative can be an autonomous group of persons representing various organizations throughout the community who unite voluntarily to meet their common cyber training goals. This group could also be formed as a working group, committee, or some other formation. Co-operative initiatives are typically used for education, work placement, economic, social and cultural needs for the community.

A cooperative training program involves mutual assistance from participating organizations throughout the community. Organizations in the community may have cybersecurity training they would be willing to share. These courses can be distributed to other organizations for them to conduct the training themselves or could be taught by the organization that created the materials, and seats in the class could be made available to others in the community. Another option for cooperative training in this level is to combine efforts to bring in hard to get and expensive training. As an example, a highly specialized or technical training class may cost $3,000 for an individual to attend the course, however, if that class was brought into the community for $15,000 and 20 organizations participated, a seat in that class would only cost $750 per person. This would make that training much more affordable for an organization.

AWARENESS ROADMAP

There are five levels to the CCSMM awareness roadmap. It begins at Level 1 – Initial which means there is very little cyber awareness in the community. That is not to say that individuals in the community do not know about cyber threats. In fact, if anyone in the community were asked if they understand cyber is a threat, universally the answer will be yes. The awareness level does not simply mean the community understands cyber is a threat, what it really means is the individuals in the community do not understand exactly what in the community can be targeted for a cyber-attack; they do not understand what the impact the attack could have; and they do not understand exactly what the cascading effects could potentially be. The awareness roadmap guides the development of this more comprehensive awareness program which takes the community to Level 5 – Vanguard, meaning awareness of the cyber threat, impacts and cascading effects has been integrated into everything the community does and the culture of cybersecurity awareness is achieved.

To begin the process of improving the awareness in the community, refer to Figure 3 to see the characteristics for the awareness dimension.

Figure 3.

LEVEL 1 Initial	LEVEL 2 Established	LEVEL 3 Self-Assessed	LEVEL 4 Integrated	LEVEL 5 Vanguard
Awareness • Minimal cyber awareness	• Leadership aware of cyber threats, issues and imperatives for cyber security and community cooperative cyber training	• Leaders promote org security awareness; formal community cooperative training	• Leaders and orgs promote awareness; citizens aware of cyber security issues	• Awareness a business imperative
Info Sharing • Minimal cyber info sharing	• Informal info sharing/ communication in community; working groups established; ad-hoc analysis, little fusion or metrics; professional orgs established or engaged	• Formal local info sharing/cyber analysis. initial cyber-physical fusion; informal external info sharing/ cyber analysis and metrics gathering	• Formal info sharing/ analysis, internal and external to community; formal local fusion and metrics, initial external efforts	• Fully integrated fusion/ analysis center, combining all-source physical and cyber info; create and disseminate near real world picture
Policy • Minimal cyber assessments and policy & procedure evaluations	• No assessments, but aware of requirement; initial evaluation of policies & procedures	• Autonomous tabletop cyber exercises with assessments of info sharing, policies & procedures, and fusion; routine audit program; mentor externals on policies & procedures, auditing and training	• Autonomous cyber exercises with assessments of formal info sharing/local fusion; exercises involve live play/metrics assessments	• Accomplish full-scale blended exercises and assess complete fusion capability; involve/ mentor other communities/entities
Plans • Little inclusion of cyber into Continuity of Operations Plan (COOP)	• Aware of need to integrate cyber security into COOP	• Include cyber in COOP; formal cyber incident response/recovery	• Integrate cyber in COOP; mentor externals on COOP integration; formal blended incident response and recovery	• Continue to integrate cyber in COOP; mentor externals on COOP integration; formal blended incident response and recovery

Awareness at Level 1: Minimal Cyber Awareness

The characteristics of a community at Level 1 recognize that most of the community has minimal cyber awareness. This is a very common place for communities to start. Remember, community awareness is not simply measuring if people know that cyber incidents are happening. The cyber awareness that is really needed is a much greater understanding of the threats, impacts and cascading effects.

The first critical step in establishing a cybersecurity program is to identify a champion. The CIAS found that those communities who had a champion were much more successful in establishing a program. The champion was the individual who got others in the community interested and engaged in the cybersecurity initiatives. This was the person who brought cybersecurity issues up in meetings and pushed the initiative forward when there were competing priorities. The champion was different in every community. Examples of potential community champions are: the fire chief, mayor, county judge, police chief, city councilman or an industry leader.

Awareness at Level 2: Leadership Aware of Cyber Threats

A community at Level 2, means the community's leadership are aware of the cyber threats, issues and imperatives for cyber security. The second characteristic is a cooperative cyber training program is initiated. Recall in Chapter 3, the Phases were introduced. The Phase contains the activities that will need to be performed to advance from one level of the model to the next. Those activities are called implementation mechanisms.

Phase 1 includes the implementation mechanisms that will increase the community's awareness from Level 1 to Level 2. First the metrics will be used to measure if the community is at Level 2.

Metrics: The metrics at this level will assess if the leadership are aware and if there is a training program initiated.

The questions to ask to transition to Level 2 are:

- Have leaders in the community been identified?
- This should include any leader in the community who should understand how a cyber incident could impact the community and be aware of the potential cascading effects? There is not a specific number of leaders that need to be identified. These leaders will have influence with specific groups in the community.
- Has a leadership cybersecurity forum or working group been created in the community?
- Have activities been identified that can be implemented to increase the leaderships awareness that will fit into their schedules?
- This could be presentations or briefings provided to a leadership forum.
- How will the leadership's awareness be maintained, and how can updates, trends and new threats be introduced?
- The leadership forum should meet periodically. This could be in a monthly or quarterly format.
- Has the community identified what types of training is needed first in the community?
- Has the community identified which organizations throughout the community could benefit from this training?

Technology: The technology needed to increase awareness to achieve Level 2 will need to be considered. Technology at this level could be used to facilitate awareness initiatives and could also support initiating a training program. Some considerations are:

- Can technology be used to provide some or all the cyber instruction or coaching needed for the leadership?
- Has a website been created to promote the cooperative cyber training program?

Training: The training leadership will need should be ongoing. Cyber threats and impacts are continually changing which means leadership will need to be updated often. The content provided will need to be focused on what they need to know. Some of the topics that may be addressed are:

- Why cybersecurity is important
- Cyber risk management concepts
- Types of attacks and evolving threats
- Cybersecurity terminology
- Situational awareness of cyber threats
- Evolving threats
- Cyber incident response
- Culture of Security

Traditional training could be used but if there are time constraints, the leadership could receive an executive cybersecurity briefing periodically.

The next thing that needs to be considered is the cooperative training program. Cybersecurity training can be very expensive and may be difficult for organizations to participate because of the expense. A cooperative training program is intended to implement a cybersecurity training capability that organizations can participate in and the cost could be shared across multiple organizations making the training much more affordable.

For a community to advance from Level 1 to Level 2 the following should be accomplished:

- Has training been developed that will inform the leadership of the cyber threat, impacts and the potential cascading effects on the community?
- Has the training been delivered to the identified leadership who should receive the information?
- Have training topics been identified for the cooperative cybersecurity training been initiated?
- Have the organizations who need the training been identified?

Processes and Procedures: The processes and procedures that should be considered will establish the leadership awareness program and the cooperative training program. They will also define how each are managed and maintained.

- Has the community established procedures to establish the leadership awareness program?
- Does the leadership awareness program have procedures defining how often training, presentations or briefings will be conducted?
- Do the procedures define how often the training will be updated?
- Has the community established procedures to establish the cooperative training program?
- Do the procedures include how training topics are determined?
- Do the procedures include describe how organizations can join the cooperative training program?

Assessments: The assessments will evaluate what has been put in place. At this level, the effectiveness of the leadership awareness program will be determined. The characteristic for the training program is to be established, so the assessment will determine if the program has been setup. The questions to consider are:

- Is there an established mechanism to assess the leadership's awareness before training and after?
- Has the community developed a training program available to organizations in the community?

Awareness at Level 3: Leaders Promote Organization Security Awareness

The awareness program has been established for the leadership in the community and the leaders are now promoting cybersecurity to ensure organizations throughout the community are aware they need to implement cybersecurity practices into their organizations and will need a cybersecurity awareness program. Consider the types of organizations that are in a community such as financial institutions, healthcare, manufacturing, education, retail, and government agencies. These organizations can be very large or may be a small or mid-sized business. The data breach reports published every year show that all of these organizations are potential targets of cyber-attacks which means all of them need good cybersecurity practices and controls in place.

The characteristics of a community at Level 3, have the leaders of the community promoting organizational security awareness and the community cooperative cyber training program is formalized.

Phase 2 includes:

Metrics: The metrics at this level will assess the increase of organizational awareness and the formalization of the cooperative training program. Questions address are:

- Has a campaign to promote cybersecurity awareness been developed by the community?
- Has a mechanism been developed to engage organizations? This could be a cybersecurity working group operated at the community level perhaps by the chamber of commerce.
- The training program has an established committee or working group that represents various organizations throughout the community to keep requirements relevant and timely.
- Are there dedicated personnel assisting with logistics and management of the established program?
- Are surveys conducted to identify cybersecurity topics, practices and techniques needed throughout the community?

Technology: The technology needed for this level will support promoting organizational awareness and the training program.

- What technologies are being used to promote awareness and training activities for organizations within the community?
  - This could be a monthly webinar, podcast or other platform that organizations can join to learn more about cybersecurity.
  - Email, social media, and websites can be utilized to market and provide information on awareness and training activities.
- What technologies might be needed to support cybersecurity topics identified in the surveys of what is needed?

Training: The training will continue to be a critical tool at each level of the CCSMM. A good way to incorporate training is to identify training that is available for low or no cost and make sure community members know how to take advantage of that training.

- What training can be conducted to support the surveys and feedback the community has received on cybersecurity needs?
- Is more detailed training needed based on feedback received from the webinars conducted?
- Have we utilized the free training resources provided by FEMA?
  - Firstrespondertraining.gov has free online cybersecurity training for individuals to take self-paced introductory, intermediate and advanced cybersecurity courses on various topics such as incident response, forensics, cybersecurity fundamentals and many more areas.
  - Instructor-led, onsite cybersecurity training can be scheduled for 20+ people per class to better prepare the community to identify, protect, detect, respond and recover from cyber-attacks and incidents. These courses are discussion based and many have hands-on activities that will build cybersecurity capabilities.
- Are there training courses organizations are willing to share?

Processes and Procedures: The processes and procedures will be needed to address the community programs that are now in place regarding how the community will introduce cybersecurity to leaders and organizations and how the training will be

- Are websites and social media being updated regularly for training and awareness initiatives that are offered throughout the community?
  - How often are they being updated and who is responsible for updating them?
- Have processes and procedures been created to address the structure and governance needs for the awareness and training programs?
- Are the processes and procedures available to everyone who needs them?

Assessments: The assessments will measure the effectiveness of the awareness and training programs.

- Does the community have established methods for collecting feedback on the how many organizations are participating in the programs?

- ○ How many organizations did the community start with and how many organizations does the community have after 6 months, 1 year and so on.
- Does the community have established methods for understanding if cybersecurity awareness is improving?

Awareness at Level 4: Leaders and Organizations Promote Awareness

A community at Level 4 has an increasing number of leaders and organizations within the community understanding the cyber threat, impacts and cascading effects. They recognize their roles in the community and recognize a cyber incident could impact the effectiveness of the overall community to do business. Organizations are educating their workforce by implementing awareness programs and enhancing existing programs.

The Verizon Data Breach Report for 2019 reports more than 100,000 breaches and of those breaches 32% were accomplished through Phishing and another 29% were from stolen credentials. To summarize, more than 60% of the breaches impacting organizations were successful because of the people. Organizations need to educate their workforce in cybersecurity threats and issues.

The workforce is a large portion of the community that will be aware of cyber security issues, but citizens include not only the workforce but also children, young adults perhaps in high school and college, stay at home parents, retired and elderly.

Level 4 characteristics for a community are the leaders and organizations are promoting cybersecurity awareness and the citizens are aware of cyber-security issues.

Phase 3 includes:

Metrics: The metrics at this level will assess if the effectiveness of established initiatives and programs and will include awareness programs for the citizens of the community.

Technology: The technology needed will support established initiatives. As the numbers of people included in the programs increase, new technologies may need to be evaluated and used. As an example, more online courses may need to be made available to fit into schedules and to allow flexibility for the amount of time spent at any given sitting.

Training: The community will have multiple training initiatives implemented at this level. Seminars, conferences, webinars, face-to-face training, podcasts, games and technical training, to name a few. Establishing an annual Community Cybersecurity Day is a great way to include the entire community to engage in cybersecurity awareness. This would be a day of speakers who focus on the different target audiences in regard to what they need to know about cybersecurity. As an example, a community could hold a one-day conference that had speakers for the community in the morning, focused on organizational security in the afternoon and held a security session for personal security in the evening for private citizens. This type of awareness activity could be established as early as in Level 2 with the intent to grow the number of participants each year.

Culture of security activities are implemented by this level to address cybersecurity for the youth that are age appropriate. Ensuring every school in the community has cybersecurity tools to teach cybersecurity such as the Cyber Threat Defender Game discussed earlier. Competitions at the middle school, high school and college levels will engage the young adults. And programs for adults not in the workforce need to be considered ideally before this level, but at a minimum should be addressed at this point.

Processes and Procedures: At this level of the CCSMM awareness dimension, the community should have a number of established programs that have processes and procedures identifying programs, how they work, how they are maintained and how they are updated.

Assessments: Each awareness initiative should be evaluated for its effectiveness, increased participation and increased awareness.

Awareness at Level 5: Awareness a Business Imperative

At this level, cybersecurity principles are integrated into most day to day activities. Everyone in the community recognizes the importance of cybersecurity and how it is incorporated. It is understood that technology alone will not solve cybersecurity issues.

Phase 4 includes:
Metrics: The metrics at this level will assess how awareness of evolving and new cyberthreats are being integrated into established programs and initiatives. Mentoring smaller communities with establishing their awareness programs would occur at this level.

Technology: Technologies that help distribute awareness training and programs to other communities can be assessed here.

Training: The training program is documented and distributed to smaller communities to help increase their capabilities and awareness. Regional awareness seminars and conferences can be established.

Processes and Procedures: Continued documenting of established programs.

Assessments: Not only are programs being assessed, but lessons learned are created from successful activities for others to use.

CONCLUSION

Increasing awareness throughout the community will begin with the leadership in the community. This is key because the leadership ultimately determine budgets and priorities for the community. With leadership understanding and support, organizations within the community can be integrated into the awareness campaign for the community. Organizations will help distribute awareness to the workforce within the community, but additional and separate efforts will need to be established in order to address the youth, retired, elderly and other adults in the community who use technology.

In order to achieve a culture of security that is understood by everyone, initiatives should be started early in the process because it will take a substantial amount of time to reach everyone in the community and to provide enough training and other awareness activities that will make an impact and change behaviors of everyone in the community. Awareness is a good place to start because it will make implementation of the other dimensions much easier, because the need will already be understood for additional programs that will address community information sharing, policy and plans for cybersecurity.

REFERENCES

A comprehensive list of cyber security competitions. (n.d.). Retrieved from Cyber Security Degrees website: https://cybersecuritydegrees.com/faq/comprehensive-list-of-cyber-security-competitions/

About stop. think. connect. (n.d.). Retrieved from STOP|THINK|CONNECT website: https://www.stopthinkconnect.org/about

Cobb, S. (2018, May 30). *Trends 2018: Critical infrastructure attacks on the rise*. Retrieved from welivesecurity website: http://www.welivesecurity.com/2018/05/30/ trends-2018-critical-infrastructure-attacks/

Code jam what's involved? (n.d.). Retrieved from code jam website: https://codingcompetitions.withgoogle.com/codejam

Connect>code>create. (n.d.). Retrieved from Youth Code Jam website: https://www.youthcodejam.org/

Crime prevention - McGruff the crime dog. (n.d.). Retrieved from AdCouncil website: https://www.adcouncil.org/Our-Campaigns/The-Classics/Crime-Prevention-McGruff-the-Crime-Dog

Critical infrastructure threats placing incident response in the crosshairs. (n.d.). Retrieved from Homeland Security Today.com website: http://www.hstoday.us/ subject-matter-areas/infrastructure-security/ perspective-critical-infrastructure-threats-placing-incident-response-in-the-crosshairs/

Cyber threat defender. (n.d.). Retrieved from CIAS website: https://cias.utsa.edu/ctd.php

Earning a certification can help you enter or advance in many careers. (n.d.). Retrieved from Careeronestop website: https://www.careeronestop.org/FindTraining/Types/certifications.aspx

Morgan, S. (Ed.). (2019). *Cybersecurity talent crunch to create 3.5 million unfilled jobs globally by 2021*. Retrieved from Cybercrime Magazine website: https://cybersecurityventures.com/jobs/

National Collegiate Cyber Defense Competition. (n.d.). In *Wikipedia*. Retrieved from en.wikipedia.org/wiki/

Security awareness statistics. (n.d.). Retrieved from INFOSEC website: https://resources.infosecinstitute.com/category/enterprise/securityawareness/security-awareness-fundamentals/security-awareness-statistics/#gref

Smokey bear. (n.d.). In *Wikipedia*. Retrieved from https://en.wikipedia.org/wiki/Smokey_Bear

Top 7 cybersecurity certifications to consider in 2019. (n.d.). Retrieved from PrepAway website: https://www.prepaway.com/certification/ top-7-cybersecurity-certifications-consider-2019/

Verizon. (2019). *2019 data breach investigations report.* Retrieved from https://enterprise.verizon.com/resources/reports/dbir/#2018DBIR

What is cyberpatriot? (n.d.). Retrieved from Air Force Association's Cyberpatriot website: https://www.uscyberpatriot.org/Pages/About/What-is-CyberPatriot.aspx

Chapter 5
Information Sharing

ABSTRACT

From the first community cybersecurity exercise the CIAS at UTSA conducted in San Antonio in 2002, information sharing has been a key element of the community cybersecurity program. Information sharing is essential in the protection and detection aspects of programs such as the NIST cyber security framework. Information sharing helps to alert other organizations to ongoing reconnaissance and attack efforts by attackers. When it comes to cybersecurity, organizations are not in competition with each other but instead are partners in a mutual defense against attackers. This has not been an easy lesson to learn, and it has taken time, but today, there are many robust information sharing programs that help various sectors and geographic regions to band together to help each other in efforts to thwart attacks against any member of the group. Information sharing is an integral part of the community cyber security maturity model and can in fact help provide a catalyst to launch an overall cybersecurity program for a community.

INTRODUCTION

A question often asked is "why would I want to share information with others? Especially my competitors?" This is a natural question that comes up when an individual is approached and asked if they want to participate in an information sharing program. As an answer to this, consider the following comment:

DOI: 10.4018/978-1-7998-4471-6.ch005

Learning from the mistakes of others sounds great. Yet it's difficult to do when those 'others' refuse to be transparent about their mistakes.

Why is intelligence sharing important? Cyber criminals find new software vulnerabilities and attack vectors every day. Cybersecurity experts are faced with an ongoing challenge to keep up. If peers open up to proactively share information–also known as [information] sharing–it can help strengthen our collective resilience and reactivity to potential threats. (Red Team, 2016)

This short quote from a 2016 blog highlights two points. First, people are often reluctant to share information with others which makes "learning from the mistakes of others" or maybe more importantly "learning from the current events impacting others" difficult to impossible. People are reluctant to share for a variety of reasons, the prime one being a concern about how the information they share will be used by others. Will providing information on a breach in one company be used by a competitor in a marketing campaign highlighting the past security problem of the first? Another issue is that of the privacy of the company and its customers. Both, however, have successfully been dealt with by information sharing organizations and it just takes some time for a new organization to trust that sharing information will not be detrimental to them.

The second point highlighted by the quote from the blog states that intelligence sharing (or information sharing) is important because of the "ongoing challenge to keep up" with cyber criminals that cybersecurity experts face. New vulnerabilities and attack vectors are discovered on a frequent basis and it is often hard for a cybersecurity professional to wade through the plethora of information presented to determine what is important to the organization. Frequently it seems like the criminal (or "hacker") community does a better job of sharing information than cybersecurity defenders.

In this chapter the topic of information sharing as it relates to a community will be discussed and the plan to implement cybersecurity information sharing within a community at the different levels of the CCSMM will be presented. It is stressed throughout this book that there is no single perfect description or plan for a community hoping to develop a viable and sustainable cybersecurity program. What will be presented in this chapter will be higher level constructs with some suggested specifics, but specific approaches must be adapted to individual communities and their local environment.

BACKGROUND

In the context of this book and in the media today, the term information sharing is generally used to mean the sharing of security, threat, and intelligence information. Information sharing in this context is not new nor is it limited to a certain sector such as intelligence gathering organizations (e.g. the CIA and NSA).

Information sharing to enhance national security and improve public safety did not begin with the post 9/11 era of counterterrorism transformation and intelligence reform. Rather, information sharing has been at the heart of a government reform movement that has sought to make the public sector more efficient and effective through the use of data.

For example, in the 1990's, the New York City Police Department implemented community policing reforms, based on sophisticated crime mapping, contributing to a substantial drop in crime. Since that time, many other police departments have adapted similar approaches.

At the federal level, the military and intelligence communities also devoted serious efforts towards closer integration. In 1986, the Goldwater-Nichols Act substantially reorganized the Department of Defense and its chain of command to enable joint service operations and achieve greater operational efficiencies. The Goldwater-Nichols Act did so by eliminating stovepipes between the different military services while preserving the distinct culture and identity of the Army, Navy, Air Force, and Marines.

During the 1990's, Director of Central Intelligence Robert Gates undertook steps toward similar reforms within the intelligence community. Despite progress, the reforms did not go deep or fast enough.

Following the September 11 attacks, a series of reviews uncovered failures of information sharing both within and between agencies, and a variety of legal, policy, and process impediments. These impediments were among the factors that resulted in the government's failure to prevent the 9/11 attacks. The National Commission on Terrorist Attacks upon the United States, commonly called the 9/11 Commission, described a number of information sharing failures and recommended a series of reforms to prevent future failures. (DNI, 2015)

Prior to the events of September 11, Presidential Decision Directive 63 (PDD 63) titled "Protecting America's Critical Infrastructures" was released. It was dated May 22, 1998 and called for the creation of Information Sharing and Analysis Centers (ISACs). A companion White Paper, "The Clinton Administration's Policy on Critical Infrastructure Protection: Presidential Decision Directive 63" dated the same day expanded on PDD 63 and explained that ISACs should be formed for each of the critical infrastructure sectors and they should

serve as the mechanism for gathering, analyzing, appropriately sanitizing and disseminating private sector information to both industry and the NIPC [National Infrastructure Protection Center]. The center could also gather, analyze and disseminate information from the NIPC for further distribution to the private sector. While crucial to a successful government-industry partnership, this mechanism for sharing important information about vulnerabilities, threats, intrusions and anomalies is not to interfere with direct information exchanges between companies and the government. (White House, 1998b)

In this companion white paper, the goal of an ISAC is clearly laid out which was to gather, analyze, sanitize, and disseminate information to industry and the government (via the NIPC). What followed was the creation of a series of ISACs such as the Financial Services ISAC (FS-ISAC), the Electricity ISAC (E-ISAC), the Communications ISAC (NCC), and the Multi-State ISAC (MS-ISAC). There are now 21 ISACs, though this number may vary with time, that are members of the National Council of ISACs (NCI). Some of these now offer membership to non-U.S. organizations and efforts to conduct more cross-sector and cross-border sharing of information has been a topic of interest to this community for a while.

As the ISACs were formed and grew in capability, and after the attacks of September 11, 2001, there was a lot of interest in improving the sharing of information between the various intelligence agencies in the U.S. and between these agencies and industry. Initially focused on sharing of terrorist threat information the issue eventually expanded to cybersecurity as well. In 2013 the White House issued Executive Order 13636 titled "Improving Critical Infrastructure Cybersecurity". This document identified a number of areas in which the process of information sharing should be improved, such as

It is the policy of the United States Government to increase the volume, timeliness, and quality of cyber threat information shared with U.S. private sector entities so that these entities may better protect and defend themselves against cyber threats. (White House, 2013).

While this executive order recognized the need for increased cooperation between the intelligence agencies and the critical infrastructures, the problem was that it focused only on the various critical infrastructures. Though these infrastructures were, as the name indicates, critical to the nation they do not represent the majority of organizations in the nation. As a result, in 2015 Executive Order 13691 "Promoting Private Sector Cybersecurity Information Sharing" was issued which directed the Secretary of the Department of Homeland Security (DHS) to select a non-government entity to become the Information Sharing Analysis Organization (ISAO) Standards Organization (SO). The ISAO SO would lead an effort to establish the standards, guidelines, best practices, and other documents that would be needed by organizations that wanted to create an ISAO. A break from the ISAC model, ISAOs could be formed based on several factors, not just sectors. They could be "organized on the basis of sector, sub-sector, region, or any other affinity, including in response to particular emerging threats or vulnerabilities." [White House, 2015] It also provided a reason for including non-critical infrastructure entities when it stated, "Organizations engaged in the sharing of information related to cybersecurity risks and incidents play an invaluable role in the collective cybersecurity of the United States." [White House, 2015] Thus, it discussed information sharing in terms of organizations instead of only referring to the critical infrastructures and federal government. A team led by The University of Texas at San Antonio and including LMI and the Retail Cyber Intelligence Sharing Center (R-CISC) was chosen to be the ISAO SO.

A little later in that same year another significant event related to information sharing occurred. In December the Cybersecurity Information Sharing Act (CISA) of 2015 was signed into law. At first there was considerable controversy over this act for fear of the government using it to obtain personal information concerning private citizens and organizations. This was eventually overcome as more details were released by DHS on how it viewed information sharing being conducted and what information they were interested in receiving.

In addition to the ISAOs (which includes the ISACs as they are a type of information sharing organization), there are a number of other entities that are involved in the sharing of cybersecurity information at some level. Some are professional organizations (such as ISSA, ISACA, and InfraGard) while others are either government entities (such as DHS with programs such as the Automated Indicator Sharing (AIS) capability) while still others may be commercial entities offering real-time threat analysis services. The information sharing ecosystem is growing and is becoming very robust.

COMMUNITY CYBERSECURITY INFORMATION SHARING

A community cybersecurity information sharing program is just what the name implies. It is a program that works to have the members of a geographic area (e.g. a community) share information related to various aspects of cybersecurity. In relationship to information sharing as exemplified by the ISACs and ISAOs, the type of information shared is generally in the context of Indicators of Compromise or IOCs. This means that if certain actions that can be detected have proven in the past to be a potential indication of a compromise (in other words, they are an indication that your system has been or is under attack and may have been breached), then you need to look into this to verify whether you system has been compromised or not. You may also want to share this information with others in case they too have been or are being attacked in a similar manner but may not have noticed it at this point. This was pretty much the original point of the information sharing ecosystem but as time has passed other information has been added to the list of things to possibly share – though the indicators of compromise are still the bedrock of the program.

Some other items that may be shared, and these are especially true for a community cybersecurity information sharing program, are best practices related to any of a number of different aspects in cybersecurity, effective awareness and training programs, or product assessments related to various security hardware or software. Organizations may also share information regarding how they have implemented information sharing programs with others who are just embarking on the process.

Information sharing is not something that organizations are immediately comfortable with doing. This is especially true for information related to compromises of security. This type of information could possibly be used for a competitive advantage by competitors of an organization thus the reason for possible hesitancy in sharing. For an organization to be comfortable with sharing this type of information it must trust that those organizations that the information is shared with will not use it in a way that would be detrimental to them. One of the best ways to establish trust is through personal contact and working together. This is often easier to accomplish in a community than it is in an information sharing organization that is geographically spread out.

There are two important points related to information sharing that should be mentioned. The first is that an organization only has to share information that it is willing to share. It does not need to include information that the organization is not comfortable sharing. While organizations need to comply with laws, such as breach notification laws, the type of information being shared in the community program is separate from the information that may be required because of a law or regulation. The second point that needs to be made about information sharing is that the programs that have been created and that are flourishing are doing so because the members have realized that when it comes to security, the "contest" is not between competing companies in a given sector, instead it is between all members of the sector and the cyber-attackers. The members of the sector are on one side and the individuals attempting to compromise the systems of one or more members of that sector are on the other side. When organizations realize that they are on the same side and that it behooves them to share, and to not abuse information that has been shared with them, then two-way information sharing is more likely to occur.

INFORMATION SHARING ROADMAP

It is time to examine the Information Sharing Domain from the 2-D model discussed earlier and break it down into its various characteristics and components. The diagram below shows the characteristics for the CCSMM Community Scope with the characteristics at each level of the model for the Information Sharing domain highlighted. The phases between the levels will help a community identify the types of activities that will need to be accomplished in order to advance from one level to the next. All of this is discussed in the sections that follow.

Information Sharing at Level 1: Minimal Information Sharing

A community at Level 1 has little to no information sharing occurring. This is the level that most communities are at when they begin their efforts to incorporate the CCSMM into the community. There may in fact be some

Figure 1.

	LEVEL 1 Initial	LEVEL 2 Established	LEVEL 3 Self-Assessed	LEVEL 4 Integrated	LEVEL 5 Vanguard
Awareness	• Minimal cyber awareness	• Leadership aware of cyber threats, issues and imperatives for cyber security and community cooperative cyber training	• Leaders promote org security awareness; formal community cooperative training	• Leaders and orgs promote awareness; citizens aware of cyber security issues	• Awareness a business imperative
Info Sharing	• Minimal cyber info sharing	• Informal info sharing/ communication in community; working groups established; ad-hoc analysis, little fusion or metrics; professional orgs established or engaged	• Formal local info sharing/cyber analysis. Initial cyber-physical fusion; informal external info sharing/ cyber analysis and metrics gathering	• Formal info sharing/ analysis, internal and external to community; formal local fusion and metrics, initial external efforts.	• Fully integrated fusion/ analysis center, combining all-source physical and cyber info; create and disseminate near real world picture
Policy	• Minimal cyber assessments and policy & procedure evaluations	• No assessments, but aware of requirement; initial evaluation of policies & procedures	• Autonomous tabletop cyber exercises with assessments of info sharing, policies & procedures, and fusion; routine audit program; mentor externals on policies & procedures, auditing and training	• Autonomous cyber exercises with assessments of formal info sharing/local fusion; exercises involve live play/metrics assessments	• Accomplish full-scale blended exercises and assess complete fusion capability; involve/ mentor other communities/entities
Plans	• Little inclusion of cyber into Continuity of Operations Plan (COOP)	• Aware of need to integrate cyber security into COOP	• Include cyber in COOP; formal cyber incident response/recovery	• Integrate cyber in COOP; mentor externals on COOP integration; formal blended incident response and recovery	• Continue to integrate cyber in COOP; mentor externals on COOP integration; formal blended incident response and recovery

sharing going on, in fact it would be surprising if there was no sharing of any sort occurring, but it is generally ad hoc and will most likely be between individuals who happen to know each other and may call or send an email to discuss an issue that is affecting one or both of them or an issue that may be in the news. There may also be organizations within the community that are part of ISACs or ISAOs and may receive sector-based information concerning issues that impact the sector they are in. Others may have a service provider that shares security information with them as well. All of these are possible, but they are not a program designed to help the community collectively but are focused on specific sectors or organizations within the community.

Information Sharing at Level 2: Informal Internal Sharing

All communities should be able to at least reach Level 2 and should strive for it or higher levels. For small rural communities, this may be as mature as their local program gets though they may be able to combine with other communities to obtain additional capabilities. A community at Level 2 will have begun to share information that will impact multiple members of the community and are focused on the community itself. The community may have one or more groups of individuals that have come together to discuss security issues impacting them. These individuals may be from multiple sectors within the community and periodically come together to discuss security issues. An example of this would be a group of CISOs from organizations around the community that come together on a monthly basis for a luncheon where they can discuss security issues affecting organizations within the community. There may be no membership fees and no vetting of members. What occurs, however, is a level of trust can be built between members of this group so that when an incident does occurs, members of the group can contact other members to discuss the best possible response and can also reach out to warn others that a similar attack might hit them.

In addition to potential informal groups such as was described above, members of the community will be part of professional security networking organizations such as ISSA and ISACA. If the community is not big enough to support a chapter of one of these organizations, individuals will be members of the closest chapters. This is particularly true for organizations such as InfraGard which will send out information to their members concerning security issues.

One aspect of information sharing is that information shared needs to be something that organizations can do something with. Receiving a lot of information that is not pertinent or useable will lead to individuals ignoring what they receive. Consequently, some level of analysis needs to take place so that only information that is important and pertinent should be shared. At Level 2 there is some attempt at analysis by individuals and organizations that are involved in information sharing.

One organization that should be present is a community ISAO. Membership in this organization should be open to any member of the community. At Level 2, the ISAO will not have a 24/7 security operations center but will have a method to communicate with all members. This may be as simple as an email list and before information is sent out to the members of the ISAO some level of analysis will be performed to ensure no personal information is revealed and to keep organizations anonymous. The ISAO should be familiar to community government officials and a subset of the membership can form a cybersecurity advisory group for the mayor/city manager if such an organization doesn't exist already.

Even though information sharing at Level 2 is often ad hoc and informal, this does not mean that going from Level 1 to Level 2 is an easy process. A community is laying the groundwork on which to establish their security program and information sharing can be used as a catalyst to do this and to keep the momentum going.

Metrics: Phase 1 consists of the activities that occur to raise a community from Level 1 to Level 2. To begin with, what metrics can be used to measure if a community is at Level 2? Metrics for this are fairly simple and binary – for each aspect of information sharing, does it exist in the community or not. Some questions to ask might include:

- Is Informal Information Sharing occurring within the community? Are there any groups of individuals who are meeting regularly to discuss security as it impacts their organizations and the community?
- Have working groups been formed by organizations such as the Chamber of Commerce to address cybersecurity needs of industry within the community?
- Has an advisory board been set up that can assist city officials on cybersecurity issues that can impact the community?
- Has a Community ISAO officially been formed? Is the ISAO communicating relevant security information to its members? Has at least some level of analysis been performed by the ISAO on information it receives to determine whether the other members need to know about this information?
- Are there local chapters of professional organizations such as ISSA, ISACA, or InfraGard within or near the community? Are members of the community participating with these organizations on a regular basis?
- Has the community joined the MS-ISAC or other similar organization and is it receiving alerts from that organization?

Technology: Next the technology needed to accomplish information sharing in the community at Level 2 needs to be present. The specific software and hardware are not important, what is important is that the software and hardware (or services contracted) provides specific capabilities. This includes the following:

- Has some method been established to allow for the dissemination of relevant information to members of a community ISAO?
- Has a website been created for the community ISAO that allows for sharing of best practices and other beneficial cybersecurity documents to members in the community? Is there a point of contact on the

website for individuals to communicate with should they want more information or want to join the ISAO?

Training: Training is always a key issue in advancing from one level to the next. There are many cybersecurity related topics for which training is needed but what we are interested in at this point is training related to information sharing only. For a community to advance from Level 1 to Level 2 the following training should be accomplished:

- Has the community ISAO developed or is it using training to inform its members of the correct procedures for sharing information? Does the training specifically outline the type of information that the ISAO is interested in receiving from its members?
- Is training available to organizations within the community on the benefits and issues related to information sharing?
- Have short training modules been created and are they being used by community officials to learn about information sharing?

Processes and Procedure: Processes and Procedures must be established to fully define how information sharing will take place in a community. A lot of this will be associated with the community ISAO as it is established and as it becomes a focal point for information security within the community. The informal groups that may have formed will most likely not have established processes and procedures as the sharing of information will be ad hoc and often between just two or a few individuals who know each other. For the ISAO, however, it will become increasingly important for it to have documented processes and procedures to follow as it matures and takes on more responsibility for the community's information sharing program. At Level 2 the questions that can be asked about processes and procedures include:

- Has the community ISAO established procedures for receiving information from members? Has it established procedures to analyze this information and to determine who it should be shared with?
- Are procedures in place in the ISAO to ensure personal information is not released through its information sharing mechanisms.
- Does community leadership have a plan for disseminating information to the community and to the state if a cybersecurity event occurs?
- Is there a protocol, such as the Traffic Light Protocol, being used to protect data according to the wishes of its original owner?

- Does the community disseminate information on who should be contacted in the event of a cyber event?

Assessments: To ensure that a community can effectively handle a cyber incident should it occur, the processes and procedures that have been developed need to be tested and exercised. There different types of assessments which can be used to identify when established processes are not sufficient or to determine if essential personnel know their responsibilities. This is true across all aspects of the CCSMM not just information sharing. Since one of the reasons for the sharing of information is to potentially provide enough information to prevent an attack from impacting at least part of the community, who people share information with, what information is shared, and when the sharing occurs needs to be examined. The type of questions to ask to determine if the community has established a Level 2 information sharing assessment program includes:

- Has the community conducted a cyber-only tabletop exercise that includes elements that will allow for the community information sharing policies and procedures to be exercised and examined?
- Does the community include cyber event information sharing into non-cyber tabletop exercises?
- Is there an established mechanism to determine if members of the community know who to report a cyber event to including when to report to law enforcement and to which agency?

Information Sharing at Level 3: Formal Internal Sharing

Communities that have more than 50,000 citizens should definitely attempt to obtain a Level 3 stature and even smaller ones should strive to incorporate some capabilities beyond those discussed for a Level 2 community. At Level 3, the local information sharing program should be formalized and should include an analysis capability. The majority of organizations in the community should be aware of the information sharing efforts (you will probably not be able to obtain 100% awareness) but the entire community does not need to be sharing information to qualify as a Level 3 community. There will always be a portion of the community that will never share information with others but will want to know about issues or events that are occurring. As time goes on, however, the percentage of organizations in the community that are active members (which means both sending and receiving information) will grow as people become more comfortable with the concept of sharing and as the ISAO proves that it can be trusted to maintain anonymity and privacy for its members.

The ISAO should share with its members, and with non-members in the community who may be willing to supply indicators of compromise, a list of the types of information that it would like to obtain. The ISAO will also perform more analysis of the information submitted so that it will be sending only relevant and useful information to its members. There will likely be different levels of sharing identified such as one level for immediate threats and another for routine cybersecurity-related information. Communities should begin to develop a Security Operations Center (SOC). Larger communities may elect to begin to establish a SOC and may have the resources to have it staffed 24/7. Having a 24/7 SOC is not a criterion for a Level 3 community – this will be up to the community. If the community does not create their own SOC, they should contract with a company to provide this service or join with another community that has a SOC or join a regional SOC should one exist.

For large communities, the sheer volume of information will make it hard to analyze so a certain level of automated sharing and analysis should be taking place. Additionally, automated feeds from other organizations such as DHS or from a service provider will become more critical and all communities at Level 3 should be a member of the MS-ISAC.

It is well understood the impact that a cyber event may have on all sectors just as cyber infrastructures are reliant upon the services of other sectors such as power and communication. At Level 3 communities should be viewing both cyber and physical events in the same way. They should not be handled separately but should be integrated and dependencies understood. At Level 3 it is not critical to have complete integration, but the community should be moving in that direction.

At Level 3 the community should be sharing and receiving cybersecurity information from more external sources. Discussed earlier were organizations such as the MS-ISAC or security service providers who deliver cyber threat analysis but the community should also be sharing with the state and with other communities. This, of course, requires these other entities to have some level of a cybersecurity program as well but even if they are only starting out, the community can share what it sees to encourage the growth of information sharing in other external entities.

Metrics: Phase 2 consists of the activities that occur to raise a community from Level 2 to Level 3. To begin with, what metrics can be used to measure if a community is at Level 3? Metrics for this continue to be fairly simple and mostly binary. For each aspect of information sharing, does it exist in the community or not. At Level 3 we do, however, start to see some questions that have a quantitative response. The questions to ask may include:

- Has a formal information sharing program been established within the community?
- Has the community formed a community ISAO?
- Does the majority of organizations within the community know about the ISAO?
    - Has a survey been conducted to determine whether organizations know about the community ISAO and do at least 50% of those surveyed respond that they do?
        § The survey should include a cross section of the size and type of organizations within the community including large and small organizations from government, industry, and academia.
- Is information concerning cybersecurity being shared with the members of the ISAO on a regular basis? Has some analysis been conducted to determine the relevance of information before it is shared?
    - Have ISAO members been surveyed to determine whether the information shared has been relevant and informative?
- Is information sharing two-way in that the ISAO is receiving information from members in addition to sending information to members?
    - Have at least 20% of the members shared information with the ISAO?
- Has a list of Indicators of Compromise that the ISAO would like to have sent to it been shared with the members of the ISAO? Has the list been made available to other members of the community who may not be a member of the ISAO but may be willing to share with the ISAO?
- Has the community begun to incorporate SOC capabilities into its overall security program?
- Is the ISAO a member of the MS-ISAC? Are other members of the community (e.g. city government, the utilities, police/fire/medical services) a member of the MS-ISAC or a sector ISAO?
- Has a survey been conducted of ISAO members to measure the level of trust with the ISAO and do the majority of the members trust that information shared with the ISAO will be appropriately protected?
- Are the advisory board and the professional organizations (mentioned in Level 2) meeting on a regular basis?

- Does the ISAO have a web site that either contains or links to best practice guides, security issue papers, and training? These can be either produced and shared by other members of the ISAO or obtained from other areas around the country.

Technology: The technology needed to accomplish information sharing in the community at Level 3 will often be an extension to the technology established at Level 2. As more members of the community begin to engage in the community information sharing program technology may change some in order to handle the increased volume of information. As automated information sharing begins to be explored systems to handle the information feeds from whatever sources will need to be established. Technology needs at Level 3 will include the following:

- Does the technology being used to share information allow for the timely dissemination of relevant information to members of a community ISAO?
- Does the technology allow for an adequate level of analysis to be performed before information is disseminated?
- Is the ISAO website established in Level 2 updated on a regular basis?
  - In a survey to the community, is at least 60% of the community aware of the website and do at least 30% view it on a regular basis?
- Is there a method for members of the ISAO to communicate in a secure manner in the event of an ongoing cybersecurity event? Is there an alternative method to communicate should the primary method not be available?

Training: Training will continue to be a key issue in advancing between levels. Again, what is important for this domain of the CCSMM is training related to information sharing only. For a community to advance from Level 2 to Level 3 the following training should be accomplished:

- Is the ISAO or other community organizations conducting training or seminars to inform community members of the community's information sharing program and how to participate?
- Do ISAO members receive training on what Indicators of Compromise are important and how they should share this information with the ISAO? Does training exist for organizations or individuals in the community who are not members of the ISAO?

- Do ISAO analysts and SOC members receive appropriate training for their mission?
- Do ISAO members receive training on how to securely communicate with other members in the event of a cybersecurity incident?

Processes and Procedures: The processes and procedures for information sharing at this level will primarily be found in the ISAO as the hub of the community's information sharing efforts. Moving from an informal program to a formal program requires established processes and procedures for the sharing of information.

- Is there a vetting process for organizations and individuals wishing to become a member of the ISAO?
- Has a process been instituted in the ISAO to verify the validity of information sent to it from both members and especially from non-members?
- Are there established processes for the correlation of separate pieces of information (analysis of information)?
- Are processes in place for the correlation of physical and cyber security events?
- Are procedures in place for establishing secure means of communication?
- If a SOC is present, are there appropriate procedures and "playbooks" established for a variety of potential cybersecurity events that SOC personnel can follow? Are there processes in place to add additional "playbooks" should they be needed?

Assessments: Assessments at Level 3 will include exercises as seen in Level 2 but with additional processes and procedures established the opportunity exists to test them. Community exercises can also include more individuals, especially from industry. Questions to ask at this level on assessments could include:

- Is there a community cybersecurity exercise in which representatives of the greater community can participate? Does information sharing play a major role in the exercise?
- Has a survey been conducted to see how many individuals and organizations within the community know who to contact in the event of a cybersecurity event?

- If a SOC is present in the community, is it tested on a regular basis to ensure that appropriate "playbooks" are in place for anticipated cybersecurity events?

Information Sharing at Level 4: External Sharing

Not every community will need to attain a Level 4 maturity level. Having said that, there are certainly elements of a Level 4 community that should be included within communities that may not incorporate all of the characteristics of a Level 3 or Level 4 community. For example, even a small, rural community that is at a Level 2 for the community overall might still want to include 2-way external information sharing as part of their ISAO operations. Communities that have significant resources and those that have been designated an Urban Area Security Initiative (UASI) community should definitely be seeking to be at least a Level 4 community.

A Level 4 community's information sharing program will still be centered on the ISAO but there should also be a community cyber Security Operation Center (SOC). For larger communities the city should have its own SOC. For smaller communities the SOC may be shared with other communities or they may contract with a service provider to offer the capabilities of a SOC. The major objective of an ISAO and a SOC are somewhat different – a significant portion of the ISAO is concerned with information sharing before an incident occurs and then in helping with the dissemination of information concerning an event when one occurs. The SOC monitors current activities and in the event of an incident can help with the incident response. This is generalizing things somewhat and both SOCs and ISAOs can do more than what was described. In fact, at Level 4 the ISAO could very well contain the community SOC as part of its organization. If it doesn't, if the city, for example, runs the SOC then the ISAO and the SOC should be working closely together. The SOC should be staffed 24/7 or provide this capability by contracting with a service provider to deliver this capability either the entire time or whenever community SOC personnel are not on duty.

The ISAO for a Level 4 community should be doing quite a bit more analysis and should have information feeds from a variety of different sources. Organizations within the community should for the most part be comfortable with sharing information with the ISAO. You will never have 100% participation, but the community as a whole should understand the importance of information sharing and in reporting if an incident occurs to them. The ISAO should also be sharing and receiving information from the state and from other communities though this can be accomplished with a tie to organizations such as the Geographically-Based Community ISAO which is an "ISAO of ISAOs" whose members are other community, county, region, or state ISAOs. The community ISAO should also be a member of the MS-ISAC and should also be part of other automated information sharing efforts such as the DHS Automated Indicator Sharing (AIS) program or the Cyber Information Sharing and Collaboration Program (CICSP).

Metrics: Phase 3 includes the activities that occur to raise a community from Level 3 to Level 4. As with the other phases, we will begin by asking what metrics can be used to measure if a community is at Level 4? At Level 4 we are going to become much more interested in not just whether a certain program exists or not but also how involved the community is with information sharing. Is a good portion of the community actively involved in information sharing or just a small subset? The questions to determine if the community is at a Level 4 of information sharing include:

- Does the ISAO have a formal information sharing analysis capability? Is cross-sector sharing of information taking place?
- What percentage of the community have joined the community ISAO?
  - All utilities should be members.
  - The city government should be a member (or members).
  - 50% of colleges and universities should be members
  - 20% of industry should be members
- In the last year, have 30% of ISAO members shared information with the ISAO?
- In a survey of the community, do 70% of the organizations surveyed know about the ISAO?
- In a survey of the community, do 70% of the organizations surveyed know who to report a cyber incident to?
- Has the ISAO provided alerts to members in the past year? (Hard to qualify how many reports should have been produced but there should not have been any "missed opportunities" to report a warning to members of the community that could have helped them avoid an incident).
- In a survey of the ISAO membership, are 70% satisfied with the level of information sharing the ISAO is conducting?

Technology: The technology needed to accomplish information sharing in the community at Level 4 will build upon the technology established at Level 3 but will include more tools to facilitate the automated sharing of information. As the number of members of the community engaging in the community information sharing program grows, technology will need to scale in order to handle the increased volume of information. As automated information sharing begins to be employed across the community the systems to handle the information feeds from whatever sources will need to be expanded. At Level 4 SOC capabilities are required which will necessitate additional tools and technology as well. Technology needs at Level 4 will include the following:

- Does the technology being used to share information allow for the timely analysis and dissemination of relevant information to members of the community ISAO?
- Are tools in place that can facilitate the near-real time automated sharing of critical information to members of the community ISAO?
- Does the ISAO have tools and the personnel to utilize them to assist in cyber threat analysis?
- Does the SOC have the tools to accept information feeds from multiple sources and to provide a near-real time picture of the cyber status of the community?
- Is the ISAO and SOC sharing information with the state and other communities (either through direct feeds or through organizations such as the GBC-ISAO and MS-ISAC)?
- Does the community or ISAO have a method to conduct online training programs?

Training: Training will continue to be a key issue in advancing between levels. At Level 4 the need for trained technical personnel will greatly increase in order to operate the SOC and ISAO to accomplish near-real-time analysis and dissemination of information. Community leaders will also need to have a certain minimum amount of training in order to be able to understand the capabilities of the SOC and ISAO at this Level and what the information they provide means to the community. For a community to advance from Level 3 to Level 4 the following training should be accomplished:

- Are SOC personnel and ISAO cyberthreat personnel trained to use the tools available to them?

- Have government, industry and academic leaders received training to understand what is presented to them by the SOC and ISAO? Have they been trained to handle cyber events impacting the community?
- Does the ISAO or some other entity provide training to community members on their information sharing program to include the use of automated information sharing?
- Do all ISAO members include user-level information sharing training in their organization's annual cybersecurity training program?
- Does the ISAO or community sponsor home cybersecurity training for its citizens?
- Has the ISAO and SOC received training on how to communicate with organizations external to the community?

Processes and Procedures: The processes and procedures for information sharing at this level will primarily be found in the ISAO and SOC as the majority of the community's information sharing efforts will reside with them. Moving from a primarily internal (i.e. within the community) program to a program that also shares information in near-real-time with external entities requires established processes and procedures to accomplish. With the potential of adding automated information sharing to the mix there is also an increased need to be able to trust the information that is being received.

- Is there an expanded vetting process for organizations and individuals wishing to participate in the automated sharing of information?
- Are processes in place to manage the handling and coordination of cyber events between the SOC, ISAO, and city officials? Between the community and external organizations?
- Do processes and procedures clearly delineate how information will be analyzed and when and how to disseminate information to ISAO member and the community – to include how automated sharing will take place?
- Does the SOC have appropriate "playbooks" for more advanced cybersecurity incidents and do all "playbooks" include communication with appropriate external entities?

Assessments: Assessments at Level 4 will include exercises as seen in Level 3 but at this level functional exercises should be considered in addition to tabletop exercises. Functional exercises should assess whether cyber personnel throughout the city know how to handle a cyber incident and who to share information with, what information should be shared, and how to do it. Operational systems do not need to actually be breached or impacted (though light scanning is a possibility). Instead, white card injects can be used to provide to operational personnel to see how they react and what they do. Exercises should include a broad cross-section of community members including government offices (including state, and federal entities if there are any within the community), the utilities, industry, and academia. It is critical that city leaders participate in these exercises to ensure they understand the impact cyber events can have on the community and to help them prepare to lead when such an event occurs.

- Have community cybersecurity exercises expanded to include more representatives of the greater community?
- Has a functional-level exercise been conducted while maintaining and not interrupting city operations? Does the mayor and other community leaders participate in these exercises? Has there been a leadership-only tabletop exercise that concentrated on the decision and emergency management leadership functions?
- Do organizations within the community conduct their own organizational exercises (at least tabletop exercises) to include
  ○ All utilities
  ○ City officials and departments
  ○ 50% of the ISAO industry and academic members
- Has at least one exercise included communication with external entities such as state officials or officials in other communities?

Information Sharing at Level 5: All-Hazard Sharing

When discussing Level 4 communities the statement was made that not everybody needs to attain that level of maturity. This is even more applicable at Level 5. It was also stated that there are elements of a Level 4 community that should be included with communities that may not incorporate all the characteristics of a Level 3 or Level 4 community. Again, this is true for Level 5. A Level 5 community serves as a model for other communities around the state. It incorporates all-hazard information sharing and analysis and has a fully integrated fusion center. Large communities may have their own fusion center while smaller communities may combine efforts or may provide information to and receive information from a state fusion center. While emergency management personnel are all trained to think in terms of all-hazard preparation, a Level 5 CCSMM community adds cyber to the mix and also involves industry, academia, and the citizens in thinking in terms of how cyber is a cross-cutting force that can impact other physical systems and that cyber is also dependent upon other elements as well. UASI communities should strive to become Level 5 communities as well as large communities with significant industry, military, or political or historical significance.

At Level 5 the SOC that was created for Level 4 will expand its capabilities and may take on additional roles such as more extensive forensics, mitigation, response, and recovery operations when a member of the community is hit with a cyber event. Additionally, a key part of being a Level 5 Vanguard community is the responsibility to reach out and to help other communities and organizations outside of the immediate community. Thus, the SOC may take responsibility for other communities nearby and may help them in discovering when an attack is underway or has occurred. The same is true with the ISAO at Level 5. It may either help other communities in forming their own ISAO or it may actually take another community into its membership and act, at least for some time, as the ISAO for the other community. The ISAO will have enrolled additional organizations as members and more members should be conducting 2-way communication. As the membership of the ISAO expands in the community, small groups of members may start to meet on their own as similar organizations will naturally gravitate toward each other. In this way the needs of the members can be better met as the ISAO sponsors these groups which can now address issues that may be of importance to a specific group but may not be of as much interest to the rest of the ISAO.

Metrics: Phase 4 includes the activities that occur to raise a community from Level 4 to Level 5. We will again begin by asking what metrics can be used to measure if a community is at Level 5? At Level 5 we will be even more interested in how involved the community is with information sharing. More organizations should now be a member of the ISAO and more members should be involved in 2-way communication. The questions to determine if the community is at a Level 5 of information sharing include:

- Is the ISAO sponsoring smaller working groups or "birds of a feather" meetings for members that have similar interests that may not be of interest to the larger membership?
- What percentage of the community has joined the community ISAO?
  - All utilities should be members.
  - The city government and its various offices should be members.
  - 65% of colleges and universities should be members

- ○ 35% of industry should be members
- In the last year, have at least 55% of ISAO members shared information with the ISAO?
- In a survey of the community, do at least 85% of the organizations surveyed know about the ISAO and SOC? A similar survey of individual citizens should show at least 70% of the individuals surveyed know about the ISAO and SOC
- In a survey of the community, do 85% of the organizations surveyed know who to report a cyber incident to.
- Has the ISAO provided alerts to members in the past year? (It is hard to qualify how many reports should have been produced but there should not have been any "missed opportunities" to report a warning to members of the community that could have helped them avoid an incident).
- In a survey of the ISAO membership, are 85% satisfied with the level of information sharing the ISAO is conducting?
- Are the ISAO and SOC helping nearby communities or have they helped these communities establish their own ISAO and SOC? Do they communicate with these other communities concerning cybersecurity issues on a regular basis?
- Have at least 25% of the citizens of the community taken the ISAO or community sponsored citizen cybersecurity training program in the last year (the number may seem low but organizations will be conducting their own cybersecurity training so a significant portion of the community will receive training that way and may not need the citizen training program)?

Technology: The technology needed to accomplish information sharing in the community at Level 5 will build upon the technology established at Level 4 but will include opportunities to help other communities to develop their own ISAO and cybersecurity program. As the number of members of the community engaging in the information sharing program grows, and as other nearby communities are added to the fold, technology will need to scale in order to handle the increased volume of information. As automated information sharing expands to other communities, there needs to be a way to maintain a separation of information that was received from one community so that it may be shared only with that one community and not others if that is the desire of the additional community. At Level 5 a SOC is also introduced which will require additional tools/technology as well. Technology needs at Level 5 will include the following:

- Does the technology allow for a separation of information gathered between different communities that may be partnering with the ISAO?
- Does the SOC have the tools to provide enhanced forensic, mitigation, response, and recovery capabilities for the community?
- Does the ISAO have the needed technology to handle real-time information sharing and dissemination to multiple levels of members?

Training: Training is always an important issue in advancing between levels. At Level 5 community and its ISAO and SOC will need to have an established training program for other communities it may now be sponsoring or partnering with. Community leaders will need to have at least a minimum amount of training in order to understand how the community can tie into the efforts of other nearby communities and how they can assist these other communities in their own cybersecurity programs. For a community to advance from Level 4 to Level 5 the following training should be accomplished:

- Is citizen training hosted by the ISAO or community and is it available to other nearby communities?
- Have government, industry and academic leaders received training to understand how they can assist other communities and how the communities can work together to address cybersecurity events?
- Is training available to other communities nearby to explain how to establish or be part of an information sharing program?

Processes and Procedures: The processes and procedures for information sharing at this level will again be primarily found in the ISAO and SOC. Moving from an internally focused program to one that is a model for other communities and that is prepared to assist and partner with other communities requires established processes and procedures. What is the process to handle information from another community and how can it be separated from the information in other communities if that is the desire? How is vetting going to occur for the other communities that may become partners? How will trust be established between communities?

- Is there an expanded vetting process that considers how to vet other communities and their organizations?

- Have processes been established to be able to maintain a separation of information obtained from different communities if that is the desire?
- Has the community developed a program that is designed to raise the level of trust between individuals and organizations in the different communities?
- Has a program been established and procedures developed that allows the community ISAO and SOC to recruit and work with other nearby communities that are just beginning to develop their own information sharing and cybersecurity programs?

Assessments: Assessments at Level 5 will include the functional, and tabletop exercises seen in Level 4 but will also include specific tabletop exercises where other communities have been invited to attend and participate. These exercises will feature events that will focus on cooperation in terms of information sharing, response, and recovery operations between the different communities represented. As the level of maturity of the cybersecurity programs in the other communities grows, these exercises could be conducted in multiple locations simultaneously to enhance the information sharing component. Exercises for the community should continually expand to include broader cross-sections of community members. As before, it is critical that city leaders participate in these exercises to ensure they understand the impact cyber events can have on the community and to help them prepare to lead when such an event occurs.

- Has the community participated in at least one cybersecurity exercise in which other nearby communities also fully participated?
- Do organizations within the community conduct their own exercises to include
  - All utilities
  - City officials and departments
  - 70% of the ISAO industry and academic members

** NOTE: The lists above are considered cumulative so that a city hoping to achieve a maturity level 4 should include not just the items listed in the Level 4 section but should also include those items listed for Level 2 and Level 3 as well.

CONCLUSION

Information sharing is an important tool in the cybersecurity fight. The U.S. government has expanded its efforts in this arena helping to promote sharing of information from federal sources such as the intelligence agencies as well as the Department of Homeland Security and encouraging the private sector to engage with the federal government and each other through organizations such as the ISAOs.

Cybersecurity Information Sharing is critical to a viable and sustainable cybersecurity program and can be used as a catalyst to jumpstart a cybersecurity program. Communities, which have been a target of cyber-attacks for several years, can create their own ISAO which can serve to expand the cybersecurity ecosystem and can help to build trust with organizations so that they become more comfortable with sharing their own information. For a community to build an effective cybersecurity information sharing program will take time and it will take funding though the path shown by the CCSMM acknowledges that most communities will not initially have a lot of funding budgeted for cybersecurity so initial efforts will need to utilize no- and low-cost activities.

At first, information sharing efforts within a community will be mostly one-way. Organizations will be in "listen mode" and will only receive information without sharing. This is natural and should be accepted. As communities advance in their CCSMM level more information sharing will be required and organizations should be encouraged to participate in two-way information sharing. A community approach actually will help with encouraging sharing as trust is needed before somebody will be willing to share potentially sensitive information and one of the best ways to establish trust is through personal relationships which are easier to accomplish within a community rather than a nation-wide sector.

REFERENCES

A brief history of the information sharing environment. (n.d.). Retrieved from Office of the Director of National Intelligence website: https://www. dni.gov/files/ISE/ documents/DocumentLibrary/Brief-History-ISE-2015.pdf

Executive Order 13636: Improving Critical Infrastructure Cybersecurity. (2013). Retrieved from https://www.govinfo.gov/content/pkg/FR-2013-02-19/pdf/2013-03915.pdf

Executive Order 13691: Promoting Private Sector Cybersecurity Information Sharing. (2015). Retrieved from https://www.govinfo.gov/content/pkg/FR-2015-02-20/pdf/2015-03714.pdf

Presidential decision directives - PDD. (1998). Retrieved from The White House website: https://fas.org/irp/offdocs/pdd-63.htm

The Clinton administration's policy on critical infrastructure protection: Presidential decision directive 63. (1998). Retrieved from The White House website: https://fas.org/irp/offdocs/paper598.htm

ADDITIONAL READING

Talamantes, J. (2016). *Why is intelligence sharing important in cyber security?* Retrieved from RedTeam website: https://www.redteamsecure.com/ why-is-intelligence-sharing-important-in-cyber-security/

Chapter 6
Policies

ABSTRACT

Local governments provide public services including police, fire departments, emergency services, and others. Operations are accomplished by following policies, laws, and regulations. Communities will need to integrate cybersecurity concepts into established community policies. Existing policies need to be reviewed for cybersecurity evaluating them for cyber integration and identifying critical services that could be disrupted or impacted by a cyber incident. Communities need to identify an authorization hierarchy that will makes decisions in regard to critical services being impacted by a cyber-attack. Roles need to be established and integrated into policies to identify existing capabilities to address cyber incidents and ultimately who will respond if needed. Public-private partnerships need to be reviewed and legal agreements crafted and signed before an incident occurs. These considerations are initial steps that can be taken as the community strives to improve its cybersecurity posture where community policies are concerned.

INTRODUCTION

Communities provide a broad range of services and have responsibilities to the organizations and citizens that reside and do business within a set geographic area representing their boundaries. "Municipalities generally take responsibility for parks and recreation services, police and fire departments, housing services, emergency medical services, municipal courts, transportation services (including public transportation), and public works (streets, sewers,

DOI: 10.4018/978-1-7998-4471-6.ch006

snow removal, signage, and so forth)" ("State and Local" n.d.). The policies that are established will reflect the long-term goals, boundaries, and guidelines the community intends to enforce in these responsibility areas. Many policies for the community are set by the legislative body such as the city or town council, the county council and the board of county commissioners. Policies establish expectations and desired outcomes for how programs and services will be accomplished within the community. Some policies that impact the non-government and non-critical infrastructure sectors may require the cooperation and acceptance of the private sector. This means the community will need to determine who is leading the cybersecurity program and may need agreement from both public and private sectors. Some options for who may oversee the cybersecurity program are, the local government, a public private partnership, or perhaps the chamber of commerce.

Community policy may also address how public private partnerships with industry will be established, how they will work and will define goals and outcomes. Community processes and functions will also have policies associated with them. As an example, public communications or public relations will establish how messages will be created, approved, and administered to reach the citizens and organizations within the community. Communities need to consider the policies that currently exist and integrate cybersecurity concepts and measures especially where cyber incidents and attacks can impact the business operations of the entire community. In this case, the communications function could be disrupted making it non-functional during a critical period of time such as during an incident, or it could be usurped and then used to distribute misinformation. Both scenarios would require a backup plan of action. Evaluating the business functions associated with this policy will drive additional processes and procedures to be created.

BACKGROUND

The terms policy, processes, and procedures need to be clarified as often they are used synonymously or are misunderstood. Policies, processes, and procedures are all different but do work together for a desired result. A policy is a high-level plan that expresses the overall goals or guidelines the community wishes to achieve. Processes and procedures support the goals by outlining what must happen and then providing the steps or detailed actions needed to accomplish the policy. This is an important concept because a **policy** is a CCSMM **dimension**. Recall that dimensions focus on specific areas of improvement that are needed in the cybersecurity program. **Processes and procedures** are **implementation mechanisms** which are used to define the main elements needed and provide steps for implementation.

Policies create and enforce how everything is done in both organizations and communities. At the community level, policies will drive and set the expectations for both the public and private sectors. It should cover what roles various organizations throughout the community will play before, during and after a cyber incident occurs that impacts the business operations of the community. Policies will also establish what the specific role and responsibilities the city government will have. Understanding the relationships and interdependencies the organizations in the community have among each other is very useful as policies, regulations and laws are examined and modified to integrate cybersecurity considerations into them.

Community cybersecurity exercises can be used to show how interdependencies and roles could be recognized. As discussed previously, the exercises focused on increasing cybersecurity awareness, understanding the importance of cyber information sharing, identifying where cyber considerations were not integrated into policy, and to test incident response capabilities and identify where gaps exist. As each of these goals is examined further, consider how policies can be used to establish roles within the community to address cyber-attacks. The community exercise referenced below was one done through a Department of Defense (DoD) initiative. The basic premise of these exercises was to see the potential impact that could occur to the military if a cyber-attack was launched against the city or community. The idea behind this is if an attacker targeted the military installation, could they impact the mission of the installation by attacking the community. The community is most likely an easier target having less defenses in place than the installation itself, and the infrastructure services that are piped into the installation are located in the community. Another aspect to this, was that some of the military installations had a cyber-related mission. If the military had intelligence that the community was targeted for attack, could the installation provide that information to the community? The results of these exercises showed that the military and community the installation resided within needed to have some form of Memorandum of Understanding (MOU) or some type of agreement that would allow formal communications between the community and the installation regarding a cyber-incident or attack. As a test after one of these exercises, one of the installations sent a request through their command to approve communication of cyber-related information to be provided to the community. It took 2 weeks for that approval to go through the chain of command. It was recognized that 2 weeks was a significant delay and would likely no longer be helpful to prevent an attack. A formal agreement put in place before an incident would provide the channels of communication to be in place before an incident occurred.

The objectives from one of these exercises is provided for context below. Names of organizations, cities and counties have been taken out. There are some objectives that specifically reference DoD, since most communities do not have a military installation, the DoD reference can be substituted with federal agencies, state agencies, and large headquarters of corporations that are located in the community. This will make the application equally applicable.

Community Cybersecurity Exercise Objectives:

- To test the response capabilities of the City and County and surrounding region to a cyber-terrorist attack.
- To recommend/develop methods for all sectors (industry, law enforcement, government, and academia) to cooperatively protect the national critical infrastructures.
- To serve as a model for other cities in preparing for a cyber-terrorist or similar event.

In meeting these objectives, it is anticipated that a number of issues will be addressed including:

- Preparing
  - How can local government and industry prepare for a cyber-attack?
  - What DoD, federal, and state roles are there in this preparation?
- Alerting
  - How can local government and industry be alerted of a possible cyber-attack?
  - What role can the DoD (Air Force, Guard, etc.) play in cyber alerts based on observed indications and warnings?
- Detecting
  - What mechanisms need to be in place to detect cyber-attacks?
  - How is coordination among the different sectors and levels of government best accomplished?
- Responding
  - How can a coordinated response among the different sectors to a cyber-attack be accomplished?

The tabletop exercise is not designed to address all of these objectives – it is aimed at the preparation and alerting phases with an emphasis on the communication channels necessary to conduct these activities.

After reviewing the above objectives, consider the questions asked in the phases of a cyber incident (Preparing, Alerting, Detecting, Responding). These questions can be used to begin discussions of what roles various organizations in the community can play in regard to a cyber-attack on the community. It will be important to have these discussions before an incident and critical to have signed agreements in place to formalize these roles. Now consider how community policy can be established to guide and encourage these conversations and how policy can be used in formalizing roles of participating organizations throughout the community. An interesting example comes from a state exercise the CIAS conducted in the 2006-time frame. In this state exercise there were three communities and a state component, made up of the state information resources department and a fusion center. One of the areas being evaluated was if the three communities would share cyber incidents with the state cell. During the progression of the scenarios, one city did finally share a cyber incident with the state. This is where it became interesting. The state information resources department reviewed the cyber information that came in and decided this information should be handled by the fusion center for analysis and distribution. The fusion center reviewed the information and recognized it contained cyber-related information and determined it should be handled by the state information resource department. This was a huge "aha" moment as both entities realized roles for cyber-related information had never been discussed nor established.

One example, that resulted from the Darkscreen exercise was the recognition that the Texas Freedom of Information Act (FOIA) laws gave access, upon request, to anyone wishing to obtain documentation on a government agency. There are instances where that would not be beneficial as some documentation may show how an agency is vulnerable to cyber-attack. FIOA provides the public the right to request access to public records of government bodies. The issue was if a state agency conducted a vulnerability assessment and a report was created that showed these vulnerabilities and areas that were not secure, anyone could request the results through FOIA and would then have a list of vulnerabilities that could be exploited. This realization came from discussions during the Darkscreen exercise and the result was an initiative to change the law to provide certain exemptions for the protection of the agency.

STRATEGIC POLICIES ON SECURITY

The strategic policies on security need to be high level, long-term, and applied community-wide. Deliberate planning used to structure activities and guidelines for implementing policies on security issues and concerns need to be in place. Recognize security includes both physical security and cybersecurity. It is important to consider both in the overall policies because cyber incidents can have physical consequences and physical destruction of a system could have direct consequences to the access of data, systems, or connectivity. The approach to include both physical and cybersecurity issues will help the community to have a more comprehensive focus on all their security needs.

On September 20, 2018, a National Cybersecurity Strategy was released by the White House. It was the first comprehensive National Cybersecurity Strategy in fifteen years. While it focused on national security it also demonstrated an interagency approach that could be useful for designing and identifying community policies for security. First it recognized the responsibility to secure the nation's critical infrastructure and manage its cybersecurity risk that is shared by the federal government and the private sector. The White House strategy addressed the following "four pillars":

- Protecting the American people, homeland and way of life, which includes a strategy for securing government systems and critical infrastructure;
- Promoting American prosperity, which encourages investments in adoption of cybersecurity technologies and innovation, and development of the cybersecurity workforce;
- Preserving peace through strength - including attributing and deterring "unacceptable behavior in cyberspace;"
- Advancing American influence including "promoting an open, interoperable reliable and secure internet."

Each of these pillars addressed areas of cybersecurity improvement that every community at some point in their maturity may want to incorporate into community policies. There are several points that could be considered in the early stages of the community's cybersecurity maturity. What follows are some ideas extracted from National Cyber Strategy that communities may wish to consider in developing security policies for the community. Some of this guidance relates directly to organizations in the community, but the information can be considered to create community policy that relates to public privacy, safety and the protection of public information.

Securing government systems and critical infrastructure: Local government agencies continuing to work toward incorporating risk management principles and protecting the critical infrastructures has been a focus since the late 1990s. Community policies that include securing and protecting systems need to be reviewed to ensure they include:

- How can the internet service providers (ISP) assist in the case of a cyber incident?
- In many cases a community will have multiple ISPs, have all the ISPs in the community been included in addressing possible cyber-attacks and incidents?
- Have cyber incident reporting channels been established?
- If so, who in the community knows what they are?
- Are all of the critical infrastructures in the community included in community exercises?
- The majority of the critical infrastructures are privately owned
- There are many very smallest and electric cooperatives (co-ops) that need to be identified.
- Do the co-ops understand what cyber threats they have? Are they protected? Can they respond to a cyber incident? How would a cyber incident on the co-op impact the greater community?

The following policies are designed more for an organization rather than a community; however, the community may consider establishing a policy that requires organizations doing business with city or county to establish these policies within their organizations. Another suggestion would be to set goals for the percentage of organizations that the community would like to have cybersecurity policies incorporated into the organizational operations.

As local governments seek to implement cybersecurity policies to protect their networks and critical information, there are policies that should not be ignored. The very first thing that should be done is to designate an employee to be responsible for cybersecurity. The following policies should be included in the cybersecurity program:

- **Acceptable Use Policy:** establishes rules that a user must agree to follow in order to be provided with access to a network or to the internet. These policies have become common practice for many organizations and require that all users physically sign an acceptable use policy before being granted network access.

- **Access Control Policy:** minimizes the risk of unauthorized access to physical and logical systems. Access control is a fundamental component of security compliance programs that ensures security technology and access control policies are in place to protect confidential information, such as customer data. An access control policy may addresses:
- standards for user access
- network access controls
- operating system software controls and requirements for creating a password
- monitoring how systems are accessed and used
- security unattended workstations
- terminating access when an employee leaves the organization
- **Remote Access Policy:** defines required methods of remotely connecting to the organizations network. This policy should address using insecure network locations such as unmanaged home networks or coffee houses.
- **Change Management Policy:** establishes the process for making changes to information technology, software development, and security services and operations. This policy ensures the organization is aware of all changes that are planned to minimize adverse impacts to services and customers.
- **Incident Response Policy:** describes the process for handling an incident and limit damages that may occur to the business operations and customers. This policy is intended to reduce recovery time and costs that may be associated with a cyber incident.
- **Business Continuity Policy:** focuses on the failure of any part of the organizations information technology platform and ensures the business can continue to operate and function uninterrupted.

Development of the Cybersecurity Workforce: Communities tend to agree that increasing the awareness of cyber incidents and attack vectors for all employees is necessary. Another common workforce development initiative a community is often involved with, is to increase the number of individuals that have technical degrees and to increase technical skills needed to assist in minimizing the lack of cybersecurity professionals that are currently in the workforce. Partnerships with community colleges, universities, technical colleges and technical training institutions are a recognized way to move this initiative forward. There are many programs that teach cybersecurity principles to middle and high school students, and more programs that encourage students to learn secure coding, network protection and incident response. These programs are beneficial but not all communities have implemented them. These efforts are building the educational pipeline to encourage more students to consider cybersecurity a career path. Communities may consider **a policy that addresses the development of the cybersecurity workforce or revising an existing workforce policy to include it**.

Unacceptable Behavior in Cyberspace: Communities are not responsible for the security of everybody within their boundaries nor are they able to dictate exactly what those entities (private) must do in cybersecurity. However, encouraging community-wide ethical practices for computer usage can discourage unacceptable behavior. Cyber ethics portrays the values and practices surrounding the use of computing technology without violating the values and beliefs of an organization and in this case the community. Cyber ethics address not only appropriate behaviors on the internet, email, and social media but it also includes principles with privacy and ensures unintended illegal actions. A community should consider a community-wide cyber ethics campaign to be included in a policy of security.

An Ethics Policy should reflect:

- The expectations of how computers will be used.
- Should reflect established ethics and core values.
- Should clearly state what the expected behaviors are when using computer resources.
- It should be clear, succinct and easy to remember.

One area not yet discussed that should be a priority for a community reviewing their existing policies, is to make sure there is a policy for continuity.

Continuity: This policy needs to require the community to develop a plan that addresses how the community will continue to provide essential services in the event of a disaster. It should also address how services that are disrupted for a period of time will be restored. In the event a community does not have a continuity policy they should implement immediately and if the community does have a continuity policy it should be reviewed to ensure cyber incidents and attacks have been addressed.

As the community reviews community policies and potentially creates new security policies, the following questions can be addressed:

- What is the formal process to document policies? What agency is responsible for this?
- How do we educate and train members of the community to understand and follow the policies?
- How often do we modify the policies?
- Do community members know where to find the policies?
- Do our policies address current cybersecurity best practices?
- How often do we measure the effectiveness of our policies? Who would be involved in this?

Key practices for policy implementation are to make sure people know about them, can access them, are trained on them, and exercised on them.

COMMUNITY CYBERSECURITY POLICIES

Integrating cybersecurity principles into community-wide policy will be a significant effort. Reviewing the policy and determining if there are cyber impact implications will be a coordinated effort of policy makers, technical staff, and decision makers. A policy maker can assist to provide the intent of a particular policy. A technical staff member can review the policy to determine if there is any technology that may be associated with the policy and may be able to provide insight as to the impacts of that technology if it were disabled or made unavailable. The decision maker may need to determine if the policy needs to be implemented, changed or eliminated. Likely these decisions will be based on recommendations from the policy makers and technical staff. Another dynamic in policy creation is to socialize any changes with key stakeholders to determine if changes will impact them and how those changes may impact them. The intent is not to create obstacles, rather to address cybersecurity concerns, and to identify areas that do not address cybersecurity that will make the community vulnerable to cyber-attack. The following are recommendations to consider as a community establishes community cybersecurity policies:

- **Establish Policies that Reflect the Community's Cybersecurity Desires:** In order to establish cybersecurity policies, the community will need to come together and define the goals or desired outcomes they wish to achieve to improve their cybersecurity posture. Creating a working group composed of key stakeholders in the community to identify the goals is one way to achieve this. The working group may decide one of their goals is to increase the number of skilled cybersecurity professionals in the community. This could be viewed in different ways. One view could be to increase cybersecurity competencies with existing information technology professionals. Another view could be to increase the number of students that become cybersecurity skilled graduates and enter the workforce.

The next step is to review existing community policies to see if this cybersecurity goal can be integrated into any of them. Perhaps the community has an Economic Development Policy that includes workforce development programs and initiatives, or the community may have some other social policy that includes partnerships with the local colleges and universities. If no policies exist, the community may consider establishing a policy that could be used.

- **Establish Policies Defining How The Community Will Implement and Maintain Awareness in the Community:** The community needs to establish goals for cybersecurity awareness of the leadership, organizations to include government agencies, critical infrastructure, and small businesses, and it needs to establish goals for cybersecurity awareness for the general public. A policy reflecting the goals for community cybersecurity awareness may establish programs and initiatives that are needed to introduce cybersecurity topics, trends, and impacts and establish roles for implementation and maintenance. The community will need to identify who in the community will own this initiative.
- **Establish Policies Defining How The Community Will Share Information Regarding Cybersecurity:** Community policies for cybersecurity information sharing may establish a community ISAO to assist in community cybersecurity sharing efforts. The community should establish policies on what types of information should be shared and which agencies and organizations throughout the community that information will be distributed to. This is also where the community can define how cyber incidents will be communicated to the public.
- **Establish Policies Defining How the Community Will Incorporate Cyber Into Plans:** The community should develop a process to review existing plans to identify where cybersecurity is applicable. The process should also include time frames to be re-evaluated to ensure the plans are current with cyber trends.

A community should consider continuity plans, incident response plans, and other emergency operating plans that can assist in responding and recovering from cyber incidents. Recovering from an incident can be challenging when there's no plan in place. Recovery teams simply won't know what to do and will instead rely on last-minute guesswork. There is a greater chance mistakes will be made, resulting in a longer and more costly recovery.

- **Establish Policies to Define How The Community Will Assess Cybersecurity and How Often:** The community should conduct risk assessments periodically. This will assist in identifying assets that are most valuable for the continued ability to provide services to the public and other partners. Once these critical systems are identified how to best protect them can be determined.

- **Establish Policies on how Public Private Partnerships Will be Established:** Cooperation between the public and private sectors is an essential aspect of our national cybersecurity strategy. These partnerships must be based on a foundation of mutual trust, and open dialogue. The community should identify which partnerships would be beneficial for the community and define how to establish and maintain those partnerships.

- **Establish Policies on How The Community Will Notify the Public on Cyber-Attacks, Breaches or Incidents Impacting Community Services or Functions:** Getting correct and up to date information to the public is critical. Misinformation can cause a great deal of confusion and in some instances could cause a panic. The community should define how the public can be informed of cyber incidents that have occurred within the community and are possibly impacting public safety or services. Multiple options are a good idea here because if the community has been impacted by a cyber-attack, information mechanisms such as websites, phones or television could be unavailable.

- **Establish Policies Defining How the Community Will Create Response Capabilities Regarding Cyber:** This policy will include the types of training needed to ensure response capabilities are learned. It should also include who should receive training and how often. Technical training can be very expensive which may limit the amount and types of training that can be obtained. No and low-cost solutions can be explored to establish innovative ways to implement the skillsets needed. As an example, a policy could include anyone who attends training will share lessons learned and course materials with others needing that training.

- **Establish Policies on Cybersecurity Requirements for Organizations Doing Business With The City or City Agencies:** Cyber breaches can occur through a vendor or partner who has access to the city network. Implementing a policy that addresses a minimum cyber hygiene could help to protect the network. The community may also want to establish what information will be reported when a cyber incident is found. Another policy that could be addressed here is to establish who will be the lead during an incident and how response activities will be carried out.
- **Establish Policies on how the Community Will Work With County Governments Regarding Cybersecurity:** Often smaller communities do not have the same level of resources and capability as a larger community. Consider creating a policy that will define how the community can work with smaller surrounding cities, counties or other jurisdictions.
- **Establish, Review or Update Policies with the State for Guidelines to Address Cybersecurity (Identify, Prevent, Protect, Respond, Recover):** Coordinate with the State to define what resources are available if the community suffers from a significant cyber incident. This would be a good place to define how to request assistance and how quickly to expect a response capability to be on-sight to assist.

CCSMM POLICY ROADMAP

The CCSMM policy roadmap begins at Level 1 – Initial. At this level, the policies that currently exist for the community do not address cybersecurity issues. Assessments are not conducted to ensure cybersecurity has been incorporated into those policies, and individuals are not tested to ensure they know how to handle the policy. The policy roadmap guides the community to Level 5 – Vanguard which means the community has implemented cybersecurity principles in everything they do, and they are conducting full-scale exercises to test both cyber and physical capabilities as they relate to each other. The ability of the community to triage, analyze and fuse cyber threat indicator capabilities are also tested. At level 5, the community is mentoring smaller communities to build relationships and improve their capabilities.

To begin the process of improving the policies in the community, refer to Figure 1 to see the characteristics for the policy dimension.

Figure 1.

	LEVEL 1 Initial	LEVEL 2 Established	LEVEL 3 Self-Assessed	LEVEL 4 Integrated	LEVEL 5 Vanguard
Awareness	• Minimal cyber awareness	• Leadership aware of cyber threats, issues and imperatives for cyber security and community cooperative cyber training	• Leaders promote org security awareness; formal community cooperative training	• Leaders and orgs promote awareness; citizens aware of cyber security issues	• Awareness a business imperative
Info Sharing	• Minimal cyber info sharing	• Informal info sharing/ communication in community; working groups established; ad-hoc analysis, little fusion or metrics; professional orgs established or engaged	• Formal local info sharing/cyber analysis, initial cyber-physical fusion; informal external info sharing/ cyber analysis and metrics gathering	• Formal info sharing/ analysis, internal and external to community; formal local fusion and metrics, initial external efforts	• Fully integrated fusion/ analysis center, combining all-source physical and cyber info; create and disseminate near real world picture
Policy	• Minimal cyber assessments and policy & procedure evaluations	• No assessments, but aware of requirement; initial evaluation of policies & procedures	• Autonomous tabletop cyber exercises with assessments of info sharing, policies & procedures, and fusion; routine audit program; mentor externals on policies & procedures, auditing and training	• Autonomous cyber exercises with assessments of formal info sharing/local fusion; exercises involve live play/metrics assessments	• Accomplish full-scale blended exercises and assess complete fusion capability; involve/ mentor other communities/entities
Plans	• Little inclusion of cyber into Continuity of Operations Plan (COOP)	• Aware of need to integrate cyber security into COOP	• Include cyber in COOP; formal cyber incident response/recovery	• Integrate cyber in COOP; mentor externals on COOP integration; formal blended incident response and recovery	• Continue to integrate cyber in COOP; mentor externals on COOP integration; formal blended incident response and recovery

Policy at Level 1: Minimal Cyber Assessments and Policy

In Level 1 of the policy dimension, the community has minimal cyber assessments and policies and procedures have not been evaluated for cyber inclusion. This level, just as it appears, means that there are existing community policies, but they have not been evaluated to determine if cybersecurity concepts need to be incorporated into them.

Assessments evaluate the community's strengths, capabilities, needs and challenges. Exercises are primarily used in communities to evaluate the community's ability to achieve specific objectives defined in the exercise. The exercise helps to identify gaps in capabilities, processes and plans.

Policy at Level 2: Initial Evaluation

At Level 2, the community is not doing assessments, but they are aware that they should. An initial evaluation to determine if cybersecurity had been incorporated in any of the policies and procedures is conducted.

Policies establish, at a high-level, the guidelines the community would like implemented. They establish expectations and limitations. The selection of the policy dimension was intended to ensure needed cybersecurity principles would be reflected. The CIAS researchers found that policies that were not cybersecurity specific were not executed consistently nor were they interpreted the same way.

- Policies must be clear to everyone in the organization and community
- Determine who will "own" them
- Have an implementation plan
- Determine technology needs
- Who should be trained on the policy
- Exercise/evaluate/update
- Determine how often

Phase 1 includes the following activities to achieve Level 2:

Metrics:
- ○ Determine how many policies currently exist
- ○ Determine how many policies currently have cyber integrated into them
- ○ Determine how many policies receive updated cyber information

Technology:
- ○ Technologies used will assist in tracking policies and training conducted

Training:
- ○ Training will provide information to raise awareness of why cyber integrated into policies is a good practice.

Processes and Procedures:
  ∘ Designate someone to be responsible for cybersecurity. This individual will manage the risk from technologies, work processes and documented policies and procedures.
  ∘ Map business functions to each policy
  ∘ Identify threats to each function and map the asset that supports the business function

Assessments:
  ∘ Assessments can be used to see the level of increased awareness of the importance of adding cyber into policies.
  ∘ Assessments can be created to ensure mapping to business processes was correct.

Policy at Level 3: Assessments and Fusion

At Level 3, the community is conducting autonomous tabletop cyber exercises with assessments that will include information sharing, policies & procedures, and fusion. The community has created an audit program that has been added into the cybersecurity program and it is being done regularly. The community is now in a position to mentor externals on policies & procedures, auditing and training.

Phase 2 activities needed to achieve Level 3 include:

Metrics:
  ∘ Track how many tabletop community cyber exercises were conducted
  ∘ Track how many and how often assessments were conducted
  ∘ Track how many and how often audits were conducted

Technology:
  ∘ Technology to conduct and analyze the tabletop and its results and consolidate after action report
  ∘ Technology needed for audits

Training:
  ∘ Training needs to be developed on topics related to audit results
  ∘ Training for new policies integrating cyber

  ◦ Training for conducting an exercise
  ◦ Training for facilitating an exercise

Processes and Procedures:
  ◦ Establish processes and procedures for how the audit program operates, how often they do audits, where they will store results and who they will report the results to.
  ◦ Establish policies on the exercise program, how often it will be conducted, where the results will be stored and who the after action report goes to.

Assessments: The assessments
  ◦ Conduct 1 exercise annually to determine how well the policies and procedures work and what the capabilities are at this level

Policy at Level 4: Assessments of Formal Info Sharing/Local Fusion

At Level 4, the community is conducting autonomous cyber exercises with assessments of formal information sharing and local fusion. The exercises involve live play and metrics assessments.
  Phase 3 activities to achieve Level 4 include:

Metrics:
  ◦ Conduct 1 more tabletop cyber exercise then the previous level
  ◦ Conduct 1 more assessment than was previously conducted
  ◦ Conduct 1 more audit than was previously conducted

Technology:
  ◦ Technology to analyze the table top results and consolidate after action report
  ◦ Technology needed for audits

Training:
  ◦ Training needs to be developed on topics related to audit results
  ◦ Training for new policies integrating cyber
  ◦ Training for conducting an exercise
  ◦ Training for facilitating an exercise

Processes and Procedures:
- ○ Update processes and procedures for how the audit program operates, how often they do audits, where they will store results and who they will report the results to.
- ○ Update policies on the exercise program, how often it will be conducted, where the results will be stored and who the after action report goes to.

Assessments:
- ○ Conduct 1 exercise annually to determine how well the policies and procedures work and what the capabilities are at this level. Extend new invitations for additional partners to participate in the exercise

Policy at Level 5: Mentor Other Communities/Entities

At Level 5 the community can accomplish full-scale blended exercises and assess complete fusion capability. The community is involved and mentoring other communities and entities.

Phase 4 activities to achieve Level 5 include:

Metrics:
- ○ Conduct 1 more tabletop cyber exercises then the previous level and conduct 1 tabletop with external community
- ○ Conduct 1 more assessments than was previously conducted and 1 tabletop with external community
- ○ Conduct 1 more audits than was previously conducted and 1 tabletop with external community

Technology: The technology needed
- ○ Technology to analyze the tabletop results and consolidate after action report
- ○ Technology needed for audits

Training: The training
- ○ Training offered on information sharing; fusion; exercise for internal and shared with external communities
- ○ Training offered on how to establish cyber policies; new policies integrating cyber and shared with external communities

- ○ Training offered on conducting a full scale blended exercise and share with external communities
- ○ Training offered on facilitating a in full scale blended exercises and share with external communities

Processes and Procedures:
- ○ Update processes and procedures for how the audit program operates, how often they do audits, where they will store results and who they will report the results to.
- ○ Update policies on the exercise program, how often it will be conducted, where the results will be stored and who the after action report goes to.

Assessments: The assessments
- ○ Conduct 1 full scale blended exercise annually to determine how well the policies and procedures work and what the capabilities are at this level. Extend invitations for additional partners to participate in the exercise

CONCLUSION

Communities offer many services to the public and establish policies enforcing the availability of those services, how they are implemented and how they operate. Cyber-attacks can impact the availability of those services which would impact the overall community. Incorporating and evaluating cybersecurity concepts into the overall policies of the community will assist in recognizing how operations should work in the event of a cyber incident and will also help to identify systems related to the business essential functions offered by a community. Once systems have been identified, vulnerabilities to those systems can be recognized and controls can be put in place to better protect them and by association protect the ability to provide the service.

The community cybersecurity exercises conducted for the DoD provided some insights into establishing agreements before an incident occurs that would allow the military installation to communicate with the community it resides in. The objectives provided in the background from one of the exercises conducted by the CIAS, offered some context to what the exercises were focusing on. These objectives can also be used to assist a community to develop their own objectives that could be used for a community cyber exercise they develop.

Some policies taken from the National Cybersecurity Strategy released by the White House on September 20, 2018, were discussed and how these policies can be referenced in designing and creating community cybersecurity policies. The national cybersecurity strategy areas reviewed were "**Securing government systems and critical infrastructure**", "**Development of the cybersecurity workforce**," and "**Unacceptable behavior in cyberspace**". Additionally, several community policies considerations were suggested for a community to review as they seek to review existing policies for cybersecurity applicability and as they develop new cybersecurity policies.

REFERENCES

The White House. (2018). *National cyber strategy of the United States of America*. Retrieved from https://www.whitehouse.gov/wp-content/uploads/2018/09/ National-Cyber-Strategy.pdf

ADDITIONAL READING

Cybersecurity council. (n.d.). Retrieved from San Antonio Chamber of Commerce website: https://www.sachamber.org/get-involved/cyber/

Hayslip, G. (2018). 9 policies and procedures you need to know about if you're starting a new security program. Retrieved August 18, 2019, from CSO website: https://www.csoonline.com/article/3263738/9-policies-and-procedures-you-need-to-know-about-if-youre-starting-a-new-security-program.html

Preparedness toolkit. (n.d.). Retrieved from FEMA website: https://preptoolkit.fema.gov/web/validate-capability

State and local government. (n.d.). Retrieved from White House website: https://www.whitehouse.gov/about-the-white-house/state-local-government/

Chapter 7
Plans

ABSTRACT

Communities have been planning for disasters for a very long time, especially for natural disasters. The capability to predict when the hurricane will hit a coastal area or island is available. Precautions are reported to the public, and preparedness activities are posted continuously. Planning for cyber incidents is a much newer activity, and it has been getting increasingly more sophisticated as time goes on. A community plans for physical events such as a hurricane, flood, or tornado because they are in geographic areas that are prone to these threats. All communities need to prepare for a cyber incident or attack. In the early 2000s, the CIAS would hear comments such as "Our county is too small" or "No one would target us, we don't have anything they would want." No matter how small the organization and no matter what the size of the community, everyone is a target today. Preparing for "when" the cyber incident happens is the best approach, and that means every municipality, county, and parish should have a plan in place to continue business and to respond to an incident.

INTRODUCTION

Communities have been coming to together for decades to plan and respond to a great number of scenarios that could be harmful or potentially dangerous to the citizens in their community or the business operations of the community. These incidents can occur from natural or human-caused events and require an emergency response to protect life and property.

DOI: 10.4018/978-1-7998-4471-6.ch007

Incidents can include major disasters, emergencies, terrorist attacks, terrorist threats, wildland and urban fires, floods, hazardous materials spills, nuclear accidents, aircraft accidents, earthquakes, hurricanes, tornadoes, tropical storms, war-related disasters, public health and medical emergencies, and other occurrences requiring an emergency response to include cyber incidents.

Determining who should respond to an incident will depend on what the incident is and its significance. It is important to note that most incidents are managed at the local level. Emergency plans for a community addresses all-hazard incidents, as previously identified, which typically require a unified response from local agencies, the private sector, and non-government organizations. Some may require additional support from neighboring jurisdictions or state governments. A smaller number of incidents require Federal support or are led by the Federal Government. An important factor for consideration is not all incidents are contained in a specific geographic area. Certain incidents such as a pandemic or a cyber event may span across jurisdictions, states or regions. This type of incident, depending on the nature of it, may be managed at the local, state, tribal, territorial, or Federal level.

BACKGROUND

One of the common findings from the combined results of the Community Cybersecurity Exercises conducted, was there were no plans that included cybersecurity threats and issues. The plans also did not address coordination and response capabilities that focused on cyber incidents. The common misconception was that anything that had to do with cyber was merely an IT problem. This way of thinking does not take into account that a cyber incident could impact an information system that contains critical information needed to provide an essential function. Emergency services are highly dependent on technology and information systems. Services such as computer-aided dispatching for law enforcement and 911 centers, emergency alert systems, event tracking, and monitoring of transportation infrastructure are all very dependent on computer systems that could be disrupted or completely taken off-line due to a denial of service cyberattack.

One of the recommendations from the community exercises was to integrate cybersecurity principles into existing plans and for those who did not have a plan, to create one. Specifically, the recommendation was:

<u>Annex to existing response plans</u>: *A cyber security annex should be developed to go along with existing emergency management/civil defense response plans to cover both the state and community levels. At a minimum the documents should include reporting procedures for suspected cyber security relevant events. This includes not just actual incidents (e.g. intrusions, attempted intrusions, denial of service attacks, etc.) but events that might be the precursor to actual attacks.*

The annex should also include the processes that will be followed when a security relevant event is reported and should outline the interface between the community, state, and federal agencies (to include the military installations within the community) in the event of a cyber incident.

The planning dimension was created to ensure cybersecurity elements are included in community plans to address incidents that could adversely impact the whole community.

COMMUNITY PLANS

Cities and counties all over the United States have suffered from cyber-attacks over the past several years. These attacks have caused massive disruptions such as loss of police video in patrol cars, municipal courts being unable to accept payments for traffic tickets, staff being locked out of systems so they are unable conduct business, 9-1-1 dispatchers unable to deploy emergency services, and access to mobile data public safety computers used by law enforcement, fire, and emergency medical agencies made unavailable. These are only some of the impacts communities have faced due to a cyber-attack. Having a plan in place to ensure operations are maintained and response and recovery methods are in place to get services back up quickly are essential.

There are several different plans that can be developed, some examples are the Emergency Operations Plan, Disaster Recovery Plan, Incident Response Plan and Continuity Plan. From a community perspective, the Continuity of Operations (COOP) plan, defines how individual executive departments and agencies will "ensure that Primary Mission Essential Functions (PMEFs) continue to be performed during a wide range of emergencies, including localized acts of nature, accidents and technological or attack-related emergencies" (FEMA). Implementing a functional annex to include cyber incident response will focus on specific responsibilities, tasks and operational actions that pertain to the portions of continuity plan.

Continuity of Operations Plan (COOP)

The National Security Presidential Directive 51 (NSPD-51) and Homeland Security Presidential Directive 20 (HSPD-20) establish a national policy on the continuity of Federal Government structures and operations. Continuity of Operations (COOP, 2011) are defined in the National Continuity Policy Implementation Plan (NCIP) and the NSPD-51/HSPD-20. The COOP plan is the continuity plan developed and utilized by communities.

COOP plans are focused on identifying essential functions and services that are provided by the community and ensure these functions and services can be continued throughout or resumed rapidly after an emergency or disaster. Partnerships with federal government agencies, non-federal government entities and with private sector owners and operators can play an important role in the continuity plan.

The continuity plan addresses the following:

- **Essential Functions:** critical activities performed by organizations, especially after a disruption of normal activities.
- **Succession:** identification of the senior agency offices during an emergency in the event any officials are unavailable to execute their legal duties.
- **Delegation of Authority:** list of positions who will make policy determinations and decisions when normal channels of direction have been disrupted.
- **Continuity Facilities:** alternate facilities used to carry out essential functions during a continuity event. This can include working from home or another mobile-office concept.
- **Vital Records Management:** identify, protect and ensure electronic and hard copy documents, information systems, software and equipment needed to support essential functions are available.
- **Human Capital:** personnel activated in an emergency to perform assigned response duties.
- **Tests, Training, and Exercises:** measures needed to ensure the continuity plan can support the execution of the essential functions throughout an event.

- **Devolution of Control and Direction:** the ability to transfer authority and responsibility for essential functions from the primary staff to other agencies and facilities.
- **Reconstitution:** process for existing primary staff and replacement personnel resume normal operations from the original or replacement facility. (*"Continuity of operations: An overview,"* n.d.).

"The plan could be activated in response to a wide range of events or situations – from a fire in the building; to a natural disaster; to the threat or occurrence of a terrorist attack. Any event that makes it impossible for employees to work in their regular facility could result in the activation of the Continuity plan" (*"Continuity of operations: An overview,"* n.d.).

Not only should a continuity plan be developed to create a roadmap to ensure services and functions continue, but they must take cyber-attacks into consideration and must be exercised to make sure they work. A perfect example of this is from the ransomware attack that occurred with the Colorado Department of Transportation (CDOT).

The Colorado Department of Transportation experienced a ransomware attack on or about February 18, 2018. A threat actor gained access to the CDOT network and installed the SamSam ransomware malware variant. On Wednesday, 21 Feb, OIT declared a security incident when the ransomware became active and infected approximately 150 servers and 2000 workstations.

CDOT had a continuity of operations plan. The issue however was that one of the provisions in the CDOT's continuity of operations plan directed workers to take their laptops to the Department of Public Health's headquarters. If this action had been successful, the infected devices could have exposed another agency's network to the malware. Fortunately, officials were able to stop the two people before they could get to the alternate location's headquarters (Statescoop).

The lesson learned identified in the after-action report stated:

Continuity of Operations Plans (COOP). Though CDOT had a thorough COOP that was instrumental in continuing its mission, these plans did not account to the challenges related to a cyber incident. Plans considered loss of infrastructure and the requirement to move people to alternate worksites, however, these plans assumed that employees would take their computers with them and be able to establish connectivity with key online applications. All State Agencies could benefit from capabilities gap analysis in their COOP for a cyber incident response. (CDOT, 2018)

While this action to move to an alternate location to conduct essential functions was appropriate for a physical event, the way a cyberattack can move throughout the network to infect additional machines was not considered. This example shows what is meant by examining policies and plans for cyber implications.

Cyber Annex for Incident Response

A community needs to have a plan in place to address how an individual hazard will be handled and as part of that plan, an individual should be able to determine the type of incident and the severity of the incident to allow for response measures to be escalated appropriately. It is important to note that each hazard should be addressed individually and considered unique. To begin the planning process the National Response Framework (NRF) can be used as a reference.

The NRF, updated in 2016, provides guides for how the community works together and how response efforts relate to all types of disasters and emergencies.

The NRF identifies the following Annexes:

- Emergency Support Function (ESF) Annexes - describe the Federal coordinating structures that group resources and capabilities into functional areas that are most frequently needed in a national response.
- Support Annexes - describe the essential supporting processes and considerations that are most common to most incidents.
- Incident Annexes - address response to specific risks and hazards. The **Incident Annexes** address the unique aspects of how the response will occur for an incident.

The annexes provide detailed information to assist with the implementation of the NRF. The graphic below, found in the NRF, indicates that each of these annexes are focused on Response. However, the NRF includes a holistic approach to the response capability which integrates the relationships among all the mission areas Prevention, Protection, Mitigation, Response and Recovery and addresses the transition between mission areas.

Response activities take place immediately before, during, and in the first few days after a major or catastrophic disaster. Recovery efforts help the community get back on its feet and focus on how best to restore, redevelop, and revitalize the health, social, economic, natural, and environmental fabric of the community. Roles and activities used for Prevention and Protection can lessen the Response efforts needed to address an incident. For example, when people proactively do things to lessen the impact of future disasters they may need fewer response resources when a disaster strikes.

Figure 1.

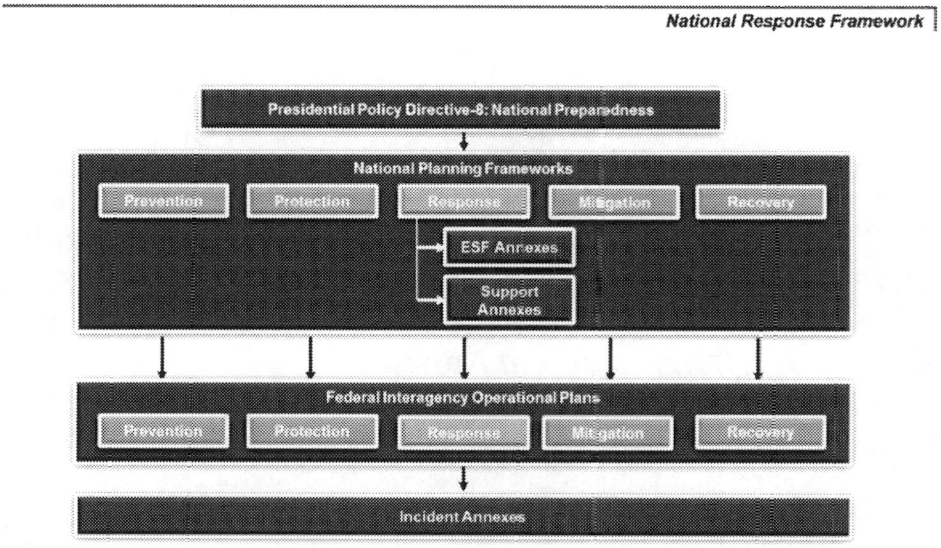

National Response Framework

The Cyber Incident Annex addresses disruptions to the Internet or other critical infrastructure information systems caused by a natural disaster with significant cyber consequences, or a deliberate attack such as malware or a distributed denial of service attack. Cyber incidents have the potential to threaten lives, property, the economy, and our national security.

Over the years, there have been many indicators to show the cyber threat is increasing in both volume and sophistication. Those indicators include:

- Increased number of public and private sector cyberattacks, and increased spending on cyber defense.
- Increased attention on cyber-crime, shopping scams and cyberbullying.
- Increased global government attention and action. Nation states are increasing their cybersecurity defenses and increasing their cyber forces.

- Increased cyber insurance policies extended.
- Increased number of Federal Government breaches.
- Future cyber-inventions that fall under the Internet of Things (IoT) banner, which include cars and homes and smart cities that are connected, cloud computing, new smartphones, big data, social media and more.

Each of these indicators identifies areas that continue to cause concern and bring more robust challenges to the cyber landscape. Communities preparing for cyber incidents by implementing a Cyber Incident Annex should consider and address any computer-generated threat.

The Cyber Incident Annex discusses policies, organization, actions, and responsibilities for a coordinated, multidisciplinary, broad-based approach to prepare for, respond to, and recover from cyber-related incidents impacting critical national processes and the national economy.

Purpose of a Cyber Incident Annex

IT infrastructure must have a high level of reliability and resiliency under any circumstance. This is important because of the increasing dependence on information technology and computer based systems. Information technology is the foundation for virtually any service, process, and capability necessary for responding to an emergency. The Cyber Incident Annex identifies the unique aspects of this hazard and integrates it into the community response plans.

The purpose for a Cyber Incident Annex is:

- To establish a standardized, flexible, and scalable foundation to prepare for and respond to a cyber threat or attack.
- To provide guidance regarding mitigation, prevention, protection, response and recovery to actual or potential cyber-related threats and attacks to participating agencies and organizations.
- To provide guidance regarding available assets and resources.
- To ensure core capabilities (Prevention, Protection, Mitigation, Response, Recovery) are consistent with Homeland Security policy and guidance.

Cyber Incident Response Plan (CIRP)

The Cyber Incident Response Plan will be integrated into the Cyber Annex. The response plan will include:

- Roles and responsibilities needed
- Define response types (Threat response, asset response, and intelligence support)
- Cyber incident response team
- Communications plan
- Equipment needs
- Mechanisms for Resources and Assistance
- Risk Assessment

Roles and Responsibilities: The roles and responsibilities will be defined. The following table was taken from NCIRP and can be used to quickly identify who is responsible for the different aspects of the CIRP. If this group is implemented into the CIRP, it can delay decision making, especially since cyber incidents can quickly spread. The group needs to be quickly come together as not to slow the response. The roles and responsibilities are based on the four (4) lines of efforts, see Table 1.

Table 1. Four lines of effort

Line of Effort	Lead SLTT Agency
Threat Response	State\Local Law Enforcement
Asset Response	State\Local Department\Division of Homeland Security State IT agency
Intelligence Support	Fusion Center\State Level ISAO
Affective Entity Response	When a significant cyber incident affect a SLTT government or agency, that government\agency will have primary responsibility for its response. When a significant cyber incident affects a private entity, the Federal or SLTT Government will typically not play a role in this line of effort, but the cognizant Sector Specific Agency(ies) can coordinate the Federal or SLTT Government efforts to understand the potential business or operational impact of a cyber incident on private sector critical infrastructure.

Once the roles are defined lead agencies to those lines of efforts need to be assigned. Then each agency's capabilities will be defined and what they will do in the Cyber Annex will be established and defined.

Response Types (Threat response, asset response, and intelligence support): each response type should be defined. Descriptions of the response types are as follows:

- **Threat response:** are those activities that "encompass many resources and capabilities from across the law enforcement and defense community. Threat response activities during a cyber incident include investigative, forensic, analytical, and mitigation activities; interdiction of a threat actor; and providing attribution that may lead to information sharing and operational synchronization with asset response activities."
- **Asset Response:** are those activities that "include furnishing technical assistance to affected entities, mitigating vulnerabilities, identifying additional at-risk entities, and assessing their risk to the same or similar vulnerabilities. These activities could also include communicating with the affected entity to understand the nature of the cyber incident; providing guidance to the affected entity on available federal, SLTT, and private sector resources and capabilities; promptly disseminating new intelligence and information through the appropriate channels; and facilitating information sharing and operational coordination with other Federal Government, SLTT government, and private sector entities. Critical asset response activities also include assessing potential risks to a sector or region, including potential cascading and interdependency effects, developing courses of action to mitigate these risks, and providing guidance on how best to utilize federal, SLTT, and private sector resources and capabilities in a timely, effective manner."
- **Intelligence Support:** are those activities that "play an important role to better understand the cyber incident and existing targeted diplomatic, economic, or military capabilities to respond and share threat and mitigation information with other potential affected entities or responders. Especially during a significant cyber incident, asset and threat responders should leverage intelligence support activities as necessary to build situational threat awareness; share related threat indicators and analysis of threats; identify and acknowledge gaps; and ultimately create a comprehensive picture of the incident."

In each response, the federal government and private sector have a role to help support the responding agency.

Cyber incident response team: The structure of an Incident response team generally falls into one of the following three categories:

- Central Incident Response Team: a single incident response team that handles incidents throughout the organization. Most effective for small organizations and for large organizations with minimal geographic diversity in terms of computing resources.
- Distributed Incident Response Teams: multiple incident response teams, each responsible for handling incidents for a particular logical or physical segment of the organization. This model is effective for large organizations and for organizations with major computing resources at distant locations. However, teams should be part of a single centralized entity so that the incident response process is consistent across the organization and information is shared among teams, which is particularly important because multiple teams may see components of the same incident or may handle similar incidents.
- Coordinating Team: an incident response team provides guidance and advice to other teams without having authority over those teams.

Communications Plan: in the event of a cyber incident it is important to have a communications plan developed. The National Incident Management Systems (NIMS) has a clearly defined communications management plan. Having solid communications will allow for a common operating picture to be established. This can only be maintained by the gathering, collating, synthesizing and dissemination of information. One of the most critical aspects of the NIMS communications plan is that is interoperable. This means that there is a common terminology for organizational structures, operational resources and facilities. There also needs to be integrated communications plans, covering common processes and technologies. More about the communications plan will be discussed in a later module.

Equipment Needs: Many incident response teams create a jump kit, which is a portable bag or case that contains materials that an incident handler may likely need during an offsite investigation. The jump kit is ready to go at all times so that when a serious incident occurs, incident handlers can grab the jump kit and go. A jump kit typically includes a laptop, loaded with appropriate software (e.g., packet sniffers, computer forensics tools). Other important materials include backup devices, blank media basic networking equipment and cables, and operating system and application media and patches. Because the purpose of having a jump kit is to facilitate faster responses, the team should refrain from borrowing items from the jump kit. It is also important to keep the jump kit current at all times (e.g., installing security patches on laptops, updating operating system media). Organizations should balance the cost of creating and maintaining jump kits with the savings from containing incidents more quickly and effectively.

Mechanisms for Resource and Assistance: incident action plans are established that identify resources that are needed. For resources that are identified and are not currently available or may not be possible to acquire, the following is a list that can be used for assistance:

- Mutual aid agreements with another community
- Emergency Management Assistance Compact (EMAC)
- For SLTT communities:
  - Regional Homeland Security offices and Fusion Centers
  - Multi-State ISAC (MS-ISAC)
  - Grant funding, including the Urban Area Security Initiative
    - Local governments that are eligible to apply and receive Urban Area Security Initiative grant funds are encouraged to include cybersecurity and training programs as part of their expenditures.

Risk Assessment: incident preparation also includes understanding risk and identifying hazards. The purpose of a risk assessments is to identify:

- Threats to organizations (i.e., operations, assets, or individuals) or threats directed through organizations against other organizations or the Nation,
- Vulnerabilities internal and external to organizations,
- The harm (i.e., adverse impact or consequence) that may occur given the potential for threats exploiting vulnerabilities; and (iv) the likelihood that harm will occur. (NIST 800-30 Revision 1)

Risk = Threat x Vulnerability x Consequence
When conducting the risk assessment, it is extremely important to:

- Identify threat sources that are relevant to organizations;
- Identify threat events that could be produced by those sources;
- Identify vulnerabilities within organizations that could be exploited by threat sources through specific threat events and the predisposing conditions that could affect successful exploitation;

- Determine the likelihood that the identified threat sources would initiate specific threat events and the likelihood that the threat events would be successful;
- Determine the adverse impacts to organizational operations and assets, individuals, other organizations, and the Nation resulting from the exploitation of vulnerabilities by threat sources (through specific threat events); and
- Determine information security risks as a combination of likelihood of threat exploitation of vulnerabilities and the impact of such exploitation, including any uncertainties associated with the risk determinations.

Once the Threats, Vulnerability and Consequence have been identified and determined the next step can be to calculate a risk score for the specific assets, processes, and systems. The scores are 0 to 10, zero being no impact/threat/vulnerability to 10, the highest impact/threat/vulnerability.

CCSMM PLAN ROADMAP

The CCSMM plans roadmap begins at Level 1 – Initial characterizing the community as having little inclusion of cyber in their Continuity of Operations Plan (COOP). This means the community does not have a plan to address cyber incidents that may impact the performance of essential functions and they do not have a backup plan to recover their data and critical systems. Additionally, the community has not evaluated what technologies support mission essential functions. The roadmap guides the community to Level 5 – Vanguard where the community has integrated cybersecurity practices into their continuity plans and are mentoring smaller communities to do the same. At this level, the community has a formal incident response and recovery plan that addresses both cyber and physical and they have considered how physical and cyber incidents can impact each other.

The planning process provides the information needed to achieve goals and to make effective decisions to maximize resources and productivity for a specific situation. In this dimension, plans will address what actions and resources are needed before, during and after a cyber incident or attack.

Figure 2.

LEVEL 1 Initial	LEVEL 2 Established	LEVEL 3 Self-Assessed	LEVEL 4 Integrated	LEVEL 5 Vanguard
Awareness · Minimal cyber awareness	· Leadership aware of cyber threats, issues and imperatives for cyber security and community cooperative cyber training	· Leaders promote org security awareness; formal community cooperative training	· Leaders and orgs promote awareness; citizens aware of cyber security issues	· Awareness a business imperative
Info Sharing · Minimal cyber info sharing	· Informal info sharing/ communication in community; working groups established; ad-hoc analysis, little fusion or metrics; professional orgs established or engaged	· Formal local info sharing/cyber analysis. initial cyber-physical fusion; informal external info sharing/ cyber analysis and metrics gathering	· Formal info sharing/ analysis, internal and external to community; formal local fusion and metrics, initial external efforts	· Fully integrated fusion/ analysis center, combining all-source physical and cyber info; create and disseminate near real world picture
Policy · Minimal cyber assessments and policy & procedure evaluations	· No assessments, but aware of requirement; initial evaluation of policies & procedures	· Autonomous tabletop cyber exercises with assessments of info sharing, policies & procedures, and fusion; routine audit program; mentor externals on policies & procedures, auditing and training	· Autonomous cyber exercises with assessments of formal info sharing/local fusion; exercises involve live play/metrics assessments	· Accomplish full-scale blended exercises and assess complete fusion capability; involve/ mentor other communities/entities
Plans · Little inclusion of cyber into Continuity of Operations Plan (COOP)	· Aware of need to integrate cyber security into COOP	· Include cyber in COOP; formal cyber incident response/recovery	· Integrate cyber in COOP; mentor externals on COOP integration; formal blended incident response and recovery	· Continue to integrate cyber in COOP; mentor externals on COOP integration; formal blended incident response and recovery

Plans at Level 1: Little Inclusion of Cyber Into Continuity of Operations Plan (COOP)

The community's characteristics at Level 1 of the planning dimension are little inclusion of cyber into Continuity of Operations Plan (COOP). The community at this level may not have a Continuity Plan at all or if there is a COOP, it has not been evaluated for cyber implications. As the cybersecurity program is established review the following FEMA guidelines:

The Federal Emergency Management Agency (FEMA, 2011) provides an overall process for preparedness that includes:

- **Identify and Assess Risk**: helps to ensure the community understands the risks it faces.
- **Estimates Capability Requirements**: helps to determine specific capabilities and additional activities that will best address the risks.
- **Build and Sustain Capabilities**: determine the best way to use limited resources to increase and sustain needed capabilities.

- **Plan to Deliver Capabilities**: reflects what the community will do to address specific risks.
- **Validate Capabilities**: helps to determine progress toward preparedness goals.
- **Review and Update**: ensure all capabilities, resources and plans are regularly reviewed and updated.

Plans at Level 2: Aware of the Need to Integrate Cybersecurity Into COOP

At Level 2 the community will be aware of the need to integrate cybersecurity into the COOP.

Phase 1 activities to achieve Level 2 include

Metrics:
- ◦ Identify and document what backup plans exist now.

Technology:
- ◦ Technologies used will assist in tracking planning activities and training conducted

Training:
- ◦ Training will provide information to raise awareness of why COOP is a good practice.

Processes and Procedures:
- ◦ A COOP plan addresses emergencies from an all-hazards approach. A continuity of operations plan establishes policy and guidance ensuring that critical functions continue and that personnel and resources are relocated to an alternate facility in case of emergencies. The plan should develop procedures for:
  - ▪ alerting, notifying, activating and deploying employees
  - ▪ identify critical business functions
  - ▪ establish an alternate facility
  - ▪ roster personnel with authority and knowledge of functions

Assessments:
- ◦ Assessments can be used to see the level of increased awareness of the importance of creating a COOP.

Plans at Level 3: COOP and Incident Response and Recovery Established

The community at Level 3 has created a COOP and included cyber into it. They have established and formalized their cyber incident response and recovery capability.

Phase 2 activities to achieve Level 3 include:

Metrics:
- ◦ Document the capabilities that exist currently with the incident response team. We will be looking to improve capabilities over time.
- ◦ Document incidents that are occurring and determine if COOP is preventing cyber-attacks.
- ◦ Determine where cyber incidents are still occurring. This will lead to an improvement plan to update policies, train and incorporate new processes into the COOP and incident response.

Technology:
- ◦ Technologies used will assist in supporting COOP
- ◦ Technologies that will assist the incident response team

Training:
- ◦ Training on COOP procedures.
- ◦ Training for incident response team to build and expand current capabilities

Processes and Procedures:
- ◦ A COOP plan addresses emergencies from an all-hazards approach. A continuity of operations plan establishes policy and guidance ensuring that critical functions continue and that personnel and resources are relocated to an alternate facility in case of emergencies. The plan should develop procedures for:
  - ▪ alerting, notifying, activating and deploying employees
  - ▪ identify critical business functions
  - ▪ establish an alternate facility
  - ▪ roster personnel with authority and knowledge of functions

- ○ Establish a cyber annex with incident response and recovery capability
  - ▪ Establish an incident response team

Assessments:
- ○ Exercise COOP.
- ○ Tests incident response team

Plans at Level 4: Cyber is Integrated in COOP; Mentor Externals on COOP Integration; Formal Blended Incident Response and Recovery

The community has integrated cyber into the COOP. They are now mentoring external communities on COOP integration and a formal blended incident response and recover program is established.

Phase 3 activities to achieve Level 4 include:

Metrics:
- ○ Document the capabilities that exist currently with the incident response team. We will be looking to improve capabilities over time.
- ○ Document incidents that are occurring and determine if COOP is preventing cyber-attacks.
- ○ Determine where cyber incidents are still occurring. This will lead to an improvement plan to update policies, train and incorporate new processes into the COOP and incident response.

Technology:
- ○ Technologies used will assist in supporting COOP
- ○ Technologies that will assist the incident response team

Training:
- ○ Training on COOP procedures.
- ○ Training for incident response team to build and expand current capabilities

Processes and Procedures:
- ○ Share COOP policies with external communities
- ○ Share cyber annex policies with external communities

Assessments:
- Exercise COOP and invite external communities to participate
- All other plans should have cyber incorporated by this level. An all hazard focus is integrated into the COOP.
- Cyber is integrated into all other annexes.

Plans at Level 5: Continued Integration of Cyber in COOP; Mentor Externals on COOP Integration; Formal Blended Incident Response and Recovery

At Level 5 the community will continue to integrate cyber into the COOP. The community will mentor communities that do not have a plan in place and will have formal blended incident response and recovery capabilities.

Phase 4 activities to achieve Level 5 include:

Metrics:
- Document and track improvements for the incident response team
- Document incidents that are occurring and determine if COOP is preventing cyber-attacks.
- Continue to track cyber incidents and assess where improvement is needed

Technology:
- Technologies used will assist in supporting COOP
- Technologies that will assist the incident response team

Training:
- Training on COOP procedures for communities with no program
- Training for incident response team to build and expand current capabilities for communities with no program

Processes and Procedures:
- Share COOP policies with communities with no program
- Share cyber annex policies with communities with no program

Assessments:
- Exercise incident response and recovery capabilities for external communities.

SUMMARY

Communities need to ensure services provided can continue in the event of a cyber incident. In this chapter community plans that need to be incorporated were discussed. The two references were a Community of Operations Plan (COOP) and a Cyber Annex. A Continuity of Operations Plan will assist the community to plan for contingencies and build capabilities in incident response and recovery. Once the community achieves a level 4 status, they will be able to share their program with communities who do not have a plan in place. This will be a force multiplier to mature communities faster and will allow them to apply practices that have been tested and found to work well.

A Cyber Annex can assist a community with incident response. A cyber incident response plan can be incorporated into the annex. The incident response plan addresses roles and responsibilities of participating community members. The plan will also address response types, who will make-up a cyber incident response team, the communications plan, equipment needs, mechanisms for resources and assistance and risk assessments.

REFERENCES

After action report released for CDOT cyber incident. (2018). Retrieved from Colorado Official State Web Portal website: https://www.colorado. gov/pacific/cobeoc/news/after-action-report-released-cdot-cyber-incident

Continuity of operations: An overview. (n.d.). Retrieved from FEMA website: https://www.fema.gov/pdf/about/org/ncp/coop_brochure.pdf

Continuity of operations planning (COOP). (2011). *Continuity of operations planning (COOP).* Retrieved from govloop website: https://www.govloop. com/community/blog/continuity-of-operations-planning-coop/

FEMA. (2011). *Continuity of Operations Plan Template and Instructions for Federal Departments and Agencies.* Retrieved from https://www.fema.gov/ pdf/about/org/ncp/coop/continuity_plan_federal_d_a.pdf

National Institute of Standards and Technology & Joint Task Force Transformation Initiative. (2012). *NIST Special Publication: Vol. 800-30 Rev. 1. Guide for conducting risk assessments.* Retrieved from https://nvlpubs.nist. gov/nistpubs/Legacy/SP/ nistspecialpublication800-30r1.pdf

National security presidential directive 51 and homeland security presidential directive 20: National continuity policy. (n.d.). Retrieved from Homeland Security Digital Library website: https://www.hsdl.org/?abstract&did=776382

ADDITIONAL READING

Freed, B. (2019). *What Colorado learned from treating a cyberattack like a disaster*. Retrieved from statescoop website: https://statescoop.com/ what-colorado-learned-from-treating-a-cyberattack-like-a-disaster/

Chapter 8
The NIST Cybersecurity Framework

ABSTRACT

With the increase in cybercrimes over the last few years, a growing realization for the need for cybersecurity has begun to be recognized by the nation. Unfortunately, being aware that cybersecurity is something you need to worry about and knowing what steps to take are two different things entirely. In the United States, the National Institute of Standards and Technology (NIST) developed the Cyber Security Framework (CSF) to assist critical infrastructures in determining what they need in order to secure their computer systems and networks. While aimed at organizations, much of the guidance provided by the CSF, especially the basic functions it identifies, are also valuable for communities attempting to put together a community cybersecurity program.

INTRODUCTION

It is a common problem among individuals attempting to secure an organization's critical computer systems and networks to struggle with where to begin. With limited budgets, where can the funds be used most wisely? Can an incremental plan be developed to ultimately arrive at the security posture desired but over a period of time that takes into consideration the need to work within budgets?

The CCSMM introduced in this text is a plan to help guide communities in the creation and maturation of their cybersecurity program. A geographic

DOI: 10.4018/978-1-7998-4471-6.ch008

community, however, is made up of a number of organizations and individuals all of whom will contribute to the security, or insecurity, of the community. This text focuses on the overall community's program and does not delve deeply into a plan for any one type of organization or sector. This is where the NIST Cyber Security Framework (CSF) enters the picture. The CSF was designed to provide guidance to the critical infrastructures on how to organize their security efforts based on a plan to manage cybersecurity risk in a cost-effective way.

The CSF contains a lot of great information and guidance. Unfortunately for many organizations, in particular smaller organizations, the amount of information contained in the CSF can be overwhelming leaving people in a similar position to where they were before reading the CSF. Recognizing this, NIST produced another document, *Small Business Information Security: The Fundamentals*, which discusses much of what is introduced in the basic core of the CSF without the overwhelming list of sub-categories and references that the CSF contains. This allows small businesses to focus their efforts in an organized manner as they go about securing their systems and networks.

For communities, the CSF also contains much information that will not be immediately useable at the community level although it will pertain to many of the individual organizations within the community. Instead, the topics introduced in the companion document for small businesses that NIST produced can help focus a community's efforts providing an extra level of guidance that will enable the community to organize their efforts. Thus, the CCSMM and the CSF can go hand-in-hand within a community to help the community address cybersecurity from different angles.

BACKGROUND

Since the 1990's, the federal government has been keenly aware of the dangers cyber events posed to the various critical infrastructures and thus focused considerable attention on securing these infrastructures. PDD 63 issued in 1998 and discussed earlier in the text was a big step forward in organizing the efforts of the various critical infrastructure sectors so that they could collectively work together to solve the challenges they each faced. Then in 2013 the White House issued Executive Order 13636 (2013) *Improving Critical Infrastructure Cybersecurity* which continued the focus on the critical infrastructures and attempted to keep things moving in a direction that would lead to more secure infrastructures. Besides addressing information sharing as was discussed in a previous chapter, EO 13636 also directed NIST to "lead the development of a framework to reduce cyber risks to critical infrastructure."

In 2014 the Cybersecurity Enhancement Act (CEA) of 2014 was signed into law. One of the things that this act did was to expand the role of NIST to "identify a prioritized, flexible, repeatable, performance-based, and cost-effective approach, including information security measures and controls, that may be voluntarily adopted by owners and operators of critical infrastructure to help them identify, assess, and manage cyber risks". (CEA, 2014) This in essence expanded upon the previous guidance in EO 13636 provided additional guidance to NIST for the creation of a framework.

In 2014 NIST released version 1.0 of the *Framework for Improving Critical Infrastructure Cybersecurity*. In 2016 revision 1 of the *Small Business Information Security: The Fundamentals* document was released which incorporated much of the basic framework from the CSF but made it more useable for small businesses. In 2017 a draft of CSF version 1.1 was released for public comment and in April of 2018 version 1.1 was officially released. This new version was compatible with the original in that it did not change the basic framework but instead expanded upon it to take into account things outside of the critical infrastructures such as their supply chains.

NIST and the federal government have been encouraging not only the critical infrastructures but government agencies to adopt the framework as part of their cybersecurity programs. They have also encouraged industry to use it as well and several large government contractors have done so and published papers on how well it has worked for them. The framework has taken hold in this government enclave but has not really caught on as well outside of government circles. This is actually somewhat disappointing as there is much useful guidance in the various NIST documents concerning the CSF. This is also true for communities. The NIST CSF can provide additional guidance beyond the steps outlined in the CCSMM that will allow communities to develop a more coordinated approach to establishing their cybersecurity program.

THE NIST CYBER SECURITY FRAMEWORK (CSF)

Before jumping into how the CSF applies to community cybersecurity programs, it will be useful to have a better understanding of what the CSF entails. The CSF was initially created for organizations that are part of the various critical infrastructures. The CSF is made up of three parts: the

Framework Core, the Implementation Tiers, and the Framework Profiles. Not all of these are going to be equally as important to a community cybersecurity program but they will be important to organizations within the community. What is involved in each of these parts is as follows:

- **Framework Core:** a set of cybersecurity activities, outcomes, and informative references that are common across sectors and critical infrastructure. Elements of the Core provide detailed guidance for developing individual organizational Profiles
- **Implementation Tiers:** provide a mechanism for organizations to view and understand the characteristics of their approach to managing cybersecurity risk, which will help in prioritizing and achieving cybersecurity objectives.
- **Framework Profiles:** will help an organization to align and prioritize its cybersecurity activities with its business/mission requirements, risk tolerances, and resources. (NIST, 2018)

A deeper investigation of each of these will be covered starting with the Framework Core. The Framework Core is the part of the CSF that people are most familiar with. As described in the CSF, the core is:

a set of cybersecurity activities, desired outcomes, and applicable references that are common across critical infrastructure sectors. The Core presents industry standards, guidelines, and practices in a manner that allows for communication of cybersecurity activities and outcomes across the organization from the executive level to the implementation/operations level. The Framework Core consists of five concurrent and continuous Functions— Identify, Protect, Detect, Respond, Recover. When considered together, these Functions provide a high-level, strategic view of the lifecycle of an organization's management of cybersecurity risk. The Framework Core then identifies underlying key Categories and Subcategories – which are discrete outcomes – for each Function and matches them with example Informative References such as existing standards, guidelines, and practices for each Subcategory. (NIST, 2018)

The functions mentioned are especially important to any effort to establish a community cybersecurity program. As mentioned above, the CSF core consists of Functions, Categories, Subcategories, and references as shown in the diagram below.

Figure 1. The NIST Cybersecurity Framework core. (NIST, 2018)

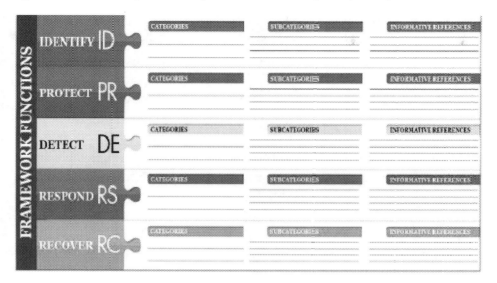

The key to the core from the perspective of a community's program are the five functions: Identify, Protect, Detect, Respond, and Recover. **Identify** simply means that an organization needs to know what resources it has, what valuable data it needs to protect, what defenses it has in place, and what remaining vulnerabilities and risks may still be present and that have been deemed an acceptable risk to an organization. It is important that organizations know what they have in order to understand what they need to be concerned with. A simple example of this might be a new vulnerability that has been discovered and that has been exploited in a specific operating system. If the organization knows what resources it has (which includes hardware and software) it will know if it should be concerned or if this is something that will not impact them because they don't have any systems running this particular operating system.

Protect means exactly what one might expect. What measures has an organization taken in order to protect its resources, data, and people? This includes not just cybersecurity but physical security, personnel security, and operational security. It includes all measures that are taken in order to maintain the security of the organization's valuable resources and data. It is interesting to note that in the earliest days of computing, computer security was primarily an issue of physical security. You controlled access to the computing device and only allowed authorized individuals to use the system. This remained the primary focus of security through the 1970's as computer systems were mostly mainframe computers with remote terminal rooms. Organizations simply controlled access to the system and the terminals in order to protect the data. Passwords were used, often not only to control access but to also control the amount of time a specific user was allowed on the system. It wasn't until the 1980's with the introduction of the IBM PC that things changed dramatically. Initially userids and passwords were still the primary means to enforce security but with the introduction of these cheap (relatively) computing devices there was a movement towards establishing networks and connecting these networks to other networks and the birth of what we now know as the Internet occurred. It is also interesting to note that the protocols used in the ARPANET, from which the Internet arose, were not devised with security in mind and this led to many security issues that were experienced in the 1980's and 1990's. Eventually in the late 1980's an operational model of cybersecurity was developed by the U.S. Air Force which promoted more than protection – it added Detection and Response.

The **Detect** function is first a realization that the security community has never been able to produce an absolutely secure computer system that works in all environments. Either a new vulnerability may be discovered in an application or an operating system, a user may make a mistake (such as providing their userid and password to somebody who asks for it), or a system may be misconfigured. Whatever the case, the ultimate result is that protection mechanisms will have failed. When this happens, the organization should have technology and processes in place to be able to detect the loss of security and what the impact of the loss has been (e.g. loss of intellectual property, theft of services, or loss of sensitive information).

When some aspect of security has been lost, the **Respond** function includes the technology and actions that an organization will take in order to react effectively to the incident. The immediate focus should be on gaining control of the system or network and preventing the loss of any additional data or services. An analogy for several of these functions might be the measures an organization takes to prevent fires in their facility, but they will also have smoke/fire detection equipment in case one occurs despite their prevention measures. When a fire is detected the immediate concern is to prevent loss of life and resources by evacuating individuals and initiating fire suppression equipment. Often this may involve the efforts of trained individuals who have practiced in advance so that they know what to do when a fire occurs. They also want to act quickly so that the fire doesn't spread to additional parts of the facility. The same is true when speaking of cybersecurity. After the incident has been contained, the focus can then shift to recovery.

The **Recovery** function involves the technology and processes that will allow the organization to first engage in its most important activities and to eventually (and hopefully shortly) return to its normal business activities. The recovery function is critical in cybersecurity as it is in other aspects of security. Processes and technology need to be identified that will allow for the rapid return to normal processing. Plans need to be in place for this to occur so that everybody knows what part they will play in recovery and to ensure the most critical activities are returned to operational status as quickly as possible.

These five functions are items that everybody involved in cybersecurity should be familiar with, no matter what their scope – organization, city, state, or nation. Categories are subdivisions within the Functions where outcomes tied to programmatic needs are grouped. The diagram below shows the list of categories associated with each of the individual functions.

Subcategories continue to further divide the categories into technical and management activities. For each one of these subcategories, a number of informative references are provided. Informative References are pointers to specific standards, guidelines, best practices, or other documents where more information can be found as to how to achieve the particular subcategory outcome. A table showing the subcategories and informative references for one category (Asset Management) in one function (Identify) is shown below.

There are a lot of similar references contained in the CSF which is one of the drawbacks to it from a small business perspective. There are simply too many subcategories and references to be able to deal with them. For the various critical infrastructures this information is very important, and it can be argued that they would be for small businesses as well, but providing somebody an encyclopedia's worth of knowledge when they are actually looking for a "how-to" guide is not going to help them and will thus probably not be used. This is why the CSF is most often being used by critical infrastructures, government agencies, and large government contractors.

As previously mentioned, there are two other parts to the CSF – the Implementation Tiers and the Framework Profiles.

Implementation Tiers provide context on how an organization views cybersecurity risk and the processes in place to manage that risk. Tiers describe the degree to which an organization's cybersecurity risk management practices exhibit the characteristics defined in the Framework (e.g., risk and threat aware, repeatable, and adaptive). The Tiers characterize an organization's practices over a range, from Partial (Tier 1) to Adaptive (Tier 4). These

Figure 2. NIST CSF Functions and Categories

Function Unique Identifier	Function	Category Unique Identifier	Category
ID	Identify	ID.AM	Asset Management
		ID.BE	Business Environment
		ID.GV	Governance
		ID.RA	Risk Assessment
		ID.RM	Risk Management Strategy
		ID.SC	Supply Chain Risk Management
PR	Protect	PR.AC	Identity Management and Access Control
		PR.AT	Awareness and Training
		PR.DS	Data Security
		PR.IP	Information Protection Processes and Procedures
		PR.MA	Maintenance
		PR.PT	Protective Technology
DE	Detect	DE.AE	Anomalies and Events
		DE.CM	Security Continuous Monitoring
		DE.DP	Detection Processes
RS	Respond	RS.RP	Response Planning
		RS.CO	Communications
		RS.AN	Analysis
		RS.MI	Mitigation
		RS.IM	Improvements
RC	Recover	RC.RP	Recovery Planning
		RC.IM	Improvements
		RC.CO	Communications

Tiers reflect a progression from informal, reactive responses to approaches that are agile and risk-informed. During the Tier selection process, an organization should consider its current risk management practices, threat environment, legal and regulatory requirements, business/mission objectives, and organizational constraints. (NIST, 2018)

There are four Tiers defined in the CSF from Tier 1 to Tier 4. Each higher tier describes an increasing degree of thoroughness and intricacy. NIST stresses that the Tiers do not represent maturity levels and recommends

Figure 3. A sample of NIST CSF subcategories and Informative References

Function	Category	Subcategory	Informative References
IDENTIFY (ID)	Asset Management (ID.AM): The data, personnel, devices, systems, and facilities that enable the organization to achieve business purposes are identified and managed consistent with their relative importance to organizational objectives and the organization's risk strategy.	ID.AM-1: Physical devices and systems within the organization are inventoried	CIS CSC 1 COBIT 5 BAI09.01, BAI09.02 ISA 62443-2-1:2009 4.2.3.4 ISA 62443-3-3:2013 SR 7.8 ISO/IEC 27001:2013 A.8.1.1, A.8.1.2 NIST SP 800-53 Rev. 4 CM-8, PM-5
		ID.AM-2: Software platforms and applications within the organization are inventoried	CIS CSC 2 COBIT 5 BAI09.01, BAI09.02, BAI09.05 ISA 62443-2-1:2009 4.2.3.4 ISA 62443-3-3:2013 SR 7.8 ISO/IEC 27001:2013 A.8.1.1, A.8.1.2, A.12.5.1 NIST SP 800-53 Rev. 4 CM-8, PM-5
		ID.AM-3: Organizational communication and data flows are mapped	CIS CSC 12 COBIT 5 DSS05.02 ISA 62443-2-1:2009 4.2.3.4 ISO/IEC 27001:2013 A.13.2.1, A.13.2.2 NIST SP 800-53 Rev. 4 AC-4, CA-3, CA-9, PL-8
		ID.AM-4: External information systems are catalogued	CIS CSC 12 COBIT 5 APO02.02, APO10.04, DSS01.02 ISO/IEC 27001:2013 A.11.2.6 NIST SP 800-53 Rev. 4 AC-20, SA-9
		ID.AM-5: Resources (e.g., hardware, devices, data, time, personnel, and software) are prioritized based on their classification, criticality, and business value	CIS CSC 13, 14 COBIT 5 APO03.03, APO03.04, APO12.01, BAI04.02, BAI09.02 ISA 62443-2-1:2009 4.2.3.6 ISO/IEC 27001:2013 A.8.2.1 NIST SP 800-53 Rev. 4 CP-2, RA-2, SA-14, SC-6
		ID.AM-6: Cybersecurity roles and responsibilities for the entire workforce and	CIS CSC 17, 19 COBIT 5 APO01.02, APO07.06, APO13.01, DSS06.03

that organizations obtain guidance from other sources such as ISAOs, other maturity models, and Federal government departments. The target Tier selected by an organization should reflect its goals and considers their threat environment, risk management practices, legal and regulatory requirements, and what is feasible for the organization. The four identified tiers and their characteristics are:

- **Tier 1: Partial**
  - *Risk Management Process – Organizational cybersecurity risk management practices are not formalized, and risk is managed in an ad hoc and sometimes reactive manner.*
  - *Integrated Risk Management Program – There is limited awareness of cybersecurity risk at the organizational level. The organization implements cybersecurity risk management on an irregular, case-by-case basis due to varied experience or information gained from outside sources.*
  - *External Participation – The organization does not understand its role in the larger ecosystem with respect to either its dependencies*

or dependents. The organization does not collaborate with or receive information such as threat intelligence, best practices, and technologies, from other entities.

- *Tier 2: Risk Informed*
  - ○ *Risk Management Process – Risk management practices are approved by management but may not be established as organizational-wide policy.*
  - ○ *Integrated Risk Management Program – There is an awareness of cybersecurity risk at the organizational level, but an organization-wide approach to managing cybersecurity risk has not been established.*
  - ○ *External Participation – Generally, the organization understands its role in the larger ecosystem with respect to either its own dependencies or dependents, but not both.*

- *Tier 3: Repeatable*
  - ○ *Risk Management Process – The organization's risk management practices are formally approved and expressed as policy.*
  - ○ *Integrated Risk Management Program – There is an organization-wide approach to manage cybersecurity risk. Risk-informed policies, processes, and procedures are defined, implemented as intended, and reviewed.*
  - ○ *External Participation – The organization understands its role, dependencies, and dependents in the larger ecosystem and may contribute to the community's broader understanding of risks.*

- *Tier 4: Adaptive*
  - ○ *Risk Management Process – The organization adapts its cybersecurity practices based on previous and current cybersecurity activities, including lessons learned and predictive indicators.*
  - ○ *Integrated Risk Management Program – There is an organization-wide approach to managing cybersecurity risk that uses risk-informed policies, processes, and procedures to address potential cybersecurity events.*
  - ○ *External Participation – The organization understands its role, dependencies, and dependents in the larger ecosystem and contributes to the community's broader understanding of risks.* (NIST, 2018)

The above is an abbreviated description of the Tiers from the CSF. It is not intended to be a tutorial or how-to document for selecting a Tier but rather as an introduction to the topic so that the concepts are understood. The term "community" is used several times in the descriptions which may be confusing. Community in this text refers to a city or town or similar geographic region. Community as it was used in the NIST CSF generally is used to mean a "community of interest" which means a group of organizations that all have something in common such as a sector (e.g. power, water, telecommunications) or it could actually mean a city though there is not a clean translation of the concepts to a city. The reason is that a city is made up of many different organizations without a single entity that controls them. The mayor of a city may suggest, recommend, or encourage organizations in the city to act in a certain way but mayors ultimately do not control all organizations within the city boundaries.

The last part of the CSF is the Framework Profile. There are actually two profiles – the Current Profile and the Target Profile. A description of what a profile is according to the NIST CSF is as follows:

A Framework Profile represents the outcomes based on business needs that an organization has selected from the Framework Categories and Subcategories. The Profile can be characterized as the alignment of standards, guidelines, and practices to the Framework Core in a particular implementation scenario. Profiles can be used to identify opportunities for improving cybersecurity posture by comparing a "Current" Profile (the 'as is" state) with a "Target" Profile (the "to be" state). To develop a Profile, an organization can review all of the Categories and Subcategories and, based on business/mission drivers and a risk assessment, determine which are most important; it can add Categories and Subcategories as needed to address the organization's risks. The Current Profile can then be used to support prioritization and measurement of progress toward the Target Profile, while factoring in other business needs including cost-effectiveness and innovation. Profiles can be used to conduct self-assessments and communicate within an organization or between organizations. (NIST, 2018)

Tiers address the organization's risk management goals while the Profiles will address the specific categories and subcategories that the organization will be addressing. These two parts go together and are part of the overall plan to help an organization develop a cybersecurity program or to improve an existing program. Notice how the description states the organization needs to determine which categories and subcategories are most important to the organization. This is a simple statement but a big challenge. Sometimes regulatory requirements may help to dictate which categories are important for the organization but in the absence of such additional guidance, determining which categories and subcategories are most important is more of a challenge – especially for smaller businesses with no full-time security personnel. The CSF goes on to describe seven steps in outlining how it can help an organization with their program.

Step 1: Prioritize and Scope. The organization identifies its business/mission objectives and high-level organizational priorities.

Step 2: Orient. Once the scope of the cybersecurity program has been determined for the business line or process, the organization identifies related systems and assets, regulatory requirements, and overall risk approach.

Step 3: Construct a hypothesis, Create a Current Profile. The organization develops a Current Profile by indicating which Category and Subcategory outcomes from the Framework Core are currently being achieved.

Step 4: Conduct a Risk Assessment. The organization analyzes the operational environment in order to discern the likelihood of a cybersecurity event and the impact that the event could have on the organization.

Step 5: Create a Target Profile. The organization creates a Target Profile that focuses on the assessment of the Framework Categories and Subcategories describing the organization's desired cybersecurity outcomes. Organizations also may develop their own additional Categories and Subcategories to account for unique organizational risks.

Step 6: Determine, Analyze, and Prioritize Gaps. The organization compares the Current Profile and the Target Profile to determine gaps. Next, it creates a prioritized action plan to address gaps – reflecting mission drivers, costs and benefits, and risks – to achieve the outcomes in the Target Profile.

Step 7: Implement Action Plan. The organization determines which actions to take to address the gaps, if any, identified in the previous step and then adjusts its current cybersecurity practices in order to achieve the Target Profile. (NIST, 2018)

Again, the goal of presenting these steps is not to provide guidance on exactly how to implement the CSF but rather to provide a basic introduction to the Framework and its various parts so that a discussion of how the Framework may apply to a community will become more apparent. The CSF is designed for organizations and any organization desiring to implement the CSF should consult the actual document for more guidance – see (NIST, 2018)

APPLYING THE FRAMEWORK TO COMMUNITIES

The Cyber Security Framework is designed to help individual organizations improve their cybersecurity programs. Even very large organizations can use the guidance it presents – in fact it can be argued that it is more applicable to at least medium-sized businesses due to the amount of information it contains and the steps an organization will have to go through to incorporate it. A community is not made up of a single organization nor even a group of similar organizations in a given sector. It also does not have management control over all entities within its boundaries. This means the creation of a community cybersecurity program is going to be fundamentally different in what it can accomplish.

One of the big differences for a community is that it can't simply mandate certain cybersecurity activities be taken by all members of the community. There may be some basic things that can be mandated by government such as breach notification laws that have been implemented by many states, but the community can't, for example, simply require all organizations to conduct user-level awareness training for the private sector. What the community has to do is to encourage organizations to conduct certain activities and to show the benefit of doing so to the organizations if they accomplish them. In certain unique instances the community may also be able to provide incentives for accomplishing specific activities such as working with an insurance company to offer members of the community reduced rates on cyber insurance if the organization accomplishes certain steps. Another potential incentive is the possible ability to use cybersecurity as a business advantage. Should an organization be faced with making a decision between two vendors, one of which has reached a certain level of cybersecurity maturity while the other has not, the organization may choose to select the organization with the proven security program. They may decide that by doing so the likelihood of a third-party security breach will be reduced which may be enough of an incentive to choose that organization. In a similar manner, the DoD, and potentially other organizations, has elected to place certain requirements on its vendors before the DoD will do business with them. Because the DoD values security so highly, and cybersecurity in particular in this case, it has elected to require its vendor to follow certain processes and procedures if the vendor wants to do business with the DoD. Obtaining compliance certificates or conducting assessments to prove that an organization has met some level of security will certainly involve a cost to that organization. In the end, however, it will be a business decision that organizations will make in deciding what cybersecurity activities to be involved in or to embrace.

Since a community is not a single, large organization, developing a cybersecurity program for a community is a challenge. In the previous chapters the phases identified activities that could be performed by the community when its organizations work together. There are a few items listed in the CCSMM levels that can be accomplished by a single organization, generally a part of the city government. An example of this would be the creation of a cybersecurity annex for the city's emergency response plans. Many items, however, will simply be things that the community as a whole will have to cooperate together on and to encourage other members of the community to join with them. An example of this would be the creation of an ISAO. Thus, the list of informative references from the CSF will have little applicability to the community as an entity but will be invaluable for organizations within the community.

What then is the community's role in terms of the CSF? As has been suggested, the role of the community will be that of encouraging its members to consider the use of the CSF, or other models or guidelines, in order to improve the cybersecurity program for individual organizations. Since many of the members of the community, in fact most of the members of the community, will not be part of the government (at any level), or the critical infrastructures, the detailed CSF may not be so easy to apply. Instead, the NIST document *Small Business Information Security: The Fundamentals* publication (Paulsen & Toth, 2016a) can serve as a tool the community can use in helping all organizations develop their individual cybersecurity programs.

As stated, the community's role will mostly be in the encouragement of its organizations. The obvious question to ask is "Who will be doing this encouraging?" In order for the CCSMM to be adopted in a community there will need to be a champion for community cybersecurity. This champion can be a city official or it can be an industry leader, but a champion is needed in order to ensure the program keeps moving forward until it is firmly rooted within the community. At the lower levels, Level 1 and Level 2, the champion may at times feel alone in their efforts to encourage the community as a whole to move forward. The list of activities previously provided in the chapters on the various dimensions should help the champion in terms of the type of things that should be encouraged at first. Once the community ISAO is created and firmly entrenched, the ISAO can become the champion for the community and can be the one that leads many of the efforts mentioned for the levels in each of the dimensions.

As organizations begin to establish their programs it can be quite daunting. For the same reason that the CCSMM was established for communities – to provide a yardstick and a roadmap – organizations need something similar to help them. The full CCSMM includes an organizational level and this is the part of the model that will most closely align with the CSF. From the whole community perspective, however, there are two essential elements that programs should consider, and that the community champion can discuss to help the members of the community. These are described in the CSF and in the companion fundamental guide for small businesses. The first of these are the six security measures outlined in the small business fundamental guide and that are shown in the diagram below

The six security measures shown in this diagram are areas of security that should be considered when any organization builds its security program. Cybersecurity is just one of these concerns. Missing any one of these measures can lead to a security event that can adversely impact the organization. When an organization embarks on the development of its security program, it should ask "what am I doing in each of these areas?" Several of these may already be in place in the organization, such as Physical Security and Personnel Security, because we are already used to thinking about them in our society. Whether the others have been considered will depend on the organization though if they are implementing the organizational scope of the CCSMM, they will be covering some of the others as well.

The second essential area was discussed in the CSF. It is the five functions which were broken down into categories and subcategories. Previously these functions were briefly described. It is time to look at them in a little greater detail.

- *Identify: Develop an organizational understanding to manage cybersecurity risk to systems, people, assets, data, and capabilities.*
  - *The activities in the Identify Function are foundational for effective use of the Framework. Understanding the business context, the resources that support critical functions, and the related cybersecurity risks enables an organization to focus and prioritize its efforts, consistent with its risk management strategy and business needs. Examples of outcome Categories within this*

Figure 4. The six security measures (Paulson & Toth, 2016a)

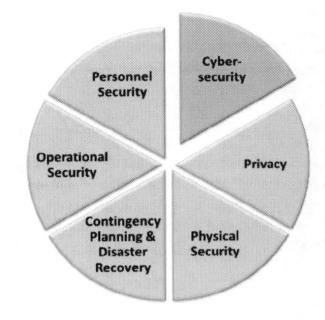

- **Physical Security** – the protection of property, e.g. using fences and locks;
- **Personnel Security** – e.g. using background checks;
- **Contingency Planning and Disaster Recovery** – how to resume normal operations after an incident, also known as Business Continuity Planning;
- **Operational Security** – protecting business plans and processes, and
- **Privacy** – protecting personal information.[2]

    Function include: Asset Management; Business Environment; Governance; Risk Assessment; and Risk Management Strategy.

- *Protect: Develop and implement appropriate safeguards to ensure delivery of critical services.*
  - *The Protect Function supports the ability to limit or contain the impact of a potential cybersecurity event. Examples of outcome Categories within this Function include: Identity Management and Access Control; Awareness and Training; Data Security; Information Protection Processes and Procedures; Maintenance; and Protective Technology.*

- *Detect: Develop and implement appropriate activities to identify the occurrence of a cybersecurity event.*
  - *The Detect Function enables timely discovery of cybersecurity events. Examples of outcome Categories within this Function include: Anomalies and Events; Security Continuous Monitoring; and Detection Processes.*
- *Respond: Develop and implement appropriate activities to take action regarding a detected cybersecurity incident.*
  - *The Respond Function supports the ability to contain the impact of a potential cybersecurity incident. Examples of outcome Categories within this Function include: Response Planning; Communications; Analysis; Mitigation; and Improvements.*
- *Recover: Develop and implement appropriate activities to maintain plans for resilience and to restore any capabilities or services that were impaired due to a cybersecurity incident.*
  - *The Recover Function supports timely recovery to normal operations to reduce the impact from a cybersecurity incident. Examples of outcome Categories within this Function include: Recovery Planning; Improvements; and Communications.* (NIST, 2018)

As an organization builds the cybersecurity portion of its overall security program, it is important for it to ask what it is doing in each of these functions. It is not enough to implement Respond and Recover activities to be prepared when a cybersecurity event occurs, the organization should be hopefully conducting activities to prevent the event from occurring in the first place. Likewise, it is not enough to perform the Identify and Protect functions because, as too many organizations have learned, no matter what you do, you need to be prepared to detect when your protection activities fail and have in place response and recovery capabilities. All five of these functions are required for a viable and sustainable organizational cybersecurity program.

These five functions are also important at the community level. As the community champion at first, and later the community ISAO, oversees the creation of the community cybersecurity program, all five of these functional areas apply to the community as well – though in a little different manner. For example:

- **Identify**: what cybersecurity resources does the community have? Who might be able to help others should an event occur? What are the potential targets in the community and who are the possible threat actors that may target them? What other resources exist in the state or nation that might be able to help when a cyber event occurs?

- **Protect**: What are the high value targets in the community doing to protect their cyber infrastructures? What processes and procedures has the community established to share information of attacks on one member that may impact another? Are organizations in the community sharing best practices to help each other protect their assets? Has the community established chapters of professional cybersecurity networking organizations (such as ISSA and ISACA)? Does the community sponsor a cybersecurity workshop or seminar on at least an annual basis that is open to all members of the community?

- **Detect**: What is the community doing to look for and share indicators of compromise? What other information sharing efforts are underway? Who else is the community communicating with in order to obtain other potential indicators of compromise? Has the community established a SOC or has it contracted with another entity to provide SOC services?

- **Respond**: What has the community done in order to enable a cooperative response to a cyber event impacting a significant portion of the community? What has the community done to be able to come together to continue functioning in the event of a cyber event? Do organizations and individuals know who to contact in the event of a cyber incident and when this contact should be made? Does the community have a Disaster Recovery Plan that includes cyber events? Has a community cyber event response plan been developed and incorporated into its overall emergency response plan? Do all individuals and organizations identified in the response plan know what their responsibilities are? Does the community examine and practice their cyber event response plan at least annually through functional or tabletop exercises?

- **Recover**: What agreements and processes are in place in the community to work together to bring the community back to its pre-event posture? Are backups made of important data to ensure that the community and individual organizations can return to normal operations as quickly as possible? Do organizations keep backup copies of data in a secure location separate from the system that is used to normally process the data? Are cooperative agreements in place to help organizations work with other organizations to speed the recovery process?

Each community will be different in terms of how they carry out plans to create a cybersecurity program but they all need to consider and include the five functional areas when making their plans. Up to this point, organizations within a community have been treated similarly and it has been stated that all organizations need to consider the five functional areas. While this is true, not all organizations need to cover the functional areas to the same level. For a community to reach a specific level in the CCSMM, organizations within the community will also have to be implementing their own cybersecurity programs. It will be hard for the community to have, for example, a viable information sharing program unless organizations within the community have reached a level of maturity that will enable them to participate in the information sharing program. This does not mean, however, that all organizations in the community must be at the same level of maturity for the community to be considered to have reached that same level. While every organization within the community should be considering cybersecurity as it applies to them, not all will need to be as mature. Small organizations that do not store personal information on the citizens in the community may not need to maintain as high of a level of cybersecurity as others that do store this sort of information. They may not be as big of a target for cyber-attacks. Still, they need to consider what would happen to their employees, customers, or the community should they suffer a cyber-attack that impacts their operations. At the same time, other organizations, such as those in the financial services sector, will need to maintain a high level of security because of the possibility of attacks on their systems. The various infrastructures that the community relies on as well as local government systems will also need to be at a higher level of security.

So, what is the relationship between the level of maturity for the community and the level of security of individual organizations within the community? This is not an easy question to answer as it should be clear by now that the level that individual organizations should attain depends on the specific organization. In general, organizations related to the individual infrastructures, their vendors, the critical city government offices and those they are connected to, and major employers in the community should be at the same level of security as the community is targeting. As for the rest of the organizations within the community, they should be at a level of security that allows them to participate in the security programs in the community (such as information sharing efforts and community cybersecurity exercises and informational events) that are part of the level of security the community is targeting.

The focus has been on the NIST *Cyber Security Framework* and its companion document, the NIST *Small Business Information Security: The*

Fundamentals documents. There are a number of other documents that may be useful for both communities and the organizations within them. NIST Special Publication 800-171 titled *Protecting Controlled Unclassified Information in Nonfederal Systems and Organizations* introduces 14 families of security requirements as shown in the diagram below:

Figure 5. Security Requirements Families (Ross et el. 2016b)

FAMILY	FAMILY
Access Control	Media Protection
Awareness and Training	Personnel Security
Audit and Accountability	Physical Protection
Configuration Management	Risk Assessment
Identification and Authentication	Security Assessment
Incident Response	System and Communications Protection
Maintenance	System and Information Integrity

Each family of security requirements includes a number of requirements related to the topic of the family. Each family has both basic security requirements and derived security requirements. The *basic security requirements* provide high-level and fundamental security requirements for that family. The derived security requirements supplement the basic security requirements and come from NIST Special Publication 800-53. NIST SP 800-171 includes a detailed discussion of both the basic and derived security requirements. The purpose of NIST SP 800-53 is to "provide guidelines for selecting and specifying security controls for organizations and information systems supporting the executive agencies of the federal government". (NIST, 2013) Neither of these documents provide step-by-step guidance for securing systems but they both provide valuable information that can be used by organizations wanting to implement a cybersecurity program. From the community's perspective, these documents provide additional information to better understand the bigger picture of what organizations need to be doing within the community and can be areas that the community's champion helps to publicize to members of the community.

CONCLUSION

The NIST Cybersecurity Framework is a valuable document containing a lot of very useful information including a number of references that will point a security professional to additional documents on a variety of security topics. It is not designed for communities or for all of the organizations within a community. Instead, it was designed to address critical infrastructure cybersecurity and has been used by them as well as government departments and agencies. Large government contractors have also utilized the information within the CSF. The CSF introduces five functions – Identify, Protect, Detect, Respond, and Recover – all of which should be part of every organization's cybersecurity program, no matter what the size. The companion publication from NIST, *Small Business Information Security: The Fundamentals*, was designed for small businesses who would not be able to address all that is found in the CSF publication. This document is also more applicable to a community as a whole. It introduces six security measures – Cybersecurity, Physical Security, Personnel Security, Operational Security, Privacy, and Contingency Planning & Disaster Recovery – all of which are pertinent to both organizational and community cybersecurity programs. A community needs to consider all six of these security measures as well as the five functions of the CSF when developing their program and when encouraging organizations within the community to improve their own cybersecurity programs.

The tie between the CSF and the CCSMM is simply that the CCSMM defines a variety of characteristics that should be part of a cybersecurity program at various levels. It is not specific in terms of identifying what has to be done for each of the five functions identified in the CSF or the six security measures in the small business document. Instead, a community or an organization that has determined it wants to attain a specific level in the model should look at the characteristics identified at that level and then determine what it can do in the five functional areas to obtain that characteristic. The CSF then can be used as a reference to find specific guidance on the variety of areas that the community has identified it needs to work on.

While this text is focused on communities, it is important for a community attempting to attain a specific maturity level as outlined in the CCSMM to ensure that organizations within the community attain a certain level of maturity as well. Not all organizations need to be at the same level as the community, it will depend on the type of organization, what assets they control, and what data they store. Essential local government offices such as law enforcement and emergency services will need to be at the same level as the community. The organizations that provide the essential services such as water, power, and communications will also need to be at the same level. Financial services, because of the information they process, will be a natural target and should be at the same level as the community as well. Employers with a large number of employees or customers as well as organizations with large financial assets, because they too will be a natural target for cyber-attacks, should also be at the same level as the community. Smaller businesses that do not control the same type of assets, are not a vendor for any of the critical community organizations, and that do not maintain a large amount of personnel information on citizens may not need to be at the same level.

REFERENCES

Executive Order 13636: Improving Critical Infrastructure Cybersecurity. (2013). Retrieved from https://www.govinfo.gov/content/pkg/FR-2013-02-19/pdf/2013-03915.pdf

Joint Task Force Transformation Initiative. (2013). *NIST Special Publication: 800-53 Rev. 4. Security and privacy controls for federal information systems and organizations*. Retrieved from https://nvlpubs.nist.gov/nistpubs/SpecialPublications/NIST.SP.800-53r4.pdf

NIST, National Institute of Standards and Technology. (2018). *Framework for improving critical infrastructure cybersecurity version 1.1*. Retrieved from https://nvlpubs.nist.gov/nistpubs/CSWP/NIST.CSWP.04162018.pdf

Paulsen, C., & Toth, P. (2016). *NISTIR 7621 Rev. 1: Small business information security: The fundamentals*. Retrieved from NIST website: https://nvlpubs.nist.gov/nistpubs/ir/2016/NIST.IR.7621r1.pdf

Ross, R., Viscuso, P., Guissanie, G., Dempsey, K., & Riddle, M. (2016). *NIST Special Publication 800-171 Rev. 1: Protecting controlled unclassified information in nonfederal systems and organizations*. Retrieved from NIST website: https://nvlpubs.nist.gov/nistpubs/SpecialPublications/NIST.SP.800-171r1.pdf

S.1353 - Cybersecurity enhancement act (CEA) of 2014. (2014). Retrieved from congress.gov website: https://www.congress.gov/bill/113th-congress/senate-bill/1353/text

Chapter 9
Building Your Community Cybersecurity Program

ABSTRACT

Communities and states are targets of cyber-attacks. Cities are popular because of generally lax cybersecurity postures and the fact that they have money. States and communities also have personal information on citizens, which can be used for identity theft. With the realization they are becoming frequent targets, communities are looking to enhance their cybersecurity programs, but many do not know where or how to start. The community cyber security maturity model is designed for this purpose – to help states and communities to develop their own viable and sustainable cybersecurity programs. There has also been considerable media attention on the NIST Cyber Security Framework. This is a program designed for organizations, and it contains a lot of good information organizations can use to enhance their cybersecurity posture. From a whole community perspective, however, it is not as useful though there are parts of it that are applicable to a community.

INTRODUCTION

Communities need cybersecurity programs. This means not just for the city government and the critical infrastructures but for all members of the community. Citizens of the community may frequent a variety of stores where they may provide their credit card information. This information is going to be used and may be stored for the logging of transactions. In most

DOI: 10.4018/978-1-7998-4471-6.ch009

communities, especially larger ones, there will also be a number of small doctor and dentist offices that have personnel health information about their patients. It is of interest to the citizens in the community that all of this information maintained by local businesses and offices follow cybersecurity and privacy best practices so that personal information is stored and transmitted securely. In addition, the businesses themselves are interested in protecting their computers and networks because they do not want to suffer a loss from a security breach or from other types of attack such as ransomware. Basically, cities and the businesses within them are becoming increasingly interested in cybersecurity. Knowing what to do in order to start a cybersecurity program within a community or to enhance an existing one is not immediately obvious. There is a plethora of vendors and service providers with tools and services that they will be willing to sell to the community and organizations within the community, but is what they are offering the right tool or service for what the organization or community needs at that time? The CCSMM provides a way to measure the current status of a community's cybersecurity program and a path for the community to follow to improve their cybersecurity posture. In its four dimensions and its five levels it provides a model for organizations and communities to follow that will also address the five functions essential to a cybersecurity program that forms the basis of the NIST Cyber Security Framework – namely Identify, Protect, Detect, Respond and Recover.

BACKGROUND

The Department of Homeland Security (DHS) has been producing the National Preparedness Report every year since 2012. This report provides a lot of interesting information regarding the nation's level of preparedness from a state perspective. Part of the report is an assessment by the states themselves as to how prepared they feel they are in a variety of areas such as Mass Search and Rescue Operations, Public Information & Warning, Fire Management and Suppression, and Health and Human Services. The diagram below shows the results for the 2017 report. This report grouped the information in a format where it is easy to see a comparison between the different disciplines. The 2018 report split the disciplines up so that there was no single chart that presented a quick way to compare the disciplines. The numbers for cybersecurity, and the placement of it in comparison to other disciplines, however, remained fairly steady – thus the reason the chart from 2017 is utilized here to illustrate the point that states are not prepared for cybersecurity incidents. In 2019 the report took on a different format and the sort of information provided in earlier years was not provided.

Since 2012, Cybersecurity has been at or near the bottom of the list in terms of the percentage of states that believe they are prepared for a cyber event. While the states' belief that their level of preparedness has increased in many of the other areas, cybersecurity has not. States realize that they are not prepared but they haven't done what is needed to change that. While the report is at the state level, it would be reasonable to assume that similar results would be obtained if cities were asked the same questions. This speaks to the need for states to develop a cybersecurity program. If the states accomplished this, would it be sufficient to handle the events that cities might face or is there a need for communities to also develop their own cybersecurity program?

When a cyber event hits a city, most are going to need assistance in dealing with it. States and the federal government have some resources that might be able to help but not in the event of a large-scale event that impacts a significant number of cities at the same time. And what if multiple attack vectors are used by the attackers or different versions of ransomware? Up until now when more than one community was hit authorities relied on the fact that the same attack vector was often used so an analysis on the one attack vector would help multiple targets. But what if there were a dozen different vectors that were used? Does the nation or state have the resources to be conducting forensic analysis on multiple tools used in the attack at the same time? Communities must adopt the position that they are going to have to be able to handle a cyber event on their own and not rely on help from the federal government or from the state. If they are the only target then help may be available and they should take advantage of it if they can, but they should not plan on having assistance available. One other option for assistance is available and that is to have contracted with a security service provider to come in and help when an event occurs. This, of course, will cost the community who will need to decide whether this is a better option or if developing their own capability would fit into their budget better. A combination of the two is also a possibility. No matter which approach a community takes, it will still need to address the other functions from the NIST CSF and will need to develop their own cybersecurity program.

Figure 1. 2017 National Preparedness Report [DHS, 2017]

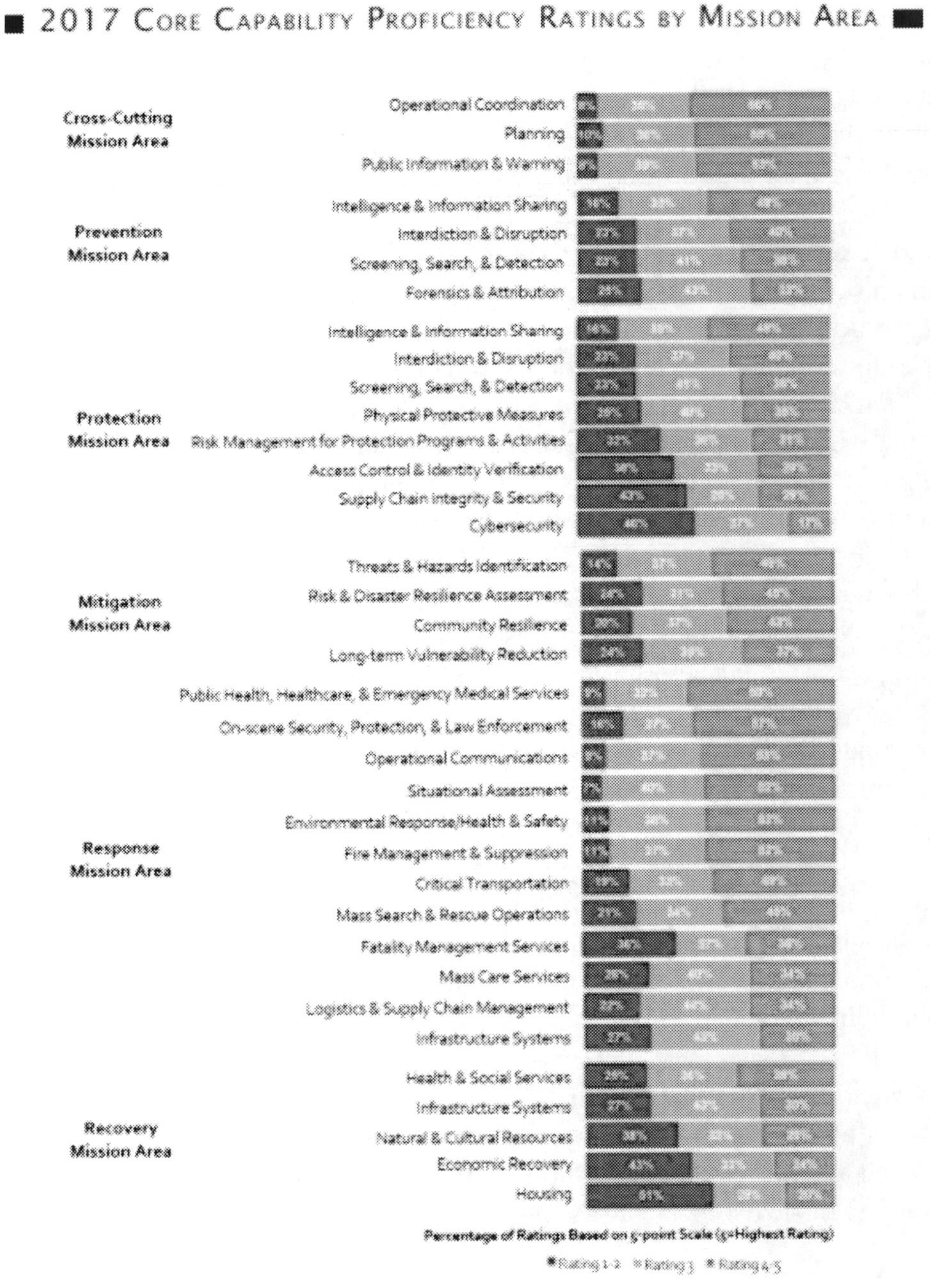

■ 2017 CORE CAPABILITY PROFICIENCY RATINGS BY MISSION AREA ■

Percentage of Ratings Based on 5-point Scale (5=Highest Rating)

● Rating 1-2   ● Rating 3   ● Rating 4-5

VIABLE AND SUSTAINABLE PROGRAMS

Two terms that have been used in relationship to the creation of community cybersecurity programs are viable and sustainable. These are critical concepts in the creation of a program. It is not especially hard to convince individuals to attend a few meetings or go to a few seminars on cybersecurity but to create a structure that will sustain community efforts for an extended period is much more difficult. The normal day-to-day responsibilities of individuals within the community will interfere with their ability to spend time helping to develop the community security program. They may be convinced of the need but realities of their other responsibilities will gradually pull them away. To be sustainable the program has to be such that it will continue despite the competition between it and the normal daily tasks that individuals will face. The program has to be designed so that it will be self-sustaining. It cannot rely on the champion previously discussed to always be around. Individuals change positions, are assigned new responsibilities and change jobs. They may move away from the community for a variety of reasons. The champion is needed to kickstart the program and to keep it going in its early days, but the champion will not always be around and the program still needs to survive if the original champion is no longer involved for whatever reason.

The program also needs to be viable in that it has to be possible for it to conduct the specified activities and to attain its target maturity level. The program needs to be designed to be flexible in order to adapt to changes in the community, regulations, and technology. It needs to also be designed to take into account the long-term costs involved in such a program. To be secure there will be a cost. It was only at Level 1 that a series of no- and low-cost items are predominant. Just like insurance and physical security, there is an ongoing cost to cybersecurity. The building of a program that is both viable and sustainable is where the CCSMM is designed to help.

The CCSMM originally started out, as the previous chapters discussed, as a 2-Dimensional model but quickly became a 3-dimensional model. The reason for this was the recognition that for a community to advance in the maturity of its cybersecurity program, the organizations within the community would also have to have a certain level of maturity in their programs. The same is true at the state level. The state needs to be at a certain level of maturity in order for communities to advance and communities need to be at a certain level for the state to advance. Consequently, both organizations and states will also ultimately need to have a viable and sustainable program that can interact with the community program. This is especially true in the dimensions of awareness and information sharing. Both of these are heavily reliant on organizations and individuals within the community participating in the program. For example, before organizations can share information on indicators of compromise, they must have an organizational program that is able to detect breaches when they occur and have the policies in place to share that information with others. Furthermore, this requires a level of awareness of the cybersecurity issues tied to information sharing and the importance of it. Organizations, and the individuals in those organizations, need to understand the benefits of an information sharing program within the community.

One way to kick off the program in a community is to develop a community ISAO. The ISAO does NOT need to immediately have a 24/7 security operations center or cyber threat analyst. The idea is to get started, not to overnight reach an advanced level of capability. The community ISAO in this case will need to be designed to be more than the simple definition of what an ISAO is. It has sometimes been referred to as an "ISAO Plus" (ISAO+). What is meant by this is that it will be involved in the sharing of information and activities that go beyond the normal sharing of indicators of compromise. It will be involved in the establishment of community policies, assessments, awareness programs, and the sharing of general information about cybersecurity. The establishment of trust between entities within the community has also been mentioned previously and an established way to do this is to have people come together to jointly work on projects and to, quite simply, get to know each other. Trust will not happen overnight but over time trusted relationships will develop.

As an example of this, in San Antonio, Texas a group was formed in 2005 known as the Security Leaders Forum (SLF). It started off slowly with just a few members, mostly Chief Information Security Officers (CISOs) or security administrators from various organizations around the community. There was no charter developed for the organization, nor were there any membership dues in order to join. The group met monthly to discuss current trends in cybersecurity and to share information between individuals struggling with the same challenges. Each month one organization would host the meeting at lunchtime at their facility and would pick the topic and speaker. It was not a sales pitch by a vendor, though occasionally a cybersecurity vendor might be asked to come and present on a specific topic (but not a specific product). Over time the members of the SLF got to know, and trust, each other and to recognize that they all were working for the same goal – more secure organizations. At one point, one of the members experienced a significant security breach. The organization was from the financial services sector and there were several other members in the SLF from other organizations within the financial services sector – they were competitors in the sector. The SLF member from the organization went to his management and obtained permission to present detailed information on how the breach occurred and what the organization learned from it. The organization recognized that this information was valuable to the other members of the SLF in order to protect their own organizations – but it was also information that could have been used by competitors to highlight the issue in the public to attempt to convince customers to switch to another financial institution. The member, however, had established a relationship with the other members of the SLF, and the other members realized the benefit of working together in combatting cyber-attacks. They understood that the sharing of cybersecurity information, especially sensitive information regarding a security breach, was more important in the long run than briefly utilizing that information for a competitive advantage. The trust that it took to open up about the incident had been established over time – several years – and the information was NOT used by others in a competitive way. It might be asked whether being part of the Financial Services ISAC would have provided the same information and the answer is that for the most part it would have. Sharing with the FS-ISAC would have provided other members of the sector with the basics of the incident and would have allowed them to take measures to avoid a similar occurrence. The difference, however, is that with an alert from the FS-ISAC the information in an alert could be anonymized so that other members of the sector would not have been able to determine (or at least to easily determine) who the target had been. In the case of the presentation made by the member of the SLF, however, the target was immediately obvious out there was also an ability to ask more detailed questions about the incident – the tactics, techniques, and specific vulnerabilities exploited and the response from the targeted organization. Additionally, most of the members of the SLF were not members of the financial services sector and would not have learned about the breach from the FS-ISAC since they were not members of it. The SLF was not set up as an ISAO at the time so there was not in place a method or processes to rapidly share the information about the incident but when it was shared it was done so in more detail than would normally occur in an alert sent out by an ISAO. The organization that had the incident was a member of the FS-ISAC but the SLF member felt the incident and their lessons learned was important enough to share more details with those that he had grown to trust.

This is an important lesson that was learned about community information sharing. As an aside, when the executive order was released on ISAOs, the SLF considered establishing themselves as an ISAO but did not as the City of San Antonio took measures to create an ISAO of its own. Instead, members of the SLF and the champion(s) for the ISAO joined together to advance cybersecurity in the city.

The CCSMM is designed to start a community off with activities that are no- or low-cost as it is recognized that communities will generally not have a considerable budget for cybersecurity. They will need time to plan for future expenses and need to have time to determine what is the most essential product or service they need to put in a budget. Having an early creation of an ISAO, which can begin by being nothing more than an informal group of CISOs in the community, allows the ISAO to become a catalyst for the further development of a community cybersecurity program.

As the community programs grows, the community should be encouraging organizations within the community to establish their own programs. This can be done using the Organization Scope of the CCSMM combined with the NIST CSF. The community program will not have an abundance of technology in its program (mostly products that will be found in the SOC and ISAO) but organizations will have quite a bit. Afterall, organizations will need to be protecting their own computers and networks, but the community isn't a single monolithic entity controlling the cyber assets of all members within the community. Thus, the responsibility for the actual securing of computers and networks will fall primarily within the organization scope.

MOVING FORWARD

If you haven't begun implementing a cybersecurity program within your community, it is time to get started. The rate of cybercrime is increasing and too many old vulnerabilities are still being exploited. Old attacks are being utilized but often in new, more sophisticated ways. You don't want to wait until your community is hit with ransomware with a price tag in the hundreds or thousands of dollars to be able to recover. Starting a cybersecurity program won't guarantee that you won't be attacked or that there won't be some vulnerability that you missed securing resulting in a breach or other cyber event. What it will guarantee is that you will become less susceptible to a number of attacks we read about almost daily and if you do miss securing a system completely or if there is a new vulnerability that is discovered that results in a breach, having a cybersecurity program will allow you to more effectively respond and recover from it.

So, what are the steps in getting started? This will vary depending on your specific environment but there are generally several items that can be accomplished to get your program moving forward. The CCSMM levels provide several things you can think about doing in the early stages but there are some very basic first steps you will probably need to take. The following is organized somewhat chronologically though, again, depending on your specific environment the order may change to better fit your own local needs. You can use these steps to get started but don't be afraid to modify them to meet your local environment.

Step 1: Find a champion. Whether this individual is in the city government offices or is an industry leader, you need somebody who is passionate about cybersecurity and your community. This person should not be planning on moving in the near future as you will really need the champion to drive things for at least 2 years – again depending on your community.

Step 2: Gather support from city and industry leaders in the community. You aren't asking for money at this point (at some point in the future support of the community ISAO may be necessary to sustain its efforts and a membership fee, based on the size of the organization, may be requested but that can be addressed later), what you are asking for is support in terms of allowing personnel to participate in the effort.

Step 3: Gather a core group of security professionals who are also interested in the project. You should have a mix of city government, industry, and individuals from the critical infrastructures. You probably don't want this initial planning group to be too large, 10-15 at most to get started. This will grow quickly as is needed to accomplish the tasks you set in motion. This can be patterned after the Security Leaders Forum in San Antonio, discussed earlier, in that one way is to just start having monthly lunch meetings to discuss the path forward.

Step 4: Pick a date in the future (probably no less than 6-9 months out and no more than 9-12 months) to plan for a city "Cybersecurity Day" with a seminar or workshop that will have three parts: 1) a session for city government employees and employees of the various critical infrastructures; 2) a session for local industry, of any size. In the future this may be split into sessions for large organizations and another for small and medium size businesses; and 3) a session for citizens of the community to let them know how to protect themselves individually in their homes. A good month to hold this meeting might be in October which is the national Cybersecurity Month. Numerous events occur around the nation sponsored by both industry, professional cybersecurity organizations, and federal agencies such as the Department of Homeland Security to raise the awareness in the nation on cybersecurity issues. Coupling the community Cybersecurity Day with the other national events that are going on can help to draw attention to both. Do not worry about this first event not being too technical, it probably shouldn't be but should be focused more on the desired community program with some pointers folks can walk away with to get started on their own cybersecurity efforts.

Step 5: Concurrent with the Cybersecurity Day, start forming your community ISAO so that it can be announced officially at the Cybersecurity Day event. You will want to have some information sessions to advertise the ISAO and its purpose before the organization is officially launched. You will need to work out a charter and decide on at least the initial goals and objectives for your community ISAO. Documents to help you in this effort can be found at the ISAO SO website, www.isao.org. Alternatively, some communities may find that forming an ISAO might be a good first step and the initial members of the community ISAO and the ISAO itself can become the champions for establishment of the community cybersecurity program. If this is the case, then the Cybersecurity Day can be used as a means to spread awareness of cybersecurity throughout the community as well as to advertise the community ISAO and the benefits of becoming a member. When it is first established, the ISAO will most likely have a small number of capabilities as defined in the ISAO guidance documents found on the ISAO SO website. This is ok, the important thing is to get it started.

Step 7: Create a community cybersecurity web site. This could be given to the ISAO itself to maintain or it could be maintained by a member of the ISAO. There are some good arguments that can be made to have the local government sponsor this website as members of the community, who may not know about the ISAO, will naturally turn to the local government when a disaster or incident occurs. No matter who maintains the website, it should have information that can be shared with the community on cybersecurity issues, events, best practices, upcoming training, etc.

Step 8: Within the first 9-18 months conduct a community cybersecurity tabletop exercise. This can be done either before or after the Community Cybersecurity Day event. If conducted before the event, it will allow you to report on at the event. If conducted after the event, it will allow you to advertise it and encourage participation in the exercise at the event. One critical item to mention on the subject of a cybersecurity exercise is that you should be trying to have community decision makers and leaders participate – not the community's IT or security personnel. IT and security employees across the community can be used to help facilitate and design the event but you want the leaders and decision makers (the individuals who can "sign a check") to be the ones who are participating in the event. The mayor, city manager, head of the EOC, leaders in industries within the city, etc. should be in attendance. It will be important to make sure that this initial tabletop exercise is kept fairly simple. Do not make it overly complex as it may then become too complicated for the non-technical city leaders to understand and so that you do not have individuals saying "that would never happen here" because they did not understand what was described. You will also have these leaders make assumptions about their own cybersecurity where they think that they are already addressing cybersecurity. You want them to realize the impact of a cyber event on the community. Remember that this exercise is supposed to address the whole-community concept and how the community can act together in responding to an event. This does not mean that specific issues that impact individual organizations can't be included (such as the need to create and maintain backup copies of essential data) but the focus of the event should not be on individual organizations alone. Another approach instead of a tabletop exercise might be to utilize the National Level Exercise 2020 community cybersecurity "game" that was developed to introduce communities to cybersecurity events. For more information on cybersecurity exercises or the NLE 2020 game, contact CIAS@utsa.edu.

Step 9: Launch a community culture of security campaign. Think of this like a Smokey Bear (often incorrectly referred to as "Smokey the Bear") or McGruff the crime fighting dog campaign. You want to start reaching the youth in your community so that they are raised with cybersecurity in mind. You want the youth to know that "they can help prevent a cyber wildfire" or that they can "help take a bite out of cybercrime." Part of this campaign should be the involvement of the community's middle and high schools in the CyberPatriot cyber defense competition and similar programs. This has grown over the last decade so that there are thousands of teams across the country registered in this event. More information on the program can be found at www.uscyberpatriot.org.

Another great activity for youth to learn about cybersecurity is the *Cyber Threat Defender Collectible Card Game* for grades 6+ and its companion game *Cyber Threat Protector* aimed at grades 3-5. These games have proven successful in introducing both youth and adults to the basics of cybersecurity. They have also served to raise interest in the field and have encouraged youth to consider a career in cybersecurity. *Cyber Threat Defender* has also been converted to a PC-based game which can be downloaded for free and has been translated to Spanish and is being translated to other languages as well. For more information on the game, both card and electronic, see www.cias.utsa.edu.

Step 10: The city should become a member of the Multi-State ISAC (MS-ISAC) and the community ISAO should become a member of the MS-ISAC and the GBC-ISAO as well. For more information on the MS-ISAC see www.cisecurity.org/ms-isac/. Once it is fully formed, the community ISAO should also consider joining the National Council of Registered ISAOs, see www.ncrisaos.org. Before becoming a member of the MS-ISAC and GBC-ISAOs, the community ISAO should be mature enough to understand what information it will receive from these organizations and be prepared to appropriately handle the information received. These organizations can provide useful resources for a community getting started on their cybersecurity program, but they may also provide information that the community ISAO may not be prepared to utilize at the moment. As the community ISAO matures, it will gradually be able to incorporate the more technical aspects of the information it receives and to appropriately handle and utilize it within the community.

Step 11: Within nine months, form a cybersecurity advisory board for the mayor and city council. This group should meet with or report to (provide a report to) both the mayor and city council on at least an annual basis and hopefully a bit more frequently. The board should help inform the city leaders on cybersecurity issues so that they can more effectively plan for cybersecurity spending and possible events. This should be a public/private effort and should also help to encourage public/private partnerships within the community on cybersecurity issues.

Step 12: By the end of the first year you should have had a meeting of community leaders to determine what level of the CCSMM is appropriate to attempt to attain and on what timeline. This then will become part of a whole-community cybersecurity plan that should be established. This plan will be adjusted over time as the program matures but will be the foundation upon which subsequent steps to a mature cybersecurity program will be based.

Step 13: Within eighteen months, create a cybersecurity annex for the community's emergency operations plans and include cybersecurity as part of the community's continuity of operations plan and exercises.

Step 14: As individual organizations establish their own programs, introduce the individual components pertinent to them such as the four dimensions of the CCSMM and the five functions in the NIST CSF. These can be topics at the first or future Community Cybersecurity Days. As the cybersecurity programs within organizations in the community will vary dramatically, the timing of this step will also vary considerably. Discussions of the components mentioned might make for a more technical talk in a technical track at the community's Cybersecurity Day and they will need to be addressed repeatedly in two ways: first since not all organizations will begin their cybersecurity programs at the same time (especially since new companies may be formed at any time); and second the specifics of what will be mentioned in a talk or discussion on the components of the model and framework will change as the programs within organizations mature.

Step 15: Since often small- and medium-sized businesses, especially newly established ones, often do not have an involved cybersecurity program (and in fact may not have considered cybersecurity beyond the most basic of protections), it is important for communities to remember them in the community's cybersecurity program. There should be a track in the Cybersecurity Day for them eventually and at least a talk in the initial Cybersecurity Day. At some point, especially in larger communities with numerous businesses that fall into the category of small- and medium-sized businesses, it may behoove you to hold a seminar or workshop specifically for these entities.

Step 16: As a related step to the one introducing the CyberPatriot Competition and the Cyber Threat Defender card game, you should consider how to introduce cybersecurity into the classroom at not just the middle and high school levels but even in elementary school (where cyber ethics and discussions on topics such as cyber bullying can be introduced). Consideration for cybersecurity in the community and 4-year college levels should also be accomplished. CyberPatriot and *Cyber Threat Defender* can serve as good tools and catalysts for programs in the public schools, but local school districts might consider developing more involved programs that could even lead to high school students obtaining one of a variety of technical network and security certifications. This is especially valuable in communities where there is a significant portion of the student population that traditionally do not consider going to college. Cybersecurity and technical certifications can lead to higher paying jobs for individuals who later may be motivated to continue their education as well. This has actually been proven to be possible in several communities around the nation.

Step 17: As the community cybersecurity program plan is established, organizations, especially the local government, should consider the financial resources that may be necessary to accomplish the various steps. Your local government may already have budgeted for increased cybersecurity measures, but often it will not have, and it will especially not have included anything for a community program. These will need to be budgeted for in the future. One thing that can greatly help facilitate individual and community programs, but that will require specific funding, are commercial services that vendors offer in areas such as cyber threat and attack detection as well as cyber event response and recovery. If the financial situation allows for these, either for organizations within the community or for the whole community program, they should be considered.

These steps will not result in a complete cybersecurity program for your community. These are only items to consider in order to initiate your program. Several of these have been discussed within the chapters on the various parts of the CCSMM and there are many more things to accomplish but to keep from being overwhelmed, consider starting with these. Some items on the list may take some research but there are publicly available sources and organizations that can provide help and training. Two organizations that can help with training and setting up your community program and ISAO are the National Cybersecurity Preparedness Consortium (NCPC) with the website www.nationalcpc.org and the Geographically Based Community ISAOs (GBC-ISAOs) organization with the website of www.gbcisaos.org. The NCPC was established specifically to provide training for SLTTs. All of the certified training programs in the DHS catalog have been paid for by DHS/FEMA and are available for free to individuals within SLTT governments and to others on a space available basis. Since some of the training is online, it is even more widely available to interested parties. The GBC-ISAOs was set up to specifically assist geographic entities (such as states and communities) in establishing their own ISAO and to facilitate information sharing between them. A third organization which your community can turn to as an additional resource is the Multi-State ISAC (their website is https://www.cisecurity.org/ms-isac/) which has previously been mentioned. It has resources that it will share with SLTTs that can be useful in establishing various programs and it also will be a source for current vulnerability and cyber intelligence data (when the community is ready to appropriately handle this type of information).

Individual communities will differ, and you will need to consider which of the above steps your community wishes to attempt and in what order. Ultimately each of these will be addressed in some fashion as you commence with the establishment of a security program for the whole community but your specific path may, and most likely will, vary from other communities. This list is also not all-inclusive as there are many other steps that can be taken but as you and the other members of your community meet you can discuss and consider what is most important for your particular situation. Use these steps only as a guide to launch your own discussion.

CONCLUSION

The nation needs to increase its cybersecurity preparedness and one of the best places to start this effort is within the cities and states across the nation. States and cities are increasingly being targeted and many will be unable to prevent successful attacks, and most are unprepared to respond to a successful attack. Most organizations within communities and states are not part of the sectors for which there is an ISAC and thus don't readily have an organization they can turn to for sharing of cybersecurity-related information or to assist in the response to a cyber event or attack. There are some efforts at the state and federal level to develop programs to assist cities in their efforts to prevent successful attacks or to respond to them when they are successful but with thousands of counties, towns and cities across the U.S. there will simply never be enough resources at the state and federal levels to help in the event of a large cyber-attack especially if it is designed to utilize multiple attack vectors taking advantage of different vulnerabilities. This means that the best plan is for states, counties, towns and cities, tribes, and territories to be prepared to handle incidents on their own if possible and if outside help is available then to utilize it. SLTTs should at the very least be prepared to handle an immediate response to the incident even if other assets (which may also include commercial entities that provide detection, response, and recovery services) are utilized. Since cybersecurity is not something that the majority of elected officials know anything about, help is needed for cities to be able to establish their own programs. Even when there are cybersecurity professionals within the city infrastructure, the majority of them have been trained on how to protect an individual organization and have no experience in bringing together the disparate parts of a community under a coordinated whole-community program. That is what the CCSMM and this text are designed to do. To provide a way forward for those interested in developing their own whole-community programs to accomplish the task. It will not be easy, nor will it be quick, but it is not impossible and it will be well worth the effort as it will help secure the assets of the community and the private information of its citizens.

A number of suggestions were made in this chapter for a community to consider as it begins its journey to establish a whole-community cybersecurity program. Every community is different though they share certain similarities. The list provided in this chapter should be considered, but then adapted to individual community needs. Communities may also find that there are other steps that they may want to take instead of, or in addition to but before some of the steps offered in this chapter. These steps are only offered as a guide to stimulate the conversation within a community as it decides to embark on a whole-community approach to a cybersecurity program. Other organizations that can provide resources and help, such as the MS-ISAC, GBC-ISAOs and the NCPC, were also mentioned and communities should utilize them and what they offer as they embark on establishing a whole-community cybersecurity program.

A final point that has been mentioned several times throughout this text and that needs to be reiterated is that the community scope of the CCSMM is not designed to secure individual organizations, nor should the community cybersecurity program be designed to address individual organizations. It is not the responsibility of local governments (nor of the governments of states, tribes, or territories) to secure the organizations that fall within their geographical boundaries. They, of course, are responsible for securing their own government assets (and possibly the utilities when they are owned by the municipality) but they are not responsible for going into organizations within the community and securing them. Most organizations would not want local or federal governments to do so either. Instead, the community scope of the CCSMM is designed to address a whole-community program intended to prepare the community to establish an overall program that will help the community, and organizations within it, to prepare for a cyber event of some sort. The community program in taking a whole-community approach will accomplish those things that will enable the community to address cyber incidents that impact more than one part of the community. It will also advance awareness and the need to address cybersecurity throughout the organizations, and individuals, within the community. It will encourage organizations to establish their own cybersecurity programs and, with assistance from other members in the community who can act as mentors for nascent organizational programs, it will help these organizations along their path to a secure cybersecurity status. In essence, a community program is designed to be the "rising tide that will lift all boats in the community."

REFERENCES

Department of Homeland Security. (n.d.). *2018 national preparedness report.* Retrieved from https://www.fema.gov/media-library-data/1541781185823-2ae55a276f604e04b68e2748adc95c68/2018NPRRprt20181108v508.pdf

Chapter 10

Incorporating Other Models and Technology Into the CCSMM

ABSTRACT

One thing about the nature of computer science in general and cybersecurity in particular is that they are both fields that are constantly changing. Whether it is because of a new version of an operating system being released, new technology that has been introduced, or a disclosure of a newly discovered vulnerability, the field is continually changing. Some changes will not have any impact on the CCSMM. Others may necessitate a change in some aspect at one or more levels. The model itself is extremely flexible and frequently does not specify the precise items that need to be covered but rather the more abstract concept that must be considered. This is true for not just changes in technology but also the introduction of new government guidance or regulations as well as the creation of other maturity models that are focused on some other aspect of cybersecurity. This chapter explores incorporating other models and technology into the CCSMM.

INTRODUCTION

The creation of the CCSMM came about after years of dealing with SLTTs and assisting in the development of their security programs. Those years were certainly not static in that what was accomplished in the early years was not

DOI: 10.4018/978-1-7998-4471-6.ch010

exactly the same as what occurred in later years. This was due to a number of factors including the introduction of new technology, regulations, federal guidance or the discovery of new vulnerabilities in software or hardware. As the model was developed, the fact that for the model to remain applicable it would need to be flexible enough to allow for these types of changes was recognized and planned for. Fortunately, when considering the community scope this is easily accommodated. For the organizational scope you will find that the requirements at each level are much more technologically specific. Instead of a general statement stating that organizations in the community need to institute some form of asset management that keeps track of hardware and software (which might be a requirement for the community scope), for the organizational scope the requirement might be for one organization to implement inventory control based on NIST SP 800-53 Rev 4, CM-8, PM-4 while another utilizes ISA 62443-2-1:2009 4.2.3.4. Since this book covers the community scope, how to address the inclusion of new technology, regulations and guidance, and other models into the CCSMM will be covered in this chapter.

BACKGROUND

The CCSMM addresses multiple ranges (or scopes) of entities. From individual citizens to the entire nation the CCSMM describes the characteristics and activities that define five different levels of maturity for security programs. This book addresses the CCSMM at the community scope. A community will consist of several different types of organizations with varying specific security requirements. Banks fall under different federal security regulations than do hospitals, for example. From a higher perspective, however, both have similar security requirements. Should one of the regulations change a specific requirement, it does not negate the usefulness of the CCSMM for the community. What it does is change an organizational requirement for entities that fall under that regulation. The overall CCSMM model would remain unchanged.

Another area in which change may occur necessitating changes in the various implementation mechanisms is technology. As new technology becomes available it will often introduce different security vulnerabilities while at the same time eliminating others. A good example of this is the switch from telephone modems for communication to wireless networks. Between the mid-1990s and the mid-2000s if you purchased a laptop computer, it most likely came with a telephone modem for you to use to connect to an Internet Service Provider so that you could browse the Internet. A decade later, however, you would find it much more difficult to find a laptop computer with a telephone modem because they had been replaced with wireless devices. The introduction of wireless connectivity to the Internet overall replaced the need to use the slower telephone modem and consequently telephone modems disappeared as wireless cards took their place. From a cybersecurity perspective, telephone modems added a specific vulnerability to networks which required cybersecurity professionals to check for. The introduction of wireless largely eliminated the need for this (with the exception of some lingering telephone connections for a few more years). Wireless, however, introduced its own vulnerabilities which had not been considered before.

OTHER INITIATIVES

As we have seen several times in this text, periodically new guidance or regulations are developed and disseminated which may require new security controls or which may introduce a new approach to addressing elements of cybersecurity. An example of this are the various Executive Orders that have been discussed. Another example is the NIST Cyber Security Framework which provided an organized approach for organizations to deal with security. What might be some other guidance or documents that might impact the way that the CCSMM is implemented.

Another item that was introduced by the DHS Cybersecurity and Infrastructure Security Agency (CISA) was the identification of 55 National Critical Functions. The definition of a National Critical Function from the DHS Website on the subject is:

The functions of government and the private sector so vital to the United States that their disruption, corruption, or dysfunction would have a debilitating effect on security, national economic security, national public health or safety, or any combination thereof. [DHS 2019]

While it seems to be closely related to the identification of the original critical infrastructures, it has a slightly different, and very important, focus. The critical functions focus "on better understanding the functions that an entity enables or to which it contributes, rather than focusing on a static sector-specific or asset world view." [DHS 2019] Thus, critical functions do not take a sector approach but rather will look across sectors to see what impacts in other sectors might occur from an attack on a critical function.

So, how does this impact a community implementing the CCSMM and how does the CCSMM adapt to it? The first thing to remember is that at the Community scope, which is the topic of this text, specific security controls and mechanisms are not addressed. A community examining these 55 functions should consider how they should be integrated into what they are already doing. Awareness activities should introduce these functions to organizations in the community through the ISAO. One significant area that examining these 55 functions should have a positive influence on is the assessment arena. These functions do not focus on a single sector but instead look across sectors which is an important element of what the community is trying to do in the first place. What impact might disruption in one sector cause to other sectors? In truth, the 55 functions play right along with the type of things that the CCSMM is already trying to accomplish – taking a whole-community approach to security. Understanding the interdependencies in a community is vital to the overall security of the community.

This example of inserting the 55 National Critical Functions into a community that has utilized the CCSMM to develop their security program is not a significant problem. In fact, if the community was accomplishing what it should be doing a number of the interdependencies should already have been discovered. The belief is that this example is not a unique one and that other initiatives and even new regulations mandated by the federal government should not have a significant detrimental impact to a community's cybersecurity program. In fact, the more the community is used to working together the more likely any new initiative will have minimal impact as the community will come together to determine ways to insert it into their community.

NEW THREATS AND TECHNOLOGY

Returning to the example of the introduction of wireless with the accompanying disappearance of the telephone modems, let's examine what would have taken place in a community that had an established cybersecurity program. Looking at this example from a CCSMM point of view, these issues are more focused in the Community scope but broadly they would also need to be considered in the framework of the five NIST CSF functions. They should have appeared during the identification function and then how to protect them should have been considered in the protection function. Both of these should be considered in the CCSMM mechanisms so that individuals could be made aware of their specific vulnerabilities, needed technology to protect against attacks aimed at them should have been implemented, policies and procedures established for handling them, metrics adopted to measure how secure they are and how well the organization is following policies regarding them, and methods to include them in assessments adopted. At the community level, the ISAO could have taken the initiative to keep members informed of the new technology and the security considerations associated with it. The ISAO would not be involved in securing the wireless networks of organizations within the community but would have taken the lead in ensuring that all members knew about this new, emerging technology and what security issues it brought with it. Members in the ISAO might have exchanged tips on wireless security and a best practice document related to it developed to disseminate to members throughout the community. The advisory board for the mayor and city council should have met with them or provided a report to let them know what this might mean for the city. This would especially be important if free wifi access was a goal of the community for all citizens. In a similar manner, information for the citizens in the community should have been created to let them know of the dangers of free wifi access in coffee shops or other locations. The questions to ask would have been "what does wireless mean to the community and how can we help ensure that it is adopted in a secure manner so as not to unduly expose the citizens or organizations within the community.

Another more current example of the introduction of a different technology issue is the current concerns about the possibility of a long-term outage of power resulting in other outages as a result of an Electromagnetic Pulse (EMP). Executive Order 13865 was issued March 26, 2019. In it, EMP is defined as:

Electromagnetic pulse'' is a burst of electromagnetic energy. EMPs have the potential to negatively affect technology systems on Earth and in space. A high-altitude EMP (HEMP) is a type of human-made EMP that occurs when a nuclear device is detonated at approximately 40 kilometers or more above the surface of Earth. A geomagnetic disturbance (GMD) is a type of natural EMP driven by a temporary disturbance of Earth's magnetic field resulting from interactions with solar eruptions. Both HEMPs and GMDs can affect large geographic areas. [White House, 2019]

The reason for the concern by the White House on the subject was described in the executive order:

An electromagnetic pulse (EMP) has the potential to disrupt, degrade, and damage technology and critical infrastructure systems. Human-made or naturally occurring EMPs can affect large geographic areas, disrupting elements critical to the Nation's security and economic prosperity, and could adversely affect global commerce and stability. [White House, 2019]

The military has been concerned with the potential catastrophic impact of an EMP for several decades. It has recently become more common knowledge with a resulting raising of the level of concern for many in the country. InfraGard, for instance, has established the InfraGard EMP Resource Center to provide a website for individuals to go to for more information on the issue. They have also established a Special Interest Group (SIG) within their organization to examine other ways that they can inform their members, and the general public, on this phenomenon and preparing for it. In very basic terms, a large EMP burst, whether man-made or natural, could result in a long-term power outage that might affect a major portion of the world. Looking at the CCSMM, then, how would this be incorporated into the model and what should the community do about it?

To start with, as with our other example, the community will not be responsible for protecting all organizations within the community from the impact of an EMP burst. What the community can do is to engage the ISAO again in an awareness campaign to inform members of the communities as well as organization within the community of the potential dangers and the risk to the community. Potentially a working group could be formed in the community to gather together guidance on protection from the impacts of an EMP burst. A "Best Practice" guide could be developed (or if one is found another community or another organization that could be adopted instead) so organizations and citizens could prepare This guidance could be provided to all members of the ISAO and to the community in general. The community advisory board should meet with, or provide a report to, the mayor and city council on the subject with recommendations for the city government on protection and response capabilities the city should consider. In terms of testing, an EMP burst might be included in an upcoming community exercise to see how well the city is prepared and to make sure the community knows about the potential issue with an EMP burst. So, as before, the city is not securing the entire community, it is taking the lead to help inform all members of the community of the threat and what they can do to prepare. It is in this way that any new technology affecting security that comes along can be addressed by the CCSMM. Remember that in most instances of a new technology, the real impact will be in the Organization scope. The community can take the lead in helping to introduce the issues to organizations and individuals and can lead groups to address ways that organizations can deal with the technology but the organizations themselves will be responsible for implementing any new security controls or mechanisms.

OTHER MODELS

If somebody conducts a search of the Internet on maturity models they will receive a number of hits with a variety of models being mentioned. There are, for example, maturity models for IT Services, the Electrical Subsector, and Industrial Control Systems. If the goal is to be able to overlay or insert another maturity model into the CCSMM, it might prove to not be straightforward. To begin with, the CCSMM is a three-dimensional model whereas most other models are two-dimensional. Overlaying any of them onto the Community Scope will not make as much sense. Attempting to do the same at the Organizational Scope makes more sense since this is where specific security controls will be found.

In the CCSMM at the Organizational Scope (which is not covered in this text), the controls that are discussed are not so specific. Instead groups or types of controls are mentioned which an organization can then address as is appropriate for the sector that they are in. Thus, a maturity model that is specifically aimed at a type of organization will easily blend with the CCSMM Organizational Scope. This can be done in one of three ways. The first is to use the CCSMM Organizational Scope as the baseline and then take the new maturity model and take the specific elements from it and insert them into the CCSMM model. What this means is that the CCSMM model will specify a type of control that should be included, then the new maturity model is checked to see if there is an entry in it for that type of control. If there is, it is inserted into the CCSMM model. When this process is done, any additional controls in the new model can be inserted into the CCSMM (as they will likely represent unique aspects for the specific sector which are not represented in the more general CCSMM model). Any items that may remain in the CCSMM model for which there was not a corresponding entry in the new model should be examined to see if they are applicable for the specific sector. If they are, then a control should be included for it, maybe borrowing from something like the NIST CSF. If the remaining item is not applicable to the sector, then it can be dropped.

The second way to address insertion of another model into the CCSMM is to use the new model as the baseline and then check to see that all general controls identified in the CCSMM have a corresponding entry in the new model. For those that may not, the entry should be examined and discarded if it is not applicable to the sector. Both this method for inserting another maturity model into the CCSMM and the previous one should basically result in very similar, if not exactly the same, models. The third way to insert another model is a slight variation on the second and simply is to remove the CCSMM Organization Scope and slide the new model into its place. For sectors that are rather unique, this may be the easiest way to do things. Whichever method is used, it should not impact the Community Scope in any significant way.

As an example of what has been discussed, consider an Industrial Control System (ICS) maturity model. Industrial Control Systems, which are generally considered more Operational Technology rather that Information Technology, have some unique characteristics and requirements. They function in arenas where reliability is essential – much more than with IT equipment. While we all would like to have our networks stay up 100% of the time, if they occasionally go down for some reason, we can live with it and there is generally little impact. In manufacturing environments, or many of our critical infrastructures, a system going down can result in a shutdown of a critical process and potentially a major disaster can ensue which in some situations could also include explosions and loss of life. Thus, the focus of ICS may be very different than the major focus of IT systems in a normal corporate environment. In terms of the CCSMM, the environment may be unique enough that it simply means that replacing the Organizational Scope with this new maturity model will be the easiest and most appropriate method.

CONCLUSION

The cyber world is constantly changing and any plan being followed to develop a comprehensive program to secure the environment needs to be able to adjust to these changes. This text mainly covered the Community Scope of the CCSMM. This scope is not concerned with specific security controls but rather addresses an overall program from a higher vantage point. As such, the introduction of new technology, new regulations or federal, state, or sector initiatives, and even different maturity models does not impact the applicability of the model to a community. The community, most likely led by the community ISAO, can address any changes by becoming the lead in making the community aware of new or changing security concerns. This is one of the missions of an ISAO in the first place and the structure and initiatives set up in developing a community cybersecurity program will not be significantly impacted by the types of changes mentioned. In the case of a more specific maturity model, this is also not a difficult issue. In fact, the security controls for two different organizations in a community may very well be considerably different from each other if the organizations are in different sectors. Specific security controls, which are found in the Organizational Scope of the model, may vary considerably and thus the Community Scope can be replaced with a specific model for one organization while a different model replaces the Community Scope for a different organization and doing this will not impact the overall community program.

REFERENCES

DHS. (2019). *National critical functions*. Retrieved from https://www.cisa.gov/sites/default/files/publications/national-critical-functions-overview-508.pdf

White House. (2019). *Coordinating national resilience to electromagnetic pulses*. Retrieved from National Archives Federal Register website: https://www.federalregister.gov/documents/2019/03/29/2019-06325/coordinating-national-resilience-to-electromagnetic-pulses

About the Authors

Gregory B. White has been involved in computer and network security since 1986. He spent 30 years with the Air Force and Air Force Reserves. He obtained his Ph.D. in Computer Science from Texas A&M University in 1995 conducting research in the area of Computer Network Intrusion Detection. He currently serves as the Director of the Center for Infrastructure Assurance and Security (CIAS) and the Geographically-Based ISOA (GBC-ISAO) and is a Professor of Computer Science at The University of Texas at San Antonio (UTSA). He has written numerous papers and is the co-author on six books on cybersecurity.

Natalie Sjelin is the Director of Training for the Center for Infrastructure Assurance and Security (CIAS) at The University of Texas San Antonio. She brings over 17 years of cybersecurity experience focused on designing and facilitating cyber security exercises, developing and delivering cyber security training, and information sharing initiatives. Her focus is working with communities to build viable and sustainable cyber security programs. Ms. Sjelin has co-authored white papers on Community Cyber Security topics and a chapter for the book, Cyber-Physical *Protecting Critical Infrastructure at the State and Local Level*. She speaks regularly for professional groups, meetings, panels and conferences across the country.

Index

2-Dimensional model 52, 55, 197
3-D Model 55-57, 71

B

Business Information 59, 172-173, 184, 189, 191
business operations 8, 17, 78, 132-133, 151

C

cascading effects 14, 19, 76, 78, 92-93, 99
city council 214-215
Community Cyber Security Maturity Model (CCSM) 4, 10-13, 32, 50-51, 55-56, 104, 193
Community Exercises 7, 13, 39, 77, 119, 152
community information 65, 101, 118, 122, 200
community plans 3-4, 19, 65, 151, 153, 169
community policies 17, 131, 136-137, 139, 141, 144, 150, 198
community's program 172, 175
Comprehensive Preparedness 2
critical infrastructures 9, 18, 28, 40, 53, 65, 67, 72, 107-108, 137, 171-173, 177, 184, 193, 212, 217
cyber event 5, 45, 48, 116, 125, 152, 195, 200, 207-208
Cyber incidents 2, 6-8, 10, 14-15, 18, 22, 27, 41, 48, 62, 64, 66, 75, 93, 131-132, 135-136, 138-139, 142, 151-152, 157-159, 163, 209

cyber threat 3-4, 12-13, 15, 24, 71, 75, 77, 85, 92, 99-100, 108, 116, 143, 157, 198
cybersecurity 1, 4-5, 7-15, 17-20, 26, 28-33, 35-53, 55-60, 62-69, 71-72, 75-80, 84-86, 91-101, 104-105, 107-109, 112, 114, 116, 120, 126-129, 131-134, 136-141, 143-146, 149-150, 152-153, 163-165, 171-177, 181, 183-185, 187, 189-191, 193, 195, 197-201, 206-210, 212-213, 218

D

data breach 96, 99

E

emergency response 49, 151-152, 184
Essential Functions 65, 78, 149, 153-154, 156, 163

H

Hazard Identification 2

I

incident response 8, 19, 40-41, 45, 49, 65, 67, 80, 120, 133, 139, 142, 154-156, 159-161, 163, 166-169
Industrial Control 216-217
information sharing 1, 13, 15-16, 20, 28, 30, 39-45, 48, 50, 52, 55, 65, 69, 71-72, 80, 101, 104-129, 133, 146-147, 172, 189, 198, 200, 206

informative references 174, 177, 179, 184
intelligence agencies 107-108, 129

M

maturity models 35, 37, 179, 210, 216, 218

N

natural disasters 1-2, 151
NICE framework 56, 63

P

private sector 49, 66, 69, 107-108, 129, 132, 136, 152, 154, 160, 183, 212

S

security awareness program 75-76, 91

Security Framework 47, 56, 63, 104, 171-173, 183, 189, 193-194, 212
Security Maturity Model 4, 10-13, 32, 50-51, 55-56, 104, 193
security measures 46, 173, 185-186, 191
security programs 10, 28, 37, 91, 189, 210-211
Software Engineering 36-37

U

unacceptable behavior 139, 150

W

whole-community program 208

Recommended Reference Books

ISBN: 978-1-5225-8876-4
© 2019; 141 pp.
List Price: $135

ISBN: 978-1-5225-8100-0
© 2019; 321 pp.
List Price: $235

ISBN: 978-1-5225-7847-5
© 2019; 306 pp.
List Price: $195

ISBN: 978-1-5225-6313-6
© 2019; 349 pp.
List Price: $215

ISBN: 978-1-5225-7628-0
© 2019; 281 pp.
List Price: $220

ISBN: 978-1-5225-5855-2
© 2019; 337 pp.
List Price: $185

Looking for free content, product updates, news, and special offers?
Join IGI Global's mailing list today and start enjoying exclusive perks sent only to IGI Global members.
Add your name to the list at **www.igi-global.com/newsletters.**

Ensure Quality Research is Introduced to the Academic Community

Become an IGI Global Reviewer for Authored Book Projects

Premier Reference Source	Premier Reference Source	Premier Reference Source	Premier Reference Source
Emerging GIS Applications for Emergency and Disaster Management	Managerial Strategies and Green Solutions for Project Sustainability	Comparative Approaches to Using R and Python for Statistical Data Analysis	Solutions for High-Touch Communications in a High-Tech World

The overall success of an authored book project is dependent on quality and timely reviews.

In this competitive age of scholarly publishing, constructive and timely feedback significantly expedites the turnaround time of manuscripts from submission to acceptance, allowing the publication and discovery of forward-thinking research at a much more expeditious rate. Several IGI Global authored book projects are currently seeking highly-qualified experts in the field to fill vacancies on their respective editorial review boards:

Applications and Inquiries may be sent to:
development@igi-global.com

Applicants must have a doctorate (or an equivalent degree) as well as publishing and reviewing experience. Reviewers are asked to complete the open-ended evaluation questions with as much detail as possible in a timely, collegial, and constructive manner. All reviewers' tenures run for one-year terms on the editorial review boards and are expected to complete at least three reviews per term. Upon successful completion of this term, reviewers can be considered for an additional term.

If you have a colleague that may be interested in this opportunity, we encourage you to share this information with them.

IGI Global Proudly Partners With eContent Pro International

Receive a 25% Discount on all Editorial Services

Editorial Services

IGI Global expects all final manuscripts submitted for publication to be in their final form. This means they must be reviewed, revised, and professionally copy edited prior to their final submission. Not only does this support with accelerating the publication process, but it also ensures that the highest quality scholarly work can be disseminated.

English Language Copy Editing

Let eContent Pro International's expert copy editors perform edits on your manuscript to resolve spelling, punctuaion, grammar, syntax, flow, formatting issues and more.

Scientific and Scholarly Editing

Allow colleagues in your research area to examine the content of your manuscript and provide you with valuable feedback and suggestions before submission.

Figure, Table, Chart & Equation Conversions

Do you have poor quality figures? Do you need visual elements in your manuscript created or converted? A design expert can help!

Translation

Need your documjent translated into English? eContent Pro International's expert translators are fluent in English and more than 40 different languages.

Printed in the United States
By Bookmasters